Niðrstigningar saga

SOURCES, TRANSMISSION, AND THEOLOGY OF THE OLD NORSE "DESCENT INTO HELL"

Niðrstigningar saga

SOURCES, TRANSMISSION, AND THEOLOGY OF THE OLD NORSE "DESCENT INTO HELL"

Dario Bullitta

UNIVERSITY OF TORONTO PRESS
Toronto Buffalo London

Toronto Buffalo London
www.utorontopress.com

ISBN 978-1-4426-9799-7

Library and Archives Canada Cataloguing in Publication

Bullitta, Dario, 1984–, author
Niðrstigningar saga : sources, transmission, and theology of the Old Norse "descent into hell" / Dario Bullitta.

(Toronto Old Norse and Icelandic series ; 11)
Includes bibliographical references and indexes.
ISBN 978-1-4426-9799-7 (cloth)

1. Gospel of Nicodemus (Icelandic version) – Criticism, Textual. 2. Sagas – Criticism, Textual. I. Title. II. Series: Toronto Old Norse and Icelandic studies ; 11

BS2860.N6B85 2017 229'.8 C2017-903590-8

The author gratefully acknowledges the Fondazione Banco di Sardegna for a generous subsidy that covered the production costs of this book.

University of Toronto Press acknowledges the financial assistance to its publishing program of the Canada Council for the Arts and the Ontario Arts Council, an agency of the Government of Ontario.

Canada Council for the Arts
Conseil des Arts du Canada

Funded by the Government of Canada
Financé par le gouvernement du Canada

Canada

Is. 25:8 cum autem mortale hoc induerit inmortalitatem
Os. 13:14 tunc fiet sermo qui scriptus est
absorta est mors in victoria

1 Corinthians 15:54[1]

Contents

Illustrations and Tables

Illustrations

Tables

Acknowledgments

I have numerous people to thank for their intellectual and moral support throughout the years of research leading to this book. First, I should like to thank Fabrizio D. Raschellà, my mentor at the University of Siena, for believing in the project from its early stages and for his attentive guidance.

I am profoundly indebted to Carla Falluomini, Zbigniew Izydorczyk, and Kirsten Wolf for their constant support and encouragement in my academic pursuits and for the invaluable advice they have provided during my work on the *Gospel of Nicodemus*.

I wish to extend my sincere gratitude to the three anonymous reviewers on behalf of the University of Toronto Press for offering highly incisive suggestions and improvements of the manuscript. I am most grateful to the University of Toronto Press – in particular, Senior Humanities Editor Suzanne Rancourt and Associate Managing Editor Barb Porter – for their assistance and commitment throughout the publishing process, and also to copy editors Beth McAuley and Kristy Hankewitz. In restituting the text of *Niðrstigningar saga*, I have consulted and made use of all the available critical editions and translations of the text, and I am greatly indebted to the works of Carl R. Unger, Philip Roughton, and Odd Einar Haugen.[1] I am especially grateful to Marteinn Helgi Sigurðsson, for providing unceasing encouragement and for making acute modifications of my translations of the Old Norse and Icelandic texts; to Zbigniew Izydorczyk and Jonathan Black, for their care in reading and commenting upon an early version of chapters 4 to 6; and to Haki Antonsson, Marco Maulu, and Andrea Meregalli, for the most fruitful discussions on the topic. I must also kindly thank scholars at the Arnamagnæan Manuscript Collection and the Dictionary of Old Norse Prose at the Department of Nordic Research (NFI), University of Copenhagen, Simonetta Battista, Helle Degnbol, Christopher Sanders (†2013), Þorbjörg Helgadóttir, Ragnheiður Mósesdóttir,

Florian Grammel, Alex Speed Kjeldsen, Gottskálk Jensson, and Annette Lassen, who have sustained my research activities in innumerable ways over the years.

I am grateful to the BnF and Glasgow UL, Special Collections for permission to reproduce the materials for which they hold copyright.

Several institutions provided financial support at various stages of the project. I am much obliged to the University of Siena, for affording me the opportunity to pursue research at the British Library, as well as to the Warburg Institute and the University College of London in Fall 2011 and Spring 2012; to the Fondazione Banco di Sardegna, for a generous subsidy that covered the production costs of this book; to the Associazione Italiana di Filologia Germanica (AIFG), for awarding me the Scardigli Prize for best publication in Germanic Philology in the Spring of 2016; and to the Jay C. and Ruth Halls Fund at the University of Wisconsin–Madison, for a visiting scholar fellowship, which allowed me to present this work at the Department of German, Nordic, and Slavic (GNS) in Fall 2016.

I feel most fortunate to have received intellectual and personal support from many other scholars, including Massimiliano Bampi, Marina Buzzoni, Odd Einar Haugen, Claudia Händl, Fulvio Ferrari, Alison Finlay, Patrizia Lendinara, Margrét Eggertsdóttir, Nicoletta Francovich Onesti (†2014), Carl Phelpstead, Svanhildur Óskarsdóttir, Paolo Trovato, and Alessandro Zironi. I also wish to reserve special thanks for Antonella Calaresu, Gabriele Cocco, Jóhanna Katrín Friðriksdóttir, Fay Lockett, Todd Michelson-Ambelang, and Natalie Van Deusen, who frequently listened to my passions and frustrations throughout years of research. I am forever indebted to my two brothers, Antonio and Luca, and to my friends and colleagues, though I cannot mention them all by name, who are a constant source of strength and fortitude.

Lastly, and most importantly, I dedicate this work to my parents, Ica and Tonino, for teaching me the beauty of history, old books, and the written word. I am in gratitude for a lifetime of love and support.

Dario Bullitta
Sassari, Sardinia, Christmas Eve 2016

Introduction

Throughout Late Antiquity and the Middle Ages, the apocryphal writings represented for clerics, theologians, and exegetes an invaluable source to consult and interrogate when the text of the biblical canon was either reticent or ambiguous. The most widely known pseudoepigraphical work among the New Testament Apocrypha was undoubtedly the *Evangelium Nicodemi* ("The Gospel of Nicodemus"), which on account of its supplementary character nearly attained the status of a "fifth gospel."[1]

In its early form, the *Gospel of Nicodemus* or *Evangelium Nicodemi*, originally called *Gesta Salvatoris* ("The Deeds of the Saviour"), consisted of two separate Latin texts, the *Acta Pilati* ("Acts of Pilate") and the *Descensus Christi ad inferos* ("Christ's Descent into Hell"). These two narratives first circulated separately and were only subsequently conflated – sometime between the fifth and the eighth centuries – to form a unique pseudo gospel depicting the Trial, Passion, and Crucifixion of Christ, and his Harrowing of Hell.[2] Its high appreciation throughout the Middle Ages can be seen through both the impressive number of surviving Latin manuscripts – over 400 today – and by the numerous medieval vernacular translations throughout Europe, the majority of which were completed early on during the process of vernacularization of devotional literature.[3]

In the context of renewed cultural contacts and the increasing exchange of clerics between Icelandic and continental centres of learning and devotion – most notably with those of northern France and the University of Paris – some exemplars of the Latin *Evangelium Nicodemi* seem to have been imported to Iceland towards the end of the twelfth century. Shortly after this acquisition, Icelandic clerics undertook the task of translating and adapting one of the Latin texts into their vernacular.

The first extant Icelandic translation of the apocryphon circulated with the title *Niðrstigningar saga* ("The Story of the Descent") and survives today in two distinct redactions.[4] As its name suggests, the Icelandic translation embraces exclusively the *Descensus Christi ad inferos*, altogether omitting the *Acta Pilati* – that is, the chronicle on the Trial and Crucifixion of Christ. This exclusion seems to have been a deliberate editorial choice, as there is evidence that the Icelandic compiler consulted and employed a Latin manuscript that contained the complete text.[5] The reasons for the omission of the *Acta Pilati* might lie in the recapitulative and repetitive nature of its text, which correlates and condenses the notable events leading to the Crucifixion of Christ, already abundantly addressed in the canonical Gospels. Its narrative might have been regarded as either less authoritative or even redundant, and its translation was, therefore, not a compelling preoccupation of the Icelandic compiler.

What undoubtedly fascinated him and urged him to translate the apocryphon in the Norse vernacular for the benefit of those illiterate in Latin was the *Descensus Christi ad inferos* and its treatment of the Harrowing of Hell.[6] Its text offers a detailed description of the afterworld and mentions, among other things, the entrance to Hell, the gates of Paradise, the hosts of angels and demons inhabiting those realms, the terrible sight of Satan, and, most notably, Christ's final victory over that Old Enemy.

Besides these suggestive portrayals, the core narrative of the *Descensus* centres on Christ's deliverance of the souls of the righteous from the imprisonment of original sin, and, therefore, it specifically addresses the main theological questions of redemption. On the occasion of a public or private reading of the text, the audience of the *Descensus*, as well as that of *Niðrstigningar saga*, might have been compelled to consider the contemporary and future implications of the story. Throughout the narrative, each member of the Christian community would accordingly be encouraged to speculate on his/her own personal path to redemption. Moreover, as a contemporary allusion to *Niðrstigningar saga* seems to suggest, the Icelandic text apparently conceals an exhortation to arduous but rewarding resistance of the temptations of the Devil.[7]

The author of *Niðrstigningar saga* was evidently educated in theology, and clear evidence will be given throughout the book that points to his inquiry and use of contemporary exegetical treatises. Despite being a precious source of information on the Harrowing of Hell, the original text of the *Descensus* remains silent, or treats only hastily or superficially, some of the most weighty theological controversies debated at the time of the composition of the Icelandic text – most crucially, the relationship between Christ's divinity and humanity. Consequently, the supplementary passages, absent in the entire Latin tradition and only subsequently introduced in the Icelandic text, should in every respect be regarded as the result of the compiler's own investigations and elucidations on contemporary theological issues. They therefore represent an invaluable historical source for the dating of the text and its contextualization.

The present volume attempts to prove that the presence in *Niðrstigningar saga* of variant readings typical of the version known as the "Troyes redaction" of the Latin *Evangelium Nicodemi*, which originated in twelfth-century France, indicates that the Icelandic compiler employed this version of the text rather than the more widely available version of the apocryphon in western Europe. Moreover, a closer analysis of the textual interpolations drawn from foreign sources reveals the compiler's acquaintance with biblical glosses and commentaries produced during the second half of the twelfth century by some of the greatest exegetes of the Paris school of theology, Peter Lombard (†1160) and Peter Comestor (†1178) in particular. Taking into account these identifications, the survey then turns to the evidence of French manuscripts dating to around 1200 and containing Parisian theological and exegetical texts that might have been brought to Iceland by students studying theology in northern France or Paris. Indeed, significantly, these texts conform to the matrix of additional biblical and theological material consulted by the compiler of *Niðrstigningar saga* to gloss, exemplify, and augment suitable passages of his copy of the Latin *Evangelium Nicodemi*. Finally, it is argued that the epilogue of *Niðrstigningar saga* was intentionally modelled on that of the *Jarteinabók Þorláks byskups in forna* ("The First Miracle Collection of Bishop Þorlákr"), written after 1199 and extant in the first section of AM 645 4to, the oldest surviving manuscript containing *Niðrstigningar saga*, and was already in circulation before the completion of the *Jarteinabók Þorláks byskups ǫnnur* ("The Second Miracle Collection of Bishop Þorlákr"), completed by the year 1210. In addition, the second section of the book includes a semidiplomatic edition of the two redactions of *Niðrstigningar saga*, which takes into account a new stemma codicum of the surviving manuscripts. Modern English translations of the edited texts are also provided.

Abbreviations

A Book of Miracles	*A Book of Miracles: MS no. 645 4to of the Arna-Magnæan Collection in the University Library of Copenhagen*, ed. Anne Holtsmark
AB	*Analecta Bollandiana*
AM	Den Arnamagnæanske Samling/Stofnun Árna Magnússonar í íslenskum fræðum
BAV	Biblioteca Apostolica Vaticana
BdA	Bibliothèque de l'Arsenal
Biskupa sögur	*Biskupa sögur*, vol. 2, ed. Ásdís Egilsdóttir
BL	British Library
BM	Bibliothèque municipale
BnF	Bibliothèque nationale de France
BNM	Biblioteca Nazionale Marciana
Bodl	Bodleian Library
BStB	Bayerische Staatsbibliothek
CCC	Corpus Christi College
CCSA	Corpus Christianorum Series Apocryphorum
CCSL	Corpus Christianorum Series Latina
CSAE	Cambridge Studies in Anglo-Saxon England
DBL	*Dansk biografisk Lexikon tillige omfattende Norge for tidsrummet 1537–1814*, ed. Carl F. Bricka
DI	*Diplomatarium Islandicum. Íslenzkt fornbréfasafn*, ed. Jón Sigurðsson et al.
DKB	Det Kongelige Bibliotek
EIMF	Early Icelandic Manuscripts in Facsimile
GkS	Gamle kongelige Samling

HAB	Herzog August Bibliothek
Heilagra manna sögur	*Heilagra manna søgur. Fortællinger og legender om hellige mænd og kvinder*, ed. Carl R. Unger
Helgensagaer	*AM 623 4to: Helgensagaer*, ed. Finnur Jónsson
Isländska handskriften 645	*Isländska handskriften No. 645 4to i den Arnamagnæanska samlingen på universitetsbiblioteket i København i diplomatariskt aftryck*, ed. Ludvig Larsson
ÍH	Íslenzk handrit. Icelandic Manuscripts, series in folio, quarto and octavo
ÍÆ	*Íslenzkar æviskrár frá landnámstímum til ársloka 1940 (1948–1976)*, ed. Páll Eggert Ólason, Jón Guðnason, and Ólafur Þ. Kristjánsson
JÁM	*Jarðabók Árna Magnússonar og Páls Vídalíns*
JS	Jón Sigurðsson Collection
Kb	Kungliga biblioteket
KLNM	*Kulturhistorisk Leksikon for nordisk middelalder*
MiAg	*Miscellanea Agostiniana*, ed. Germain Morin
MRTS	Medieval and Renaissance Texts and Studies
MS	*Maríu saga. Legender om Jomfru Maria og hendes jertegn*, ed. Carl R. Unger
NkS	Ny kongelige Samling
ONP	*Ordbog over det norrøne prosasprog. A Dictionary of Old Norse Prose*
PG	*Patrologiae Cursus Completus, Series Graeca*, ed. Jacques-Paul Migne et al.
PL	*Patrologiae Cursus Completus, Series Latina*, ed. Jacques-Paul Migne et al.
PLS	*Patrologiae Cursus Completus, Series Latina Supplementum*, ed. Adalbert Hamman et al.
Postola sögur	*Postola sögur. Legendariske fortællinger om apostlernes liv, deres kamp for kristendommens udbredelse samt deres martyrdød*, ed. Carl R. Unger
SÁM	Stofnun Árna Magnússonar á Íslandi
SPK	Staatsbibliothek Preußischer Kulturbesitz
StB	Stiftsbibliothek
SSFS	Samlingar utgivna av Svenska Fornskriftsällskapet
SUGNL	Samfund til udgivelse af gammel nordisk litteratur
TC	Trinity College
TNL	*The Nordic Languages: An International Handbook of the History of the North Germanic Languages*, ed. Oskar Bandle et al.

TONIS	Toronto Old Norse-Icelandic Series
Two Old English Apocrypha	*Two Old English Apocrypha and their Manuscript Source. The Gospel of Nicodemus and the Avenging of the Saviour*, ed. James E. Cross
UB	Universitetsbiblioteket
UL	University Library
ÖNB	Österreichische Nationalbibliothek

Niðrstigningar saga

1 The Latin *Evangelium Nicodemi* in Medieval Europe

In spite of being one of the most influential religious narratives on devotional and secular literature and on the visual arts of the Middle Ages, as well as possibly representing the best known New Testament apocryphon along with the *Gospel of the Pseudo-Matthew*, much of the earliest textual history of the *Evangelium Nicodemi* has yet to be written.[1]

The intrinsic composite nature of its most common and best known textual form throughout medieval and modern times seems to have resulted from the merging and conflation of two separate narratives, the *Acta Pilati* ("Acts of Pilate") and the *Descensus Christi ad inferos* ("Christ's Descent into Hell"). These texts seem to have originated and circulated independently for an unascertained time before being combined together – sometime between Late Antiquity and the High Middle Ages – to form a single pseudoepigraphical gospel depicting the history of Christ's Passion and his legendary Harrowing of Hell. In one of the concluding lines of the text, the composition of the original Hebrew gospel is allegedly ascribed to Nicodemus, the Pharisee and covert disciple of Christ, who, according to John 19:32–42, assisted Joseph of Arimathea in the atonement and entombment of Christ's corpse.[2] On account of this attribution, the text came to be known in the Low Middle Ages and early modern times as *Evangelium Nicodemi* ("The Gospel of Nicodemus"), although its first title in manuscripts ranging from the ninth to the thirteenth centuries is *Gesta Pilati* ("Deeds of Pilate").[3]

The text of the so-called *Acta Pilati* constitutes the first sixteen chapters of the *Evangelium Nicodemi* and relates to the events leading to the Crucifixion and to the wondrous outcomes, which took place in Galilee. The narrative starts with Christ's Trial before Pilate, continues with his Crucifixion, Entombment, and Resurrection before moving on to his apparition to the disciples in Galilee, and ends with Christ's miraculous liberation of Joseph of Arimathea from his imprisonment. The original text of the *Acta Pilati* was in all probability composed in Greek between the second and the fourth centuries and translated remarkably early into Arabic, Aramaic, Armenian, Coptic, Georgian, and Syriac.[4] In his edition of the Greek text, which is regrettably transmitted exclusively in later manuscripts dating from the twelfth century, Constantin von Tischendorf identified two main recensions: a shorter version, designated as Greek A and transmitted in fifteen manuscripts, and a longer redaction, Greek B, which survives today in some thirty codices.[5] Tischendorf also demonstrated that Greek B was only subsequently amplified with additional narrative material and that, therefore, Greek A must represent the oldest redaction of the two.[6]

A typical text of Greek A opens with a prologue dating Christ's Passion to the years of the Emperor Tiberius (†AD 37), which is at times preceded by an additional prologue attributing the discovery of the Hebrew apocryphon and its subsequent translation into Greek to a certain Ananias, a praetorian guard in Jerusalem during the reign of the Emperor Theodosius II, nicknamed the Calligrapher († AD 450).[7]

The first extant Latin translation of the *Acta Pilati* survives in the so-called *Codex Vindobonensis* (Vienna, ÖNB, Cod. lat. 563, ff. 122–77), a voluminous manuscript composed of six codicological units, palimpsested with various patristic texts at the Benedictine Abbey of Neuwiller-lès-Saverne in Alsace during the first half of the eleventh century.[8] The *scriptio inferior* of section four contains remarkably old texts, such as the oldest surviving fragments of the Latin *Infancy Gospel of Thomas* and portions of the *Gospel of Matthew* from the *Vetus Latina*. In the same section are also extant chapters I–VI, IX–X, and XIII–XVI of the Latin *Acta Pilati*, which make up two-fifths of the entire text.[9] Elias A. Lowe has dated the Latin uncial of section four to the fifth century and suggested as a possible place of composition an unidentified scriptorium in northern Italy.[10] The text of the *Acta Pilati* in the Vienna palimpsest is clearly derived from Greek A, as it maintains the prologue of the first type, where the newly converted Praetorian Guard (here transliterated as Aeneas) is mentioned as the discoverer and first translator of the pseudo gospel, and the prologue of the second type, which dates Christ's Passion to the nineteenth year of rule of the Emperor Tiberius.

If some important omissions relate the first surviving witnesses of the *Evangelium Nicodemi* to the Vienna palimpsest, their greatest departure from it is represented by their inclusion of the *Descensus Christi ad inferos*. Its omission in the Vienna palimpsest remains yet unclarified. A Greek version of the *Descensus* may have already been in circulation as far back as the second century, since numerous Greek homilists (most eminently Eusebius of Alexandria) were acquainted with the same theme of catabasis. Nevertheless, none of their homilies seem to be specifically indebted to the text of the *Descensus*.[11] It is consequently possible that the Vienna palimpsest never included a Latin translation of the *Descensus Christi ad inferos*.

From the fifth century onwards, the text of the Latin *Acta Pilati* must have undergone substantial revisions under the hand of learned scribes and copyists, who were interested in additional apocryphal details concerning the life of Christ. Its most noteworthy acquisition may well be represented by the *Descensus Christi ad inferos*, which comprises the last eleven chapters of *Evangelium Nicodemi*. Its text was in all probability appended to the *Acta Pilati* as a sequel narrative to the Passion and Resurrection of Christ, providing it with the glorious and wondrous events of Christ's immediate afterlife, namely, his Descent and Harrowing of Hell.

The narrative of the *Descensus* starts with the encounter of the Jews and Joseph of Arimathea with Carinus and Leucius, the two sons of Simeon the Elder, who were long dead and in terrible pain, dwelling in the darkness of Hell before being liberated by Christ. They begin relating with fear their experience and testifying that on the very day Christ was crucified, a great light illuminated the whole realm of Hell, announcing Christ's imminent and much awaited arrival. At the sight of this divine light, the patriarchs and prophets who had been long imprisoned in Hell – most notably, John the Baptist, David, Micah, Habakkuk, and Isaiah – rejoiced greatly and began recalling the words and psalms they pronounced when alive on earth, predicting the coming of the Messiah. Inferus (a personification of Hell) disputes Christ's divinity with Satan and warns his old companion of the immense and almighty powers of Christ. After this debate, in a hasty passage, Christ descends into Hell, defeats Satan, and frees the souls of the righteous from the bondage of sin. Starting with Adam, Christ delivers the patriarchs and prophets to the archangel Michael, who finally guides them to the eternal bliss of Paradise.

All known medieval manuscripts transmitting the Latin *Evangelium Nicodemi* have been catalogued by Zbigniew Izydorczyk, who counts a total of 436 medieval codices, including the Vienna palimpsest.[12] Besides Latin A and Latin B, Izydorczyk has identified two more recensions, labelled as Latin C and Latin T, based on common features of lexicon, style, and literary motifs. It should be noted that these exclusively represent the main possible subgroups of Latin manuscripts, as there still exist a remarkable number of hybrid compilations into which two or more textual typologies of the pseudo gospel were conflated.[13]

Latin A

The most extensively diffused version of the Latin *Evangelium Nicodemi* was undoubtedly Latin A, which numbers today roughly 387 codices out of the 436, making up to almost nine-tenths of the entire tradition. Latin A consequently represents the Majority Text within the surviving manuscripts, a nomenclature borrowed from Biblical philology.[14] Previous research regarded the so-called *Codex Einsidlensis* (Einsiedeln, StB, 326, ff. 11r–29v), a manuscript produced in Fulda in the tenth century and edited by Hack C. Kim, hereafter referred to by the letter K, as the best representative witness of Latin A. To facilitate the comparison of the texts, edited and unedited Latin and vernacular versions of the apocryphon will be assigned the chapters and paragraph numbers employed by Kim in his edition of K.[15]

One of the main characteristics of the Majority Text is the omission of the first prologue, mentioning Aeneas as the occasional, fortuitous discoverer of the pseudo gospel; another, on the other hand, is the inclusion of the prologue of the second type, dating Christ's Passion to the years of the Emperor Tiberius, identical to that transmitted in the Vienna palimpsest:

> Factum est in anno XVIII imperatoris Tyberii Caesaris, imperatoris Romanorum, et Herodis filii Herodis imperatoris Galileae, anno XVIIII principatus eius, VIII Kal. Aprilis, quod est XXV dies mensis Martii, consolatu Rufini et Rubellionis, in anno quarto ducentesimae secundae Olympiadis, sub principatu sacerdotum Iudaeorum Ioseph et Caifae, et quanta post crucem et passionem Domini historiatus est Nichodemus, acta a principibus sacerdotum et reliquis Iudaeis, mandauit ipse Nichodemus litteris ebraicis.[16]

> (It happened in the eighteenth year of the Emperor Tiberius, ruler of the Romans, and of Herod, son of Herod, ruler of Galilee, in the nineteenth year of his rule, on the eighth calends of April, which is the twenty-fifth day of March, in the consulate of Rufinus and Rubellio, in the fourth year of the two hundred and second Olympiad, under the rule of the Jewish priests Joseph and Caiaphas, that Nicodemus recorded what happened after the Crucifixion and Passion of the Lord, and what was done by the high priests and the rest of the Jews. Nicodemus wrote it himself in the Hebrew script.)[17]

Besides the prologue, the most noteworthy characteristic of the Majority Text is, as mentioned above, its inclusion of the *Descensus Christi ad inferos*, which is altogether missing from the Vienna palimpsest, as well as in the earliest Greek manuscripts, and consequently in all Oriental recensions derived directly from the Greek text. All of these texts transmit the *Acta Pilati*.

Izydorczyk suggests the fifth century as a reasonable *terminus post quem* for the merging of the two texts. Before this time, he maintains, the Majority Text could not have acquired the two interpolated sections central in the development of its plot – the Latin *Vita Adae et Evae* and the pseudo-Augustinian *Sermo* CLX *De Pascha* II – since neither of them were yet available.[18]

The Old Testament apocryphon *Vita Adae et Evae*, which relates Seth's legendary journey to Paradise in search of the Oil of Mercy, is woven into the end of paragraph XIX.1, where Michael's prophecy of the coming of the Messiah is reported almost verbatim.[19]

> Nullo modo poteris ex eo accipere nisi in nouissimis temporibus quando conpleti fuerint V milia et D anni. Tunc ueniet super terram amantissimus Dei Filius Christus qui faciet resurgere corpus Adae et conresuscitare corpora mortuorum ac sanare omnem infirmitatem. Et ipse ueniens in Iordane baptizabitur. Cum autem egressus fuerit de aqua Iordanis, tunc de oleo misericordiae suae unguet omnes credentes in se, et erit oleum illud misericordiae in generationem qui nascendi sunt ex aqua et spiritu in uitam aeternam. Amen. Tunc descendens in terram amantissimus Dei Filius Christus.[20]

> (In no way can you receive [the Oil of Mercy] from Him until future times, when 5,500 years shall be completed. Then shall come upon earth the beloved Christ, Son of God, who shall resurrect the body of Adam, and with him the bodies of the dead, and heal all the sickness. And He shall be baptized in the Jordan, and when He shall come out of the waters of the Jordan, He shall anoint with the Oil of His Mercy all of those who believed in Him, and the Oil of Mercy shall be among the generation of those who are born from the water and the spirit in eternal life. Amen. Then shall descend upon earth the most beloved Christ, the Son of God.)

The pseudo-Augustinian *Sermo* CLX *De Pascha* II, which along with the *Evangelium Nicodemi* represents the other great medieval source relating to Christ's Descent and Harrowing of Hell, supplies the Majority Text with a series of dramatic rhetorical questions addressed to both Christ and Satan and voiced with fear by the infernal legions once they realize that Christ is about to overcome them.[21] These utterances are scattered in paragraphs XXII.1, XXIII.1, and XXIV.1.

> Unde es tu, Iesu, tam fortis homo et splendidus maiestate, tam preclarus sine macula et mundus a crimine? Ille enim mundus terrenus qui nobis subiectus fuit semper usque nunc, qui nostris usibus tributa persoluebat, numquam nobis talem mortuum hominem transmisit, numquam talia munera Inferis destinauit. Quis ergo es tu qui sic intrepidus nostros fines ingressus es? Non solum nostra supplicia

nos uereris, insuper et omnes de nostris uinculis auferre conaris. Forsitan tu es ille Iesus, de quo princeps noster Satan dicebat quod per tuam mortem crucis totius mundi potestatem accepturus esses.[22]

(Whence are you, Jesus, so strong a man and splendid in majesty, so clear without stain and clean from crime? For that earthly world, which has always been subject to us until now, and paid the tribute to our use, has never sent us a dead man, never sent such a gift to Hell. Who are you who enters dauntlessly our borders? Not only do you not fear our tortures but you also try to take away all men from our bonds. Perhaps you are the same Jesus of whom our Prince Satan said that, through your death on the Cross, he would acquire power over the whole world?)

Ecce iam iste Iesus diuinitatis suae fulgore fugat omnes tenebras mortis, et firmum carcerem confregit, et eicit captious, soluit uinctos. Et omnes qui sub nostris solebant suspirare tormentis insulant nobis, et deprecationibus eorum expugnantur imperia nostra et regna nostra uincuntur et nullum iam nos reueretur genus hominum. Insuper et fortiter nobis comminantur qui numquam nobis superbi fuerunt mortui, nec aliquando potuerunt laeti esse captiui. O princeps Satan, omnium malorum impiorum et refugarum pater, quid haec facere uoluisti? Quia qui a principio usque nunc fuerunt disperati salutem et uitam, modo nullus eorum hinc iam solito mugitus auditur, nec ullus eorum personat gemitus, nec in alicuius eorum facie lacrimarum uestigium inuenitur. O princeps Satan, possessor clauium inferorum, illas tuas diuitias, quas adquisieras per lignum preuaricationis et paradysi amissionem, nunc per lignum crucis perdidisti et periit omnis laetitia tua. Dum istum Christum Regem Gloriae suspendisti, aduersus te et aduersum me egisti. Amodo cognosce quanta tormenta aeterna et suplicia infinita passurus eris in mea custodia sempiterna. O princeps Satan, auctor mortis et origo superbiae, debueras primum istius Iesu causam malam requirere. Et in quo nullam culpam congouisti quare sine ratione iniuste eum crucifigere ausus fuisti et ad nostram regionem innocentem et iustum perduxisti, et totius mundi noxios, impios et iniustos perdidisti?[23]

(For now, this Jesus dispels all the shadows of death by the lightning of His divinity and has broken the strong bonds of the prisons and let out the prisoners and freed those who were bound. And all of those who used to sigh under our torments, they now insult us, and at their prayers, our realms and our kingdoms are overwhelmed and conquered, and no nation reveres us any longer. And moreover, the dead who were never haughty against us and the prisoners who could never be happy, they now threaten us strongly. O Prince Satan, father of all the evil and impious, and the fugitives, what did you want to do? Those who from the beginning until now have been desperate for salvation and life, now none of their usual lowing is heard from this place, none of their groans resound, and no trace of tears can be found on their faces. O Prince Satan, owner of the keys of Hell, the wealth you had acquired through the wood of prevarication and the entrance to Paradise you have now lost through the wood of the Cross, and all your gladness has died. When you hung that King of Glory, you acted against yourself and me. Henceforth, recognize how many eternal torments and infinite tortures you are going to suffer in my everlasting custody. O Prince Satan, author of death and origin of pride, you had to seek for a cause of sin in this Jesus. And when you recognized no fault in Him, why did you dare to crucify Him without a reason and bring Him, innocent and just, to our regions, and why have you lost the guilty, the criminal, the godless, and the unjust of the whole world?)

Aduenisti redemptor mundi; sicut per legem et prophetas tuos predixisti, factis adimplesti.[24]

(O Redeemer of the world, you have come just as you have predicted through the law and your prophets, you have [now] fulfilled with facts.)

The *terminus ante quem* date for the merging of the *Acta Pilati* with the *Descensus Christi ad inferos* is represented by the transcription and completion of the first nine Carolingian manuscripts transmitting a text of the Majority type in the ninth century. Among them, the five witnesses of French origin seem to have played a fundamental role in the course of the early dissemination and circulation of the text throughout western Europe.

Laon, BM Suzanne Martinet, 265 (ff. 2r–35r) is a miscellaneous codex preserving mostly sermons and saints' lives and was one of the numerous manuscripts consulted by the Irish scholar Martianus Hibernensis (†875), as noted in some marginalia of the codex.[25] Martianus was director the Cathedral School of Laon during the third quarter of the ninth century, where, among other subjects, he also taught Greek.[26]

Saint-Omer, Bibliothèque d'agglomération de Saint-Omer, 202 (ff. 1r–13r) is a voluminous homilary written in the Benedictine Abbey of Saint Bertin in the French province of Saint-Omer during the third quarter of the ninth century. James E. Cross has recognized it as being the very source text underlying the first Old English translation of the Latin *Evangelium Nicodemi*, which dates back to the eleventh century.[27] A paleographical survey of the several Old English marginal glosses transmitted in the homilary has sought to prove that the manuscript was in Exeter during the episcopacy of Leofric (†1072).[28]

London, BL, Royal 5 E. XIII (ff. 82r–100r) is a collection of theological texts containing works by Cyprian and Bede and extracts from the apocryphal

Book of Enoch. It was written in Brittany during the ninth century and, as some corrections and annotations in Old English indicate, was already exported to England by the tenth century, where it was preserved at Worcester Cathedral Priory.[29]

Paris, BnF, nuov. acq. lat. 1605 (ff. 4r–16v) is a manuscript written at Fleury Abbey towards the end of the ninth century. It preserves various hagiographical and homiletic texts, most notably the *Passio sancti Christophori*, the *Gospel of Pseudo-Matthew*, and sermons by Augustine, and it was written at Fleury Abbey towards the end of the ninth century. A note (f. 110r) places the manuscript in England at Ramsey Abbey in Huntingdonshire during the second decade of the eleventh century, where it was owned by Abbot Whitman (†ca. 1047).[30] The codex may have been subsequently taken back to its place of origin by Abbot Whitman himself during his travel to Jerusalem in 1020, as it is was once part of the manuscript collection of the BM of Orléans (now Médiathèque).[31]

A fifth fragment, consisting of four leaves transmitting sections of *Evangelium Nicodemi* – today Munich, BStB, Clm 29275 (olim Clm 29163) – was, according to Bernhard Bischoff, written in France. It has, however, been part of the manuscript collection of Weihenstephan Abbey, in the Freising district of Bavaria, since the early Middle Ages.[32] Clm 29275 may, within reason, represent one of the first exemplars of the Majority Text, which by the end of the ninth century was imported to Bavaria, where there must have been considerable subsequent copying.

Providing testimony of this high appreciation of the *Evangelium Nicodemi* in Bavaria are two more Carolingian witnesses that transmit a text of the Majority type, also written in the diocese of Freising before the year 900: a voluminous palimpsest, Berlin, SPK, Theol. lat. oct. 157 from Tegernsee (the *Evangelium Nicodemi* is on pp. 205–73 of the *scriptio superior*), containing writings of Augustine and Alcuin, and two leaves in twelve strips, Munich, Universitätsbibliothek, 2° Cod. ms. 87a, transmitting Augustine's *De civitate Dei* along with small sections of *Evangelium Nicodemi*, possibly compiled in the Benedictine Abbey of St Blasien in the Black Forest.[33] A ninth voluminous manuscript, Bern, Burgerbibliothek, 582 (ff. 46r–75v), containing Adamnán of Iona's *De locis sanctis* and an *Itinerarium Antonini Placentini*, was copied in the St Gallen scriptorium towards the end of the ninth century.[34]

To judge from the combined evidence of the very first surviving witnesses of the *Evangelium Nicodemi*, the centre of composition and dissemination of the Majority Text (in the form it has been transmitted up to the present) can be identified with the prestigious ninth century Carolingian scriptoria of northern France. The fervid intellectual activities of these centres of learning represented the cultural excellence of the Carolingian Renaissance; it is consequently understandable that already by the end of the same century, some French codices transmitting the Majority Text were exported to Bavaria and Switzerland and that a considerable number of them were acquired and consulted by English scribes throughout the tenth and the very beginning of the eleventh centuries, where the Latin text was both copied and transported into the vernacular. Moreover, the fact that two of these French exemplars were simply borrowed by the English scriptoria and were subsequently returned to their respective continental ateliers of provenance may corroborate the hypothesis that the demand for these French exemplars in those decades was considerably high.

The cathedral schools of northern France during the middle of the ninth century may have been the ideal place for the assemblage and composition of the Latin *Evangelium Nicodemi* in the form we know it today. As a matter of fact, the translation of the original Greek text into Latin required a good knowledge of the Greek language and a considerable availability of Latin and Greek apocryphal and homiletic material, including the Latin *Acta Pilati*, the Greek *Descensus Christi ad inferos*, the Latin *Vita Adae et Evae*, and the pseudo-Augustinian *Sermo* CLX *De Pascha* II. Such requirements were easily fulfilled by the late Carolingian libraries, and the task of translating such texts from Greek to Latin may well have been undertaken by some of the Irish monks, who, around the middle of the ninth century, were active in the Irish monastic colonies of northern France. Besides the Frankish Hilduin at the Abbey of Saint Denis (†855) near Paris, a considerable number of these Irish scholars and masters were active on the Continent, most notably Johannes Scotus Eriugena (†877) at the palace school of Aachen, Sedulius Scotus (†850) at the cathedral school of Liège, and the aforementioned Martianus Hiberniensis (†875) at the cathedral school of Laon. All well-read in Greek, they were already in those decades successfully teaching Greek to the new generations of young clerics in their respective cathedral schools and abbeys – not least with the production of some of the first pedagogical material for the study of Greek language, such as Greek-Latin glossaries – and were themselves transcribing and translating Greek biblical, patristic, and homiletic literature into Latin.[35]

It should also be noted that the two writings with which the Latin Majority Text was interpolated earlier in its history, the Latin *Vita Adae et Evae* and the pseudo-Augustinian *Sermo* CLX *De Pascha* II, which subsequently became two of its most evident and distinguishing features, were integral parts of the insular apocryphal and homiletic repertoire. They were already circulating abundantly in Ireland and the British Isles in the eighth century where they were employed for the composition of new devotional texts.[36]

The eight surviving exemplars dating to the tenth century further testify to the great availability of the Majority Text in northern France in the following decades. In fact, five of them are without doubt of French provenance, and virtually all are from the northern regions. Copenhagen, DKB, GkS 1335 4to (ff. 1r–20rb) was, according to Bernhard Bischoff, written between the eighth and the ninth century in an unknown scriptorium of eastern France;[37] Orléans, Médiathèque, 341 (olim 289) (pp. 415–44) was written at Fleury Abbey; Paris, BnF, lat. 5327 (ff. 35v–55r) was written in France, although its exact place of composition is yet unknown. Two more manuscripts transmit only the incipit of the text on their final leaves – Paris, BnF, lat. 2825 (f. 137v), from the Benedictine Abbey of Saint-Amand-les-Eaux; and Chartres, Médiathèque l'Apostrophe, 34 (olim 109) (f. 118v), probably written at the Abbey of Saint-Père-en-Valleé in Chartres, was destroyed in the 1944 bombing.[38] Besides the five French witnesses, three more codices from the tenth century survive: the above-mentioned *Codex Einsidlensis* (Einsiedeln, Stiftsbibliothek, 326, ff. 11r–29v), written at Fulda Abbey; a manuscript written between northern Italy and Einsiedeln Abbey, Einsiedeln, Stiftsbibliothek, 169 (olim 468) (pp. 69–102); and again another voluminous manuscript from Tegernsee in Bavaria, today Munich, BStB, Clm 19105 (ff. 51v–95v).[39]

Latin B

A secondary, considerably different, recension of the Latin *Evangelium Nicodemi* has been referred to in previous studies as Latin B.[40] Its main characteristic is the inclusion of a prologue of the first type, as the one transmitted in the Vienna palimpsest, attributing the discovery of the apocryphon to the otherwise unknown Aeneas, which in some codices is introduced by a homiletic prologue reading: "Audistis, fratres karissimi, quae acta sunt sub Pontio Pilato preside temporibus Tiberii caesaris" ("You have heard, O dearest brothers, what has happened under Pontius Pilate, ruler in the times of the Emperor Tiberius"). The *Acta Pilati* text is considerably abridged in comparison to a typical text of the Majority type. Within the *Descensus Christi ad inferos*, the redactor often intervenes to mould the original plot to his taste, by adding for instance the otherwise unattested arrival of the Good Thief in Hell and omitting altogether the encounter of the patriarchs with Enoch and Elijah in Paradise.[41]

Its text seems to have originated and circulated in northern Italy, as eleven of its twenty-five surviving manuscripts indicate. The first two witnesses date to the eleventh century: one – Padua, Biblioteca Antoniana, 473 Scaff. XXI (ff. 138v–147v) – was written in an unknown location of northern Italy, and another – Munich, BStB, Clm 17181 (ff. 103r–112r) – in Schäftlarn Abbey in

Bavaria. Six manuscripts date from the twelfth century: three of them were compiled in Italy, one in Spain, one at the Abbey of Saint Victor in Paris, and one in either Austria or Bavaria.[42] Only two manuscripts survive from the thirteenth century, both transcribed in the British Isles;[43] whereas from the fourteenth century, four manuscripts written in Italy, two in England, and one in Spain survive.[44] The pattern is similar among the eight surviving manuscripts from the fifteenth century, as three of them, representing the majority, are from Italy, two from England, and the two from Czech Republic, whereas only a single manuscript is from France.[45]

Latin C

A further subgroup directly derived from the Majority Text has been recently identified by Zbigniew Izydorczyk and labelled as Latin C.[46] This textual typology seems to have originated in Spain during the ninth century, soon after a text of the Majority type was exported from northern France and became available there. Its Spanish origins are suggested both by the provenance of its two oldest manuscripts and by a certain textual detail ascribable exclusively to Spain, first brought into attention by Izydorczyk, who highlights the unusual anthroponym for the Good Thief, Lismas, clearly a misreading of Dismas. This name is otherwise only documented in an illustration of a codex better known as the *Girona Beatus* (Girona, Museu de la Catedral, Núm. Inv. 7 11), a finely illustrated manuscript transmitting the *Commentaria in Apocalypsin* of the theologian Beatus of Liébana (†ca. 800) produced around 975 in the monastery of San Salvador de Tábara, in the province of León.[47]

The text of Latin C is further characterized by the presence of the prologue of the second type, as that of the Majority Text, and by new fictional details, such as the inclusion of the name of Pilate's messenger, Romanus, and a suggestive scene that shows Christ dining with Lazarus after resurrecting him.[48] Nevertheless, its most significant innovation is the inclusion of an additional and final chapter, here referred to as Tischendorf's chapter XXVIII, to distinguish it from chapter XXVIII of the Majority Text, which transmits the regular epilogue of the narrative, the so-called *Epistola Pilati*.[49] This additional chapter relates how the Jews were summoned and interrogated by Pilate in their own synagogue after Christ's Resurrection. Pilate asks the high priests to show him their Bible and whether there was any particular passage in it, which could have foreseen the coming of Christ among their people. They confess that indeed they had found a reference in the first book of the Septuagint and that they had understood that the sum of the measurements of Noah's ark, five and a half cubits (instructed to Noah directly from God), was a divine sign indicating that 5,500 years would have to pass from the construction of the Ark of the Covenant to the coming of their Messiah, a computistical chronology derived from Hippolytus of Rome's *Commentarii in Danielem* 4:23–4.[50]

As already mentioned, the two oldest manuscripts transmitting a text of type C are from the Iberian Peninsula. Barcelona, Archivo de la Corona de Aragón, Ripoll 106 (ff. 122r–136r) is a theological miscellany compiled at the Benedictine monastery of Santa Maria de Ripoll during the second half of the ninth century, a time when tight relationships were kept with the late Carolingian scriptoria of northern France, especially those of Fleury, Saint-Germain-des-Prés, and Laon. This cultural ascendant is especially evident in the presence among the Ripoll manuscript collections of codices transcribed in those abbeys or in the transcription in Ripoll manuscripts of texts typical of those areas.[51] A second manuscript, Lisbon, Biblioteca Nacional, Alcobaça CCLXXXV/419 (ff. 175vb–188ra) was produced in the Cistercian Abbey of Santa Maria of Alcobaça in Portugal during the second half of the twelfth century. In the following centuries, the text reached northern France, Prague, and Italy, as indicated by the other five surviving witnesses.[52]

Latin T

Leaving aside Latin B, whose traits are markedly different, by the beginning of the twelfth century there must have been two similar versions of the Latin *Evangelium Nicodemi* circulating in northern France: the Majority Text, which by that time must have been present in the territory with a considerable number of exemplars, and Latin C, imported from Spain, with its new appealing inclusions. A scribe working at one of these scriptoria, allured by the details and anecdotes of both texts and possibly unable to judge which of the two versions was more authoritative, decided to assemble a third composite, or better, "hybrid" text, which fuses together textual features of the Majority Text and Latin C.

This version was first identified by Zbigniew Izydorczyk, who named it after its oldest and most representative witness: Troyes, Médiathèque du Grand Troyes, 1636 (ff. 90r–104v). Troyes 1636 is a composite miscellaneous manuscript written in the twelfth century in an elegant protogothic script for the newly funded Abbey of Clairvaux, established around the year 1115. It contains thirteen lives and passions of various universal and local saints and martyrs.[53]

Two of the most evident characteristics of Latin T are found in its prologue of the second type inherited from the Majority Text, although its readings are considerably more unstable. Indeed, the first is a scribal error, which transfigures the year of the Passion of Christ from the regular *anno nonodecimo* (the nineteenth year) of the reign of the Emperor Tiberius – that is, AD 33 – into the ostensibly corrupted *anno nonagesimo* (ninetieth year) – that is, AD 104. Its second feature is the inclusion of an additional sentence which allegedly ascribes the commission of the first translation of the original Hebrew gospel into Latin to the Emperor Theodosius I, known as "the Great" (†395). This clause is absent in the Majority Text, Latin B, and Latin C. It survives solely in manuscripts pertaining to Latin T and, consequently, in all the vernacular translations deriving from it.

> Factum est in anno nonagesimo imperii Tyberii Cesaris imperatoris Romanorum et Herodis filii Herodis regis Galilee anno nonagesimo principatus eius octauo Kalendas Aprilis quod est uicesima prima die mensis Martii consulatu filii Vellionis anno quarto ducentesimo secundo Olimpiadis sub principatu sacerdotum Iudaeorum Ioseph Anne et Cayphe post crucem et passionem Domini Nostri Ihesu Christi hystoriatus est Nichodemus acta Saluatoris ad principes sacerdotum et reliquos Iudeorum. Ipse Nichodemus scripsit litteris hebraicis. Theodosius autem Magnus imperator fecit ea transferri de hebreo in latinum.[54]

> (It happened in the ninetieth year of the Emperor Tiberius, ruler of the Romans, and of Herod, son of Herod, king of Galilee, in the ninetieth year of his leadership, on the eighth calends of April, which is the twenty-first day of March, during the consulate of the son of Vellio, in the fourth year of the two hundred and second Olympiad, under the leadership of the Jewish priests Joseph, Annas, and Caiphas, that Nicodemus documented what happened after the Crucifixion and Passion of the Lord, the Deed of the Saviour, of the high priests and of the rest of the Jews. This same Nicodemus wrote it in Hebrew letters, then the Emperor Theodosius the Great had it translated from Hebrew into Latin.)

In general terms, it may be asserted that whereas the redactor of Latin T draws extensively on Latin C throughout the *Acta Pilati*, he restores the *Descensus Christi ad inferos* from the Majority Text. This is possibly because its narrative is more complete and exhaustive than that of Latin C, which towards the end of the pseudo gospel becomes considerably abridged. The text of Latin C is retained again in the epilogue of the apocryphon, as all the manuscripts of Latin T transmit Tischendorf's chapter XXVIII.

Latin T seems to have originated in northern France (possibly in an area between Reims and Paris) in the first half of the twelfth century and to have circulated there for almost two centuries before being disseminated and copied throughout northern Germany, as the provenance of its other sixteen copies indicate.[55] Although it is a secondary, considerably smaller tradition, T has left a remarkable vernacular legacy. Beside *Niðrstigningar saga*, whose text was composed in the turn of the thirteenth century and therefore represents the oldest (though not verbatim) surviving translation of T, its text underlies, roughly in this chronological order, Old French, Old Catalan, Middle English, Old Swedish, Middle Low German, Middle Dutch, Early New High German, and Welsh translations and adaptations of the pseudo gospel.[56] Latin T was translated into Old French in the thirteenth century, and its text survives in three manuscripts from the thirteenth to the fifteenth century.[57] An Old Catalan paraphrase of Latin T is embedded into a poem on the Passion of Christ entitled *E la mira car tot era ensems*, transmitted in a manuscript from the second half of the fourteenth century.[58] The Old French translation was subsequently employed for the composition of two Middle English prose translations: the first is preserved in a manuscript written at the end of the fifteenth century and the second in the editio princeps of the text dated 1507.[59] Variant readings of Latin T are also found in the so-called Middle English *Stanzaic Gospel of Nicodemus*, preserved today in London in four manuscripts from the first half of the fifteenth century.[60] Indebted to Latin T is also the Old Swedish translation, which survives in three manuscripts from the end of the fourteenth to the beginning of the sixteenth century.[61] The considerable presence of manuscripts transmitting Latin T in northern Germany gave birth to a Middle Low German prose version, extant in four manuscripts from the middle of the fifteenth to the first decade of the sixteenth century.[62] One of the four Middle Dutch translations of the *Evangelium Nicodemi* is clearly derived from T. Its text, only recently identified by Werner J. Hoffmann and designated as D, is transmitted in two manuscripts from the end of the fifteenth to the beginning of the sixteenth century.[63] The text of Latin T also underlies a single Modern High German undated translation, which survives in the first German printed edition of the text, which was published several times during the sixteenth century.[64] Finally, a Welsh translation of Latin T is extant in a manuscript copied between the fourth quarter of the eighteenth century and the first quarter of the nineteenth century.[65]

The cause of the remarkable fortune of Latin T may reasonably be its additional textual features and anecdotes, which mould the original plot making it all the more exhaustive and therefore engaging to audiences. Consequently, in spite of having circulated less widely, on account of these additions, its narrative might have been considered more complete and even more authoritative than that transmitted by the Majority Text.

Iceland

The earliest evidence of the dissemination and knowledge of the *Evangelium Nicodemi* in medieval Scandinavia is represented by an Old Norse translation and adaptation of the Latin text that came to be known as *Niðrstigningar saga*, or "The Story of the Descent."[66] As promptly clarified by its title, the Old Norse text includes only the second section of the apocryphon, the *Descensus Christi ad inferos*, and begins with Carinus and Leucius's narration (chapter XVIII.1) three paragraphs after the actual beginning of the *Descensus* (chapters XVII.1, XVII.2, and XVII.3). Consequently, the text of the *Acta Pilati* is entirely omitted. Nevertheless, the Norse compiler seems to have had access to a manuscript transmitting the entire text of the Latin *Evangelium Nicodemi*, proven by the presence of readings typical of a prologue of the second type, which in *Niðrstigningar saga* is anaphorically appended to the narrative of the Harrowing of Hell.[67]

Niðrstigningar saga survives in five Icelandic manuscripts. The four medieval codices – AM 645 4to (ff. 51v–55v) from the years 1220–50, AM 623 4to (ff. 1r–5v) from around 1325, AM 233 a fol. (28ra–28vb) from 1350 to 1360, and AM 238 V fol. written between 1400 and 1500 – are all housed in Copenhagen at Den Arnamagnæanske Samling. Reykjavík, Landsbókasafn Íslands, JS 405 8vo (ff. 2r–10r) written between 1780 and 1791, is the sole modern copy to transmit the medieval text. The place of origin and possible date of composition of *Niðrstigningar saga* have been subject to controversial debate in previous scholarship. On account of some alleged "Norwegianisms" of the text, Eugen Mogk, Didrik Arup Seip, and Hans Bekker-Nielsen have sought to prove that the text of *Niðrstigningar saga* was compiled in twelfth-century Norway.[68] Nevertheless, this theory has been subsequently disregarded, as the words in questions were either misreadings present in Unger's transcription of the oldest surviving witness of the text, AM 645 4to, in *Niðrstigningar saga* I[69] or were archaic scribal practices, dating to the beginning of the thirteenth century, still in use in Icelandic manuscripts.[70]

On the other hand, Magnús Már Lárusson pointed out that the surviving manuscripts of *Niðrstigningar saga* are exclusively Icelandic and that this may be taken as evidence for the possible place of origin of the text. Without giving reasonable evidence for his suggestion, he further maintained that Jón Ögmundarson of Hólar (†1122), the first bishop of the northern diocese, may have been the compiler of the text; in this connection, he recalled Jón's famous erudition and his reputation as one of the first translators of hagiographical literature into Icelandic.[71] Otto Gschwantler and Ian J. Kirby have also relied on Magnús Már Lárusson's unfounded hypothesis for the dating of the Old Norse text to the first two decades of the twelfth century.[72] However, as shall be seen, evidence of the composition, dissemination, and fruition of *Niðrstigningar saga* are all unambiguously Icelandic.

The text of *Niðrstigningar saga* has been hitherto related and compared to the Majority Text of the Latin tradition.[73] Nevertheless, despite the overall agreement of readings, lexicon, and style, the Majority Text does not fully represent the Old Norse rendition, which instead seems to share important readings with the text of Latin T. As mentioned above, Latin T was in all probability not available in Europe before the twelfth century, as indicated by the complete absence of surviving copies – both in its direct Latin tradition and in its indirect vernacular transmission. *Niðrstigningar saga* consequently stands today as the oldest vernacular translation of T and may owe its existence to one of the Icelandic clerics studying or travelling through France in the second half of the twelfth century.[74]

During the time of composition of *Niðrstigningar saga*, apart from a copy of Latin T, from which the *Niðrstigningar saga* is derived, Iceland also owned an exemplar of the Majority Text. This is today transmitted only fragmentarily in Reykjavík, Þjóðminjasafn Íslands, 921, a single double-column leaf written in Iceland during the thirteenth century, which was only recently fortuitously gathered from a book binding.[75] This was not the text employed by the Icelandic compiler, but it is plausible that he – much like other European scribes engaging in the translation of the apocryphon – was acquainted with the Majority Text and nevertheless preferred T on account of its textual features and thoroughness in the description of events.

The second section of this book offers a semidiplomatic edition of the two redactions of *Niðrstigningar saga*. An older version represented by AM 645 4to, which, despite a considerable degree of textual corruption, was chosen as *codex optimus* on account of its remarkable early age and, more importantly, because it is the sole surviving medieval manuscript transmitting the text in its entirety. The apparatus of the edited text includes all the variant readings of three manuscripts pertaining to the older redaction, namely, AM 623 4to, AM 233 a fol., and JS 405 8vo. The second, considerably younger redaction of *Niðrstigningar saga* is edited on the basis of AM 238 V fol. alone, whose text underwent a second meticulous revision based on another Latin exemplar of the *Evangelium Nicodemi* transmitting a text of the Majority type. Latin and Icelandic variant texts have been assigned the chapters and paragraphs numbers given by Hack C.

Kim to the *Codex Einsidlensis* in order to facilitate immediate confrontations of the texts.[76]

A second independent Old Norse translation of the Latin *Evangelium Nicodemi* survives in Copenhagen, Den Arnamagnæanske Samling, AM 655 XXVII 4to (ff. 6r–9v), a much-neglected homiliary written around 1300. The text was first identified by Hallgrímur J. Ámundason in 1994 and was only recently mentioned by Stephen Pelle in his article on the Latin sources of two Icelandic homilies transmitted in that manuscript.[77] The text in AM 655 XXVII 4to does not share any textual feature with *Niðrstigningar saga*, as the extant translation exclusively embraces the section of the *Acta Pilati* that reports the story of Joseph of Arimathea. This relates to Joseph's arrest and imprisonment on behalf of the Jews for having buried the body of Christ and to his subsequent, miraculous release from prison, which was accomplished by Christ himself.[78] Although all possible collations of their readings are hindered by the fact that no portion of the translation in AM 655 XXVII 4to overlaps with the text of *Niðrstigningar saga*, in reasoning with purely stylistic and textual evidence, the two texts seem to be unrelated.[79] Extracts of the *Evangelium Nicodemi* are often found embedded in homiliaries, and the reason for the insertion of this section of the *Acta Pilati* into AM 655 XXVII 4to may be ascribable to its extracanonical nature. The story of Joseph of Arimathea is indeed one of the most borrowed passages of the Latin text, and it is often found interwoven into homilies, either quoted verbatim or adopted to various degrees into a different narrative.[80]

In reasoning with the age of the first surviving Latin manuscripts in Scandinavian soil and that of the first vernacular translations, the *Evangelium Nicodemi* seems to have been imported to Iceland between the end of the twelfth and the beginning of the thirteenth centuries, whereas evidence of its fruition in continental Scandinavia post-dates the Icelandic texts of more than a century.[81] An Old Danish *knittel* verse adaptation of a Middle Low German original, which displays features of the Majority type, survives in a single manuscript written in the Lund area around 1315.[82] As seen above, the Old Swedish translation transmits readings typical of Latin T and was compiled at Vadstena Abbey during the last decades of the fourteenth century.[83] There currently seems to be no direct or indirect evidence of the circulation of the vernacular *Evangelium Nicodemi* in Norway, and although it is highly likely that the text was also known in some vernacular form during Middle Ages, supposed Old Norwegian translations of the *Evangelium Nicodemi* remain to present only a matter of speculation.[84]

Besides *Niðrstigningar saga*, whose text enjoyed considerable circulation and influence throughout the Icelandic Middle Ages and beyond, the core narrative of the *Evangelium Nicodemi* was also the subject of a poetical exercise on the verge of Reformation. A sixteenth-century poetic version of the pseudo gospel known as *Niðurstigningarvísur* ("Verses of the Descent"), mainly ascribed to Jón Arason (†1550), the last Catholic bishop of Iceland, survives in a remarkably large number of postmedieval manuscripts.[85] It has been noted that the affinities between the *Niðurstigningarvísur* and the *Evangelium Nicodemi* are exclusively thematic, rather than of pure textual nature. On the other hand, the *vísur* (short for *Niðurstigningarvísur*) may well have been influenced by the text of *Niðrstigningar saga*, but these relations are extremely difficult to determine, since there seems to be no direct verbal similarities between the two works. The single exception is a reference at the end of stanza 27 – "upp ǻ krossin ormuren skreid / ok andlatz beid / salina suelgia uilldi"[86] ("up on the Cross the serpent crept / and for death abode / willing to swallow the soul") – which describes Satan crawling up the Cross in the shape of a serpent, on the verge of swallowing up the soul of Christ. This scene corresponds to the fourth interpolation of *Niðrstigningar saga*, which describes the entrapment of Satan on the cross.[87] In this connection, Finnur Jónsson has reasonably advanced that the text of the *Niðurstigningarvísur* does not necessarily revert to that of *Niðrstigningar saga* in terms of direct textual borrowings and that the scenes of the *vísur* presumably indebted to *Niðrstigningar saga* may in fact simply be based on distant memories of the text.[88]

After the Reformation, the *Evangelium Nicodemi* continued to enjoy considerable popularity in Iceland, as witnessed by two translations into Modern Icelandic, which have been only recently investigated by Kirsten Wolf. A younger rendition was compiled by Magnús Grímsson (†1860), the celebrated first collector of Icelandic folktales in the middle of the nineteenth century, whereas an older translation, which survives in two redactions, A and B, dates from the eighteenth century.[89] Both translations seem to have been compiled anew from an unknown exemplar of the Latin *Evangelium Nicodemi* and are consequently unrelated to *Niðrstigningar saga*.

2 The Manuscript Tradition of *Niðrstigningar saga*

Niðrstigningar saga is transmitted in four medieval Icelandic manuscripts and fragments housed at the Arnamagnæan Collection of Copenhagen: AM 645 4to (ff. 51v–55v), from 1220 to 1250; AM 623 4to (ff. 1r–5v), from around 1325; AM 233 a fol. (28ra–28vb), from 1350 to 1370; and AM 238 V fol., from 1400 to 1500. The medieval text has also survived in a single postmedieval Icelandic manuscript, JS 405 4to (ff. 2r–10r), from 1780 to 1791, housed in Reykjavík at the National and University Library of Iceland as part of the Jón Sigurðsson Collection. (See Figure 1.) The description of the manuscripts is followed by a listing of their items, giving modern foliation, rubrics, incipit, explicit, and reference to relevant and most recent editions.[1]

AM 645 4to

AM 645 4to, dating to the second quarter of the thirteenth century, is among the earliest medieval miscellanies to transmit Latin hagiographical texts in Icelandic translation. *Niðrstigningar saga* is extant in full in its oldest known textual form; AM 645 4to also represents the oldest surviving witness transmitting the first redactions of the *vitae* and *passiones* of the apostles Andrew, Bartholomew, James the Greater, and Paul, as well as those of Saints Clement of Rome and Martin of Tours.[2] The lives of Peter and Matthew, notably some of the first devotional accounts to be translated into Old Norse, are found here in secondary textual forms.[3]

AM 645 4to is a parchment manuscript consisting of sixty-six leaves, measuring approximately 21.1 by 13.7 centimetres, composed of two distinct codicological units. The first unit comprises folios 1r–42v, with twenty-three to thirty-four lines to the page; it begins defectively with the *Jarteinabók Þorláks*

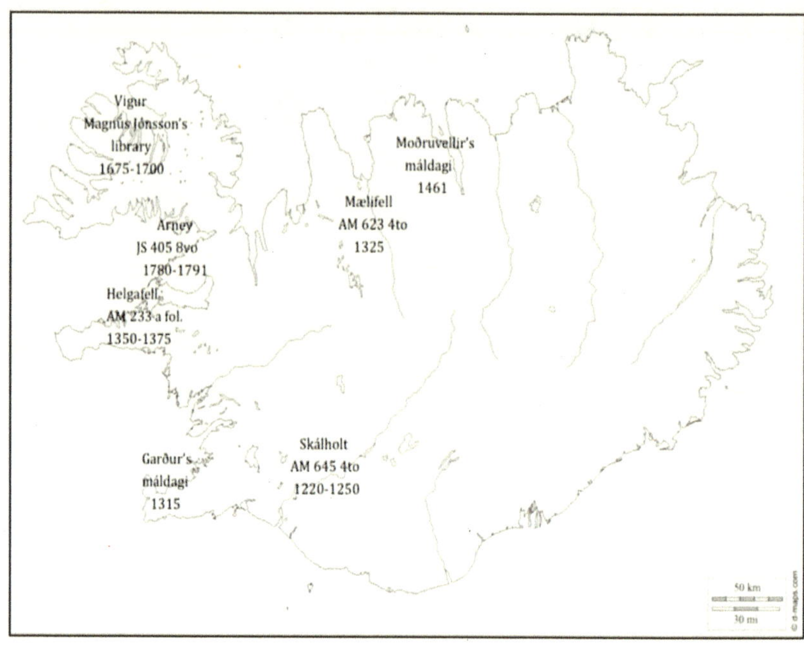

Figure 1. Mapping of the manuscripts of *Niðrstigningar saga*

byskups in forna and covers up to two thirds of *Andréss saga postola*. The second section includes folios 43r–66v with thirty to thirty-five lines per page; it preserves the remnant text of *Andréss saga postola* and ends defectively with *Marteins saga byskups*. The manuscript is in good condition overall, although in several places, most notably on folios 52v and 53r (in correspondence to *Niðrstigningar saga*), its text is almost illegible due to wear. The lower margins are frequently damaged, the upper margins are torn, especially on folios 17, 19–22, and 24, and there are holes in folios 22 and 41. The initials are written with black ink in the first unit and in red ink in the second.

The greatest study of the manuscript was undertaken by Anne Holtsmark, who recognized the hands of three scribes, A, B, and C, in its compilation. The first scribe (A) wrote the first codicological unit, which includes the *Jarteinabók Þorláks byskups in forna* (ff. 1r–11v), *Klements saga* (ff. 11v–24v), *Pétrs saga postola* (ff. 25r–30r), *Jakobs saga postola* (ff. 30r–33r), *Barthólómeuss saga postola* (ff. 33r–35v), *Matheuss saga postola* (ff. 35v–41r), and *Andréss saga postola* (ff. 41r–43r). Two hands are recognizable within the second section. The first (B) transcribed *Páls saga postola* (ff. 43r–51v) and

Niðrstigningar saga (ff. 51v–55v), and the second (C) transcribed the entire *Marteins saga byskups* (ff. 55v–66v). The writing of C changes from that of B in terms of the breadth of letters, which become progressively more spaced, and possibly in the adoption of a different use of accents.[4] Holtsmark's conclusions disagree with Carl R. Unger's first description of the manuscript. He believed that the two units were written by two scribes. Her conclusions have more recently been questioned by Odd Einar Haugen, who, in his survey of the scribal practices of AM 645 4to, also identifies a single hand within its second codicological unit.[5]

The script of AM 645 4to is a "praegothica" with few recognizable Anglo-Saxon features, such as the usage of insular *f* and insular *y*, which is exclusive to the second section of the codex (and makes its first appearance in Iceland around the year 1200), and finally *ð*, which is used indiscriminately in initial and central positions.[6] Other distinguishing features are the use of the *m* rune for the word "maþr" ("man"), the cross symbol (+) for the word "cross" ("cross"), and the redundant use of Latin abbreviations for Icelandic words – for instance, *sīt* "sicut" ("as") for "svá," *dīx* "dixit" ("said") for "sagði," *fr.* "fratres" ("brother") for "broðir," and *d.* "dominus" ("Lord") for "drottinn."

The first scholar to date the manuscript was Kristian Kålund, who suggested that it was compiled during the first half of the thirteenth century.[7] A more thorough survey was undertaken by Harald Spehr and Hreinn Benediktsson, who dated the first codicological unit to approximately 1220,[8] and by Didrik Arup Seip, who dated the second unit to the second quarter of the thirteenth century.[9] Anne Holtsmark mainly agreed with their views and suggested the diocese of Skálholt as place of origin.[10]

The first section of AM 645 4to transmitting the so-called *Jarteinabók Þorláks byskups in forna* ("The Ancient Miracle Collection of Bishop Þorlákr," item 1 of the codex) may be a direct copy of the very codex containing the collection of miracles of Saint Þorlákr. This was first collected and then read aloud before a great crowd at the Althing of 1199 at the request of Bishop Páll Jónsson, nephew and successor of Þorlákr at the see of Skálholt.[11] This identification is suggested in miracle forty-one of the *Jarteinabók in forna*, which serves as a small epilogue to the forty miracles allegedly performed by Saint Þorlákr before 1199: "Á Alþingi þessu enu sama lét Páll byskup ráða upp at bœn manna jarteinir ens sæla Þorláks byskups, þær er hér ero skrifaðar á þessi bók"[12] ("At that same Althing, Bishop Páll had the miracles of the blessed Bishop Þorlákr, which are here written in this book, read aloud at the request of people"). As recorded in the Icelandic annals, the year in question was 1199, when after the public declamation of Þorlákr's miracles, Bishop Páll instituted the "Þorláksmessa" ("Þorlákr's mass") to be celebrated on 23 December. In AM 645 4to, six other miracles follow miracle forty-one, suggesting that the antigraph of AM 645 4to was concluded soon after 1199, possibly during the winter of 1200.[13]

The provenance of the manuscript remains obscure, although a note on a slip records the oral account of Guðbrandur Björnsson (†1733), son of Björn Magnússon (†1697), *sýslumaður* ("governor") of Munkaþverá (northern Iceland) between 1662 and 1688, who remembers that the volume was preserved in the monastery when he was a child:[14]

> Postula sögur, 4to. med æde gamla og vanda skrift seiger Gudbrandr Biörnsson vered hafa i sinu Barndæmi ä Munkaþverä, og hafi þær einginn lesid gietad. firi utan einn mann þar ï Eyafirdi. Þad eru, liklegast þær eg ä.[15]

> (*Postola sögur* in 4to [format] with a very old and difficult script. Guðbrandur Björnsson says it was in Munkaþverá during his childhood and that nobody was able to read from it except for a man there in Eyjafjörður. These are most probably those [leaves] in my possession.)

Content of AM 645 4to

1 1r–11v "oc ętloþo at moca þann dag allan … / … oc enn sęla Thorlac biscop." Oldest (defective) redaction of the *Jarteinabók Þorláks byskups in forna*. [*Biskupa sögur*, vol. 2, 103–40; Jón Helgason, ed., *Byskupa sǫgur*, vol. 13.2, 121–57; *A Book of Miracles*, 1r–11v; *Isländska handskriften 645*, 1–33.]

2 11v–24v "Iulius hét inn fyrste keisare yfer ǫllom heime … / … hverso hann of mętte sva lengi føzlolaust of lifa þar." Oldest (defective) recension of *Klements saga*. [Helen Carron, ed., *Clemens saga*, 2–52; Dietrich Hofmann, ed., *Die Legende von Sankt Clemens*, 236–75; *A Book of Miracles*, 11v–24v; *Isländska handskriften 645*, 33–74; *Postola sögur*, 126–51.]

3 25r–30r "manna. Siþan gerþi Petrus fǫr braut af Iorsalalande … / … þeim er meþ Feþr oc Helgom Anda liver oc riker oc allar alder allda." Abridged (defective) version of the second redaction of *Pétrs saga postola*. [Foote, "A Fragment of Text in AM 235 fol."; *A Book of Miracles*, 25r–30r; *Isländska handskriften 645*, 74–90; *Postola sögur*, 201–11.]

4 30r–33r Rubric "Passio Sancti Jacobi apostoli." "Iacobus postole Domini Nostri Ihesu Christi frater Iohannis evangeliste … / … þess er vegr er oc dyrþ of allar alder allda." Oldest redaction of *Jakobs saga postola* (*ins eldra*). [*A Book of Miracles*, 30r–33r; *Isländska handskriften 645*, 90–9; *Postola sögur*, 524–9.]

5 33r–35v Rubric "Passio Bartholomei apostoli." "Indialønd ero .iii. eitt þat er ligr hia Blalande … / … enn siþan fór hann til Goþs þess er liver

ok riker of allar allder allda. Amen." Oldest (defective) redaction of *Barthólómeuss saga postola*. [*A Book of Miracles*, 33r–35v; *Isländska handskriften 645*, 99–108; *Postola sögur*, 757–62.]

6 35v–41r Rubric "Passio sancti Mathei apostoli." "Tveir fiolcunger menn voro a Blalande Zareos oc Arfaxáþ ... / ... meþ Helgom Anda huggar⟨a⟩ nu oc ei of allar allder alda." Second redaction of *Matheuss saga postola*. [Ólafur Halldórsson, ed., *Mattheus saga postula*, 4–83; *A Book of Miracles*, 35v–41r; *Isländska handskriften 645*, 108–24; *Postola sögur*, 813–23.]

7 41r–43r Rubric "Passio sancti Andree apostoli." "Heilagr postole Andreas fór of alt Gricland ... / ... ðeim er hann georði i borganne at vilia Guþs." Oldest (defective) redaction of *Andréss saga postola*. [*A Book of Miracles*, 41r–43r; *Isländska handskriften 645*, 124–30; *Postola sögur*, 349–53.]

8 40r–51v Rubric "Sancti Pauli apostoli." "Saulus var grimr viþ lęrisveina Christz oc toc hann rit de principibus Iudeorum ... / ... meþ sigri til Guþs svasem sact er i annari søgu." Oldest redaction of *Páls saga postola*. [*A Book of Miracles*, 40r–51v; *Postola sögur*, 216–36.]

9 51v–55v Rubric "Niþrstigningar saga." "Karinus oc Leutius fratres syner Simeonis ens Gamla segia sva fra niþrstigningo Crisz ... / ... oc varþ þar monnom alldat umb per omnia secula seculorum. Amen." Older redaction of *Niðrstigningar saga*. [Present volume, 133–53; Odd Einar Haugen, ed., "Niðrstigningar saga," 250–6; Odd Einar Haugen, ed., *Stamtre og tekstlandskap*, vol. 2, 17–28; *A Book of Miracles*, 51v–55v; *Heilagra manna sögur*, vol. 2, 1–8.]

10 55v–66v Rubric "Sancti Martini episcopi." "Martinus var æzcaþr af Ungara lande enn hann var føddr a Langbarþa lande ... / ... þat er þegia er betra enn fra at segia." Oldest (defective) redaction of *Marteins saga byskups*. [*A Book of Miracles*, 55v–66v; *Heilagra manna sögur*, vol. 1, 554–74.]

AM 623 4to

On account of its conservatism in the script and of the fairly early dates of the texts transmitted, AM 623 4to in the Arnamagnæan Collection in Copenhagen, dating to around 1325, seems to be a copy of a remarkably older exemplar. Among its texts, especially worthy of note, are the *fabella* of Saint Alexis, which is preserved here in *codex unicus*, and the *passio* of the Forty Armenian Martyrs, which is otherwise transmitted only in AM 655 4to fragment XXIII 4to, dating from the middle of the thirteenth century. The text of *Niðrstigningar saga* is transmitted fragmentarily as the first item of the codex. The lost beginning due to a lacuna in the manuscript corresponds to fifty lines in AM 645 4to and amounts to around one-fifth of the entire text.[16]

AM 623 4to is a parchment manuscript consisting of thirty-one leaves measuring approximately 16.8 by 12.4 centimetres, beginning and ending defectively. There are thirty to thirty-five lines to the page. The text becomes progressively more dense towards the end of the codex. The parchment is marred with small holes (especially on ff. 10, 15, 23, and 30), possibly due to mildew. The lower margin of folio 31 is trimmed. The initials are written with red ink.

The whole manuscript was written by a single scribe in a clear protogothic script. Finnur Jónsson has recognized a different hand in five lines towards the end of the manuscript, on folio 30r/26–30 (in correspondence to *Sjau sofanda saga*), and Hreinn Benediktsson has noticed how in these lines the script seems to display more distinct gothic features.[17] AM 623 4to was dated to the thirteenth century by Kristian Kålund and Carl R. Unger.[18] Finnur Jónsson held AM 623 4to to be compiled after 1250 but also noticed how, on account of the conservatism in the script, it should be a direct copy of a much older antigraph.[19] Subsequently, Hreinn Benediktsson also shifted the date of composition to the middle of the thirteenth century.[20] Today the widely accepted date of composition is the one suggested by the register of the *ONP*, which, following an oral communication of Ole Widding from 1984, dates the manuscript to around the year 1325.[21]

AM 623 4to may have connections with one of the manuscripts available in the impressive library of the cloister of Möðruvellir as recorded in the *máldagi* ("inventory") of 1461. Among the manuscripts written in the vernacular *þessar norrænu bækr* ("these Norse books"), the inventory also mentions a codex transmitting *Niðrstigningar saga* along with a translation the *Septem dormientes* (*Sjau sofanda saga*), whose text otherwise survives today only as item 6 of AM 623 4to.[22]

> þetta a einne bok. laurencius saga. teodorij saga. johanes oc pauli. mag(n)us. halvardz. marie magdalene oc marte. gesta saluatoris. septem dormiencivm. jterata passio christi. barbare. luce. s(ancta) agnes. sancte juliane. sancte eusstake.[23]

> (This in one book: *Lárentíuss saga erkidjákns*, *Theódórs saga*, *Tveggja postola saga Jóns ok Páls*†, *Magnúss saga Eyjajarls*, *Hallvarðs saga*, *Mǫrtu saga ok Maríu Magðalenu*, *Gesta Salvatoris* [*Niðrstigningar saga*], *Septem dormientes* [*Sjau sofanda saga*], another [text] on the *Passio Domini* [possibly *Flagellatio Crucis*, part of the so-called *Kross saga*], *Barbǫru saga*, *Lúcíu saga*, *Agnesar saga*, *Júlíǫnu saga*†, and *Plácíduss saga*.)
>
> † Refers to a text that has not survived.

The presence of this high variety of texts in a single manuscript is possibly due to the great availability of religious writings at Möðruvellir scriptorium, where new miscellanies were compiled from older manuscripts of different provenance.

On the history of AM 623 4to, Árni Magnússon notes on folio 25 of his catalogue, AM 435 a 4to, that the manuscript was owned by Björn Þorleifsson (†1710), the Bishop of Hólar, who received it from the Provost Ari Guðmundsson (†1707) of Mælifell in Skagafjörður:[24] "4to minori. Codex pervetustus, sed mutilus. Kominn til min fra Mag. Birne Þorleifssyne, enn til hans fra Sera Ara Gudmundzsyne ä Mælefell" ("Very old but defective codex in 4to format. [The codex] has arrived to me from Bishop Björn Þorleifsson, and to him from Reverend Ari Guðmundsson of Mælifell").

Content of AM 623 4to

1 1r–5v "til þin. Ec emc til þess settr at lita hvers manz hag … / … Per omnia benedictus Deus. Amen." Older (defective) redaction of *Niðrstigningar saga*. [Present volume, 133–53 (variant readings in the apparatus); Odd Einar Haugen, ed., *Stamtre og tekstlandskap*, vol. 2, *Tekster og tabellar*, 29–36; *Helgensagaer*, 9–14; *Heilagra manna sögur*, vol. 2, 9–14.]

2 6r–15r "Domitianus keisari framþi ena mesto styriolld nest eptir Neronem … / … Nu varþveiti oss Guþ Almattigr sa er lifir oc rikir meþ feþr oc helgom anda of alldir allda. Amen." Third redaction of *Jóns saga postola*. [*Helgensagaer*, 9–25; *Postola sögur*, 455–65.]

3 15r–19r Rubric "Passio .xl. militum." "Sa varþ atburþr at þvi ⟨er⟩ men segia at tiþ Licinii konongs … / … Nicallus. Pricus. Sacerdón. Edicius. Þeodulus. Mellitus. Gaius. Valerianus." Oldest redaction of *XL riddara saga*. [*Heilagra manna sögur*, vol. 2, 211–19.]

4 19r–26r Rubric "Passio Blasii eposcopi." "Licinius het konungr í Austrriki sa var magr Constantinus ens mikla … / … þess er meþ Feþr oc Helgom Anda lifir oc rikir of allar alldir allda. Amen." Second redaction of *Blasíuss saga*. [*Helgensagaer*, 39–47; *Heilagra manna sögur*, vol. 1, 256–64/8 and 265/29–269.]

5 26r–29r Rubric "Febella Alexis confessoris." "A dǫgom Arkadii oc Honorii keisara var einn gǫfogr maþr … / … þeim se vęgr oc velldi lof oc riki in secula seculorum. Amen." Oldest and only redaction of *Alexíss saga*. [*Helgensagaer*, 47–53; *Heilagra manna sögur*, vol. 1, 23–7.]

6 29r–31v Rubric "VII dormiencium." "A þeim dǫgom er Decius var keisari þa for hann i margar borgir … / … Oc allir undraþosc oc kendi engi hann. En þo treis." Oldest (defective) redaction of *Sjau sofanda saga*. [*Helgensagaer*, 54–9; *Heilagra manna sögur*, vol. 2, 236–40.]

AM 233 a fol.

Along with the *vitae* of John the Baptist, Mary, and six female saints, AM 233 a fol., preserved at the Arnamagnæan Collection in Copenhagen, dating to the third quarter of the fourteenth century, also transmits fragments of the older redaction of *Niðrstigningar saga* alongside the legend known as *Inventio Crucis* (also part of *Kross saga*), which relates the finding of the True Cross in Jerusalem. Approximately one-quarter of the original text of *Niðrstigningar saga* survives, corresponding to seventy-five lines in AM 645 4to.[25]

AM 233 a fol. consists of thirty-one double-column leaves measuring approximately 38.5 by 32.4 centimetres, with forty-seven lines per column, and that is all that remains today of the original voluminous manuscript. Folios 4, 5, 6, 9, 10, 13, and 14 (mostly in correspondence to *Maríu saga*) are especially damaged and torn. Folio 4 is composed today of several parchment strips; folios 5, 6, and 10 have been cut apart, and of the original folios 13 and 14, only the upper and lower parts, respectively, remain. There are two lacunae on folio 15 (in correspondence to the end of *Fídesar saga, Spesar ok Karítasar* and the beginning of *Katrínar saga*, which are therefore missing), and another lacuna on folios 27 and 28 (in correspondence to the beginning of *Margrétar saga*). The manuscript is written in a gothic script, and initials are written either in red or green ink. There are a total of six illuminations, including a great illustration depicting either Christ or John the Baptist on folio 1r (at the beginning of *Jóns saga baptista*) and five illuminated initials: *A*, depicting John the Baptist (f. 1v); *D*, with Mary and the Child along with Saint Anne and Joachim (f. 5r); *Þ*, with Fides, Spes, and Caritas and the Emperor Hadrian (f. 15v); *A*, with Mary of Bethany, Martha, and Lazarus (f. 19v); and *K*, depicting Saint Agatha (f. 26).[26]

Three different hands have been recognized: the first scribe wrote folios 1va–12rb – that is, *Jóns saga baptista* and almost the entire *Maríu saga* – and *Niðrstigningar saga* on folios 28ra–29vb. A second, lesser-trained scribe was responsible for the transcription of folios 15–7, while folios 13 and 14, transmitting *Maríu jartegnir*, derive from a separate manuscript, only subsequently bound into AM 233 a fol.[27] Stefán Karlsson dated the section compiled by the first scribe to the middle of the fourteenth century; Ólafur Halldórsson demonstrated that the first hand of AM 233 a fol. is identical with that of the so-called *Skarðsbók Jónsbókar* (AM 350 fol.) from around 1363, while the second hand is possibly the same as the first hand of *Codex Scardensis* (SÁM 1 fol.), dated to the years 1350–75.[28] Both manuscripts were written in the monastery of Helgafell (Snæfellsnes), and on account of these connections, Halldórsson proposed the Augustinian monastery of Helgafell as the possible place of composition.[29]

In terms of date and area of composition and in consideration of the typology of the texts transmitted, AM 233 a fol. shows important similarities to a manuscript transmitting *Niðrstigningar saga* mentioned in the *máldagi* of the parish church of Garður (Suðrness), dating from 1318. A manuscript containing *María saga* along with *Niðrstigningar saga* is recorded among the first (and possibly most precious) possessions of the parish church. It is listed after the livestock and the liturgical vestments, and before all other liturgical books:

> þętta j kuikfie. viij kýr. xij. ær. hundradz hokull. messufot ein. oc hokull vm framm. alltaris stein. mariu sogu ok nidurstigningar sogu. artijda riim. sequentiu bok. oc vorbok ad song. lesturbok vm sumarid. kluckur. iiij. krossa. iiij. mariu skript. thomas lýkneski.[30]

> ("This [much] in cattle: eight cows; twelve ewes; a priest's cope worth one hundred [and twenty ells of wadmal]; one set of liturgical vestments and an additional priest's cope; an altar stone; *María saga* and *Niðrstigningar saga*; a liturgical calendar for the anniversary [of the dedication of the church]; a book with sequences; a gradual for the spring; a lectionary for the summer; four bells; four crosses; a painted image of Mary; a statue of [Saint] Thomas.)

Mary, along with the apostles Thomas and John, was the patron saint of the Church of Garður, where she was consequently held in very high consideration. Holy depictions of her were carefully preserved and contemplated, and her *vita* and miracles were read aloud during public functions throughout the year, most notably on the occasion of her festivity on 15 August.[31] The manuscript transmitting *María saga* and *Niðrstigningar saga* mentioned in the *máldagi* may represent one of the predecessors of AM 233 a fol. This association is plausible because of the geographical proximity of the two manuscripts. AM 233 a fol. was compiled in the area of Helgafell (some 200 kilometres away from Garður) between the years 1350 and 1375, roughly fifty years after the recording of the *María saga* manuscript among the possessions of the Church of Garður.

Content of AM 233 a fol.

1 1va–5ra Rubric "Bref Grim Prests" "Virduligum Herra Runolfi abota i Veri sendir Grimr prestr qveðio Guds sina ok sina sanna vínattu ... / ... Þat lati ser soma oss at veita Almattigr Guð sa er með Feðr ok Helugum Anda lifir ok rikir um endalausar alldir verallda. Amen." Second (defective) redaction of *Jóns saga baptista*, compiled by the priest Grímr Hólmsteinsson (†1298). [Variants of the text are available in *Postola sögur*, 849–52, 873–85, and 925–31.]

2 5ra–12vb Rubric "Her byriar upp lifssǫgu hinar helguztu ok dyruztu Drottningar Meyar cy lifrar ok Guds modir. Fru Sancte Marie hinar milldztu nest Gudi." "Drottníng hímins ok iardar sæl ok dyrdlig mær María moðir Dróttins Ihesu Cristi ... / ... Þessir stafir er ero í nafni Marío segir engillinn merkia." Variant (defective) text of *Maríu saga*. [*MS*, 1–7.] 6ra–12vb "Sialfum Gudi til sæmdar ok hans signadur modir ... / ... þickia i ordi enn sannliga satt i g." Variant text of *Maríu jartegnir*. [*MS*, 243–9, 266–8, 275–6, 291–7, 302–6, 444–5, 521–7, 533–4, 554–5, 598–9.]

3 13ra–14rb "munu þer rikia ... / ... hans modur Marie nu ok at eilifu. Amen." *Maríu jartegnir*. [See item 2 above.]

4 15va–15vb "Þa er um allan heim heilugh kenning gudligs sads runnit med vaxandi milldi kraptaverkanna fra blotum skurðgoða ... / ... boðorð þinn. Enn ór sárum." Younger (defective) redaction of *Fídesar saga, Spesar ok Karítasar*. [Kirsten Wolf, ed., "Saga af Fídes, Spes, Caritas," 56–8; *Heilagra manna sögur*, vol. 1, 369–72.]

5 16ra–19rb "Liberalis heita. Hun kunni margar tungur at skilia ... / ... sa er lifir ok rikir um allar alldir verallda. Amen." Oldest and only (defective) redaction of *Katrínar saga*. [*Heilagra manna sögur*, vol. 1, 401–21.]

6 19va–25vb Rubric "Af Martha." "Hin sæla Martha var gǫfug at kýni enn gǫfgari at godum sidum ... / ... Ok þa er þeir hofðu lengi." Second (defective) redaction of *Mǫrtu saga ok Maríu Magðalenu*. [Natalie Van Deusen, "The Old Norse-Icelandic Legend," 258–301; *Heilagra manna sögur*, vol. 1, 513–51.]

7 26ra "Tak þu heilsu þína. Eptir þat leid hun fra henna at syn himins ... / ... þeim er lifir ok rikir med Fedr ok Syni ok Helgum Anda einn Guð um allar alldir verallda. Amen." Second (defective) redaction of *Agnesar saga*. [*Heilagra manna sögur*, vol. 1, 22.]

8 26ra–27rb Rubric "Her byriar upp sogu sellar Aghattu meyar." "Kuincianus Sikileyiar iarl fretti goða siðu heilagrar Agathe meyiar ... / ... at rikianda Drotni Vorum Ihesu Christo er með Feðr ok Helgum Anda lifir ok rikir einn Guð um allar alldir verallda amen." Second redaction of *Agǫtu saga*. [*Heilagra manna sögur*, vol. 1, 7–13.]

9 27rb Rubric "Prologus firir Margreta sogu." "Siðan er Vór Drottinn Ihesus Christus hafdi til himins stigit til feðrs sins Almattigs sendi hann postola sína ... / ... þa leipti sæl Margret fæti." Older (defective) redaction of *Margrétar saga*. [*Heilagra manna sögur*, vol. 1, 474–6.]

10 28ra–28vb "cipes vestras et elevamini porte eternales ... / ... per omnia benedictus Deus in secula seculorum." Older (defective) redaction of *Niðrstigningar saga*. [Present volume, 133–53 (variant readings in the apparatus); Odd Einar Haugen, ed., *Stamtre og tekstlandskap*, vol. 2, *Tekster og tabellar*, 37–40; *Heilagra manna sögur*, vol. 2, 14–17.]

11 28vb–29vb Rubric "Her hefr upp ok segher fra þvi hverss⟨u⟩ fanzt kross Drottins Vars Ihesu Christz ok fra þeim ufridi er Romveriar giordu kristnu folki um alla verolld." "I þann tíma er lidit var fra higatburd Cristz .cc. vetra var Dioclecianus keisari yfir heimi … / … Nu hefir þu cross þinn latid upp taka til oþurftar mer." Second (defective) redaction of *Kross saga* (*Inventio Crucis*). [Svanhildur Óskarsdóttir, "Universal History in Fourteenth-Century Iceland," 294–5; Mariane Overgaard, ed., *The History of the Cross Tree*, 58; *Heilagra manna sögur*, vol. 1, 301–8.]

AM 238 V fol.

AM 238 V fol. is unquestionably the most obscure witness of *Niðrstigningar saga*, as its history is still unknown. *Niðrstigningar saga* alone is transmitted here in a secondary revised version, and its text amounts to around a third of the original translation, corresponding to ninety-three lines in AM 645 4to.[32] Later in chapter 4, it is argued that the underlying Latin text employed for this correction displays features of the Majority Text rather than the readings typical of the source text Latin T, with which the older redaction of *Niðrstigningar saga* shares several important readings.[33]

AM 238 V fol. is a single parchment leaf measuring approximately 20.5 by 16.8 centimetres, with thirty-nine lines on folio 1r and thirty-six on folio 1v, written in a hybrid Gothic, semicursive script. Carl R. Unger has dated the fragment to the fifteenth century, yet a specific paleographical study on AM 238 V fol., which could help reveal a more precise date of transcription and place of origin, remains a desideratum.[34]

Content of AM 238 V fol.

1 1r–1v "Þessi er Son minn elskuligur vidur þann er mier likadi vel … / … Hann sa þa takn þau er voru i Iorsalaborg ⟨at⟩ Drottin Varn ⟨var⟩ i andlati ok jamskiott." Younger (defective) redaction of *Niðrstigningar saga*. [Present volume, 154–7; Odd Einar Haugen, ed., *Stamtre og tekstlandskap*, vol. 2, 41–5; *Heilagra manna sögur*, vol. 2, *Tekster og tabellar*, 17–20.]

JS 405 8vo

Although it is the only postmedieval manuscript transmitting *Niðrstigningar saga*, JS 405 8vo has a high stemmatic value as a direct copy of a medieval manuscript. Moreover, next to AM 645 4to, it is the only manuscript to transmit the text in its entirety (see Table 1). Evidence that its antigraph may have

Table 1. Extant text of *Niðrstigningar saga* in its manuscripts

	AM 645 4to	AM 623 4to	AM 233 a fol.	AM 238 V fol.	JS 405 8vo
Prologue	x				x
XVIII.1	x				x
XVIII.2	x				x
XVIII.3	x			x	x
XIX.1	x	x		x	x
XIX.2	x	x		x	x
XX.1	x	x		x	x
XX.2	x	x		x	x
XX.3	x	x		x	x
XXI.1	x	x	x	x	x
XXI.2	x	x	x		x
XXI.3	x	x	x		x
XXII.1	x	x			x
XXII.2	x	x			x
XXIII.1	x	x			x
XXIII.2	x	x			x
XXIV.1	x	x			x
XXIV.2	x	x			x
XXIV.3	x	x			x
XXV	x	x	x		x
XXVI	x	x	x		x
XXVII.1	x	x	x		x
XXVII.2	x	x	x		x

been a medieval parchment manuscript is suggested by its first two items: the oldest redaction of *Niðrstigningar saga* and *Viðræða líkams ok sálar*, here titled *Bernharðs leiðsla*, a remarkably old text that is also found in the *Old Norwegian Homily Book* (AM 619 4to, ff. 75v–78r) from around the year 1200, where it is wrongly entitled *Visio Sancti Pauli apostoli*.[35]

JS 405 8vo is a paper manuscript consisting of 104 pages measuring approximately 16 by 9.8 centimetres, with twenty-four to twenty-eight lines per page. Its text was written in Arney (western Iceland) in a neo-Gothic script by a single scribe, Ólafur Jónsson (†1800), between 1780 and 1791; it is in remarkably good condition.[36] The manuscript was later owned by Þorvaldur Sívertsen (†1863) from Hrappsey (an island not far from Arney), as recorded on folio 1: "Bókin er frá Þorvaldison af Sivertsen í Hrappsey" ("The book belongs to Þorvaldur Sívertsen in Hrappsey").[37] In his introductory colophon on folio 1r, Ólafur writes that the collection was compiled from old, torn, and possibly loose leaves containing various sagas and texts:

> Einn litill sagnapese og byriar á Nidurstigningu Drottins Vors Jesu Kristi til helvitis og um nafnid Jesu. Samannskrifadur af gǒmlum og funum sagnablǒdum epter þvi sem riettast hefur ordid af Olafe Jónssyne á Arney árid 1780.
>
> (A little collection of sagas, which begins with the story of the Descent into Hell of Our Lord, Jesus Christ [*Niðrstigningar saga*], and [a text] about the name Jesus [Bernard of Clairvaux, *Sermones in Cantica Canticorum*, *Sermo* XV]. Compiled from old and decaying leaves of sagas as precisely as possible by Ólafur Jónsson in Arney in 1780.)

After the translation of some miscellaneous narrative material, which includes extracts from the German *Volksbücher*, Apuleius's *Asinus aureus*, and Isidore of Seville's *De aetatibus hominum* (all possibly translated from Danish), Ólafur Jónsson also translated about a third of Hans Hanssen Skonning's *Collegium philosophorum*, a 1636 collection of philosophical apothegms and anecdotes concerning the lives of Greek and Latin philosophers with the addition of some medieval and early modern thinkers in Aarhus, as he states in the concluding lines of JS 405 8vo, on folio 103v:

> Ei hef eg sied meir af þessari bók, og er þad inntakid ur 12 hennar fyrstu kapitulum, enn hun hefr inne ad halda 38 kapitula. Bokin er samanntekin ur griskum og latinskum sagnameisturum af Hans Hanssyne Skonning \`i hans Collegio Philosophorum/ bygjandi til Aarhus anno 1636. Er svo þetta sticki endurklórad á Arney árid 1791 af Olafe Jónssyne.
>
> (I have not seen more from this book, and this is the summary of its first twelve chapters, but it contains thirty-eight chapters. The book is assembled from Greek and Latin authors, [extracted] from Hans Hanssen Skonning in his *Collegium philosophorum*, published in Aarhus in the year 1636. This collection was transcribed in Arney in the year 1791 by Ólafur Jónsson.)

In a letter dated 28 May 1728 and addressed to the descendants of Páll Vídalín (†1727), co-author of his *Jarðabók* ("Land Register"), Árni Magnússon claims to be repaid a debt contracted with him by Páll. He therefore compiles an inventory of eighteen books still in Páll's family's possession that he would like to acquire in order to extinguish the debt. Several manuscripts in Páll's collection once belonged to his father-in-law, Magnús Jónsson (†1702), a wealthy landowner in Vigur. Item 6 in Árni's list is a manuscript written by Priest Magnús Ketilsson (†1709), a relative of Magnús Jónsson (who was later chaplain in Desjarmýri) who worked on his estate as a scribe,[38] that begins with *Niðrstigningar saga* and, like JS 405 8vo, also contains fragments of *Bernharðs leiðsla*.[39]

> Bök i qvarto, med hende S^{ra} Magnuss Ketelssonar. þar ä er Nidurstigningar Historia Christi, Duggals leidsla, Bernhardi leidsla fragm: Formäle til Ste Margretar Sǒgu, drauma rädningar, Tungls alldrar, Nockud ur Blǒndu, edur rẏme vidvykiande, of fäein æfentẏr. Bokenn er komenn frä Vigur.[40]

> (Book in quarto format in the hand of Reverend Magnús Ketilsson. It contains the *Niðrstigningar* history of Christ; *Duggals leiðsla* and a fragment of *Bernharðs leiðsla*; the preface to *Margrétar saga*; interpretations of dreams; the phases of the moon; parts of *Blanda* or material concerning [astronomical] computation; and a few exempla. The book comes from Vigur.)

As suggested by Jón Helgason, this manuscript is identical to item 28 of another inventory of Páll Vídalín's library that was reconstructed from memory by his foster son Jón Ólafsson from Grunnavík (†1799). In his inventory, Jón specifies that one of the short tales contained in the manuscript concerned Psyche and the three daughters of the king. The fairy tale is perhaps identical with the so-called *Gullasni*, item 7 of JS 405 8vo, extracted from books 4 and 5 of Apuleius's *Asinus aureus*, relating to Psyche and her sisters:

> bök med hende S^{ra} Magn(usar) Ketelss(onar). Þar ä Nidurstign(ingar) historia. Duggalsleidsla. Fragment af S. Bernhardi leidslu. miked stycke aptan af Rimbeiglu. Tungls alldrar. Nockrer vidburder i ǒdrum londum. Æfentir af Psyche kongsd(ottur) 3^{m} gydium under Jordunne etc.[41]

> (Book in the hand of Reverend Magnús Ketilsson. It contains the story of *Niðrstigningar saga*; *Duggals leiðsla*; fragments of *Bernharðs leiðsla*; a great section from the last part of *Rimbegla*; the phases of the moon [*Blanda*]; a few events in other lands [*Ævintýr um eina stúlku er gaf sig djöflinum*; *Einn fáheyrður atburður*; *Einn tilburður frá 1570*]; exempla about Princess Psyche and three goddesses beneath the earth [*Gullasni*], etc.)

It is consequently reasonable that, towards the end of the eighteenth century, Ólafur Jónsson employed a manuscript similar to that owned by Magnús Jónsson for the compilation of the first section of JS 405 8vo. Besides being the only two postmedieval manuscripts of the tradition and being remarkably close both in date of composition and place of origin, they boast important affinities in terms of the typology of texts transmitted. For example, in addition to *Niðrstigningar saga*, they also share *Bernharðs leiðsla* and *Gullasni*, two otherwise very uncommon texts. It is also worth noting that in his list, Árni refers to *Niðrstigningar saga* with the appellative of "historia Christi" ("History of Christ"). This additional title may indicate that the text included in the manuscript owned by Magnús Jónsson contained the same lengthy introduction, which survives exclusively in JS 405 8vo, indicated below as item 1 of the codex. Its text (extracted from the Gospels) describes Christ's last hours on the cross, the miracles attending the death of Christ, and Joseph and Nicodemus's preparation of Christ's body for burial.

Content of JS 405 8vo

1 2r–3r "Wier vilium æ vísa góder brædr fyrir ydr um nockur stórmerke Vors ens liúfa Lausnara píningar … / … Sídan er ecke almennelega þess getid hvad Kristr vann í Guddómenum þá er hann stie nidr ad leysa mannkinid. Enn þo finnst svo skrifad i annálum ad tveir menn segia frá nidrstigningu Dróttins oc munum ver þa her greina ef Gudi vill." Additional Introductory chapter to *Niðrstigningar saga*, a harmonization of passages in the Gospels describing Christ's crucifixion and entombment (Luke 23:39–46; Mark 15:33–6; Luke 23:46; Matthew 27:51–2; John 19:38–42). [Odd Einar Haugen, ed., *Stamtre og tekstlandskap*, vol. 2, *Tekster og tabellar*, 46–8.]

2 3r–10r "Karinus er madr nefndr annar Leusius syner Simeonis … / … þa skulum ver so segia. Dírd sie Gude Fødr oc Syne oc Heløgum Anda oc svo sem hun var ad upphafe er enn nu oc iafnann oc um allar alder. Amen." Older redaction of *Niðrstigningar saga*. [Present volume, 133–53; Odd Einar Haugen, ed., *Stamtre og tekstlandskap*, vol. 2, *Tekster og tabellar*, 48–59.]

3 10r–11v "Svo seger hinn heilage Bernhardus ad nafnid Jesus þad upplyse lof giðrdina … / … viltu upplýsast þá er hann liósed viltu nærast þá er hann fædslan etc." Excerpts of Bernard of Clairvaux, *Sermones in Cantica Canticorum, Sermo* XV. [The Icelandic text is unedited; the Latin text is available in PL 183, 843D–848C.]

4 11r–16r Rubric "Her biriast Bernhardi leidsla." "Einn vis og vellærdr madr Bernhardus ad nafne var i einum stad á Einglande … / … hvðria ad

sǫnnu veiti hann oss med syninum oc Heilǫgum Anda. Amen." *Bernharðs leiðsla.* [This text, here entitled *Bernharðs leiðsla*, is the Old Norse translation of the Latin poem *Nuper huiuscemodi* (also known as "Royal Debate"), possibly through mediation of its Anglo-Norman rendition known as *Un samedi par nuit*. The same Old Norse translation is transmitted (fragmentarily) in the *Old Norwegian Homily Book* (ca. 1200) under the mistaken title *Visio Sancti Pauli apostoli*.[42] (Gustav Indrebø, ed., *Gamal norsk Homiliebok*, 148–53. The Icelandic text transmitted in JS 405 8vo is edited in Ole Widding and Hans Bekker-Nielsen, eds., "A Debate of the Body and the Soul," 280–9.)]

5 16v–17v Rubric "Ævintu⟨r⟩ um eina stúlku er gaf sig djǫflinum." "Svo bar til i þeim stad er Printzlaw nefnist í Berlinum um striðstið … / … So ad andlítid horfde á bak aptur, þángad sem fyre var hnackin oc so aumkunarlega hefur hun ut endat sitt vesæla líf. Giætum vor fyrer Guds sakir. Amen." *Ævintýr um eina stúlku er gaf sig djöflinum.* [This is possibly an exemplum extracted from one of the *Teufelsbücher* by the Gnesio-Lutheran theologian Andreas Musculus (†1581). See for instance Johannes Janssen, *Geschichte des deutschen Volkes*, vol. 8, 238. The same text, still unedited, is also extant in Reykjavík, Landsbókasafn Íslands, 714 8vo (ff. 72r–72v) from 1790.]

6 17v–19r Rubric "Einn fáheyrdur atburdr." "Var so til ut í Italia á dogum þess virdviglega keisara Rudolphi anno 1578 … / … þá Gidinga dómurin ad Guds ráde vard eydelagdr af Tito oc Vespaciano. Gud gefe oss ollum i Trúnem vaka, so mun oss ecke víst saka." *Einn fáheyrður atburður.* [The source is unknown.]

7 19r–23v Rubric "Apuleius skrifar eina dæme sǫgu i sinne fiórdu og fimtu bók sem han kallar Gullasna sohjódande." "Konungr oc Drottning voru þa fordum, er atta sier dætr þriár…. / … Af Psyche lærum vier, ad margr hvǫr sie ordfolk til sinar cigin olucku, oc so sem Psyche systr reindu, ad vond rad verda þeim optast vest sem vit gefa. Ender." *Gullasni.* [Excerpts from the fourth and fifth books of Apuleius's *Asinus aureus*. The Icelandic text is unedited.]

8 24r Rubric "Einn tilbu⟨r⟩dur sem skede 1570." "I Líneborg var mikid fólk samann i eine kró til dryckiuskapar Jonsmessu kvǫld … / … oc litid sticke af ǫdrum skorsteine þess sama húss var komid út ad valbitorum hálfa mílu frá Kaupenenhafn." *Einn tilburður frá 1570.* [The source is unknown.]

9 24v Rubric "Um aldrdóm mannsins." "Soó er ritad ad sex eru aldar mannsins á jardríki. Hinn fyrste aldr mannsins heiter Infantia … / … A hinum siǫtta aldre sníst mannsins líf i daudann sorg oc sút og mǫrg hatur

fáande oc full scidinda etc." *Æviskeið mannsins*. [A translation of Isidore of Seville's *De aetatibus hominum*, extracted from the eleventh book of the *Etymologiae*. The Icelandic translation is unedited.]

10 Rubric 25r–56v "Nockrar eptertakanlegar smáhistoríur samantíndar til fródleiks 1783." "Ad foreldranna elska er stærre til barn\n/a enn barnanna til foreldranna, þad kann madr skynia af þrem historiu sem skede i Fianderen … / … Merker þiónsins skiótleik ur einum stadi i annan sjúlfbóndanum til gagns og ábata." *Eftirtakanlegar smáhistoríur*. [A translation of ninety-four short stories including quotations of numerous Greek and Latin authors from Antiquity (e.g., Herodotus, Plutarch, Aristippus, and Valerius Maximus), Late Antiquity (e.g., Sozomenus, John Xiphilinus, and Caesarius of Arles), the Middle Ages (e.g., Saxo Grammaticus), and the Renaissance (e.g., Iovianus Pontanus). The source is unknown and the Icelandic text is unedited.]

11 Rubric "Nockur spekmæle heidinna manna og vísdómsfullra spekinga saman hendt úr griskum oc latinskum bókum." 57r–103v "Um Gud seger so Arestotelis … / … þa má ecki þar fyrer forkreinkia lög oc riett oc hann undir fótum tróda. Tantum." *Spekmæli heiðinna manna og vísdómsfullra spekinga*. [A collection of aphorisms, proverbs, and commonplaces ascribed to eminent Classical philosophers and extracted from Hans Hanssen Skonning, *Collegium philosophorum*. The Danish collection was first published in Aarhus in 1636. The Icelandic text is still unedited.][43]

Table 2. Dissemination of the manuscripts of *Niðrstigningar saga*

	Manuscript	Date	Scriptorium/Region	Scribe
1	AM 645 4to	1220–1250	Skálholt (Suðurland)	–
2	Garður's máldagi	1315	Garður (Suðurnes)	–
3	AM 623 4to	1325	Mælifell (Skagafjörður)	–
4	AM 233 a fol.	1350–1375	Helgafell (Snæfellsnes)	–
5	Möðruvellir's máldagi	1461	Möðruvellir (Hörgárdalur)	–
6	AM 238 V fol.	1400–1500	–	–
7	Magnús Jónsson's library	1675–1700	Vigur (Vestfirðir)	Magnús Ketilsson (1675–1703)
8	JS 405 8vo	1780–1791	Arney (Vesturland)	Ólafur Jónsson (1722–1800)

3 The Manuscript Filiation of *Niðrstigningar saga*

This chapter looks into the manuscript filiation of *Niðrstigningar saga*. To facilitate constant comparison and testing of their readings, reference to the five manuscripts of *Niðrstigningar saga* will hereafter, and in the apparatus, be made through the letters A, B, C, D, and E as follows: A = AM 645 4to; B = AM 623 4to; C = AM 233 a fol.; D = JS 405 8vo; and E = AM 238 V fol.

Agreement of the Two Redactions

The complicated relationships between the manuscripts of *Niðrstigningar saga* have already been surveyed in several studies. Gabriel Turville-Petre has observed that regardless of the high variance of the texts transmitted in A, B, C, and E, they should be considered as deriving from a single ancient translation. In order to support this argument, he makes reference to the presence of the two sections of text, previously considered as the "first" and "second" interpolations.[1] As a matter of fact, the text of *Niðrstigningar saga* contains a total of four interpolations, surveyed in chapter 5 in order of appearance in the text. They all derive from foreign narrative material and are consequently absent from the entire Latin tradition of the *Evangelium Nicodemi*. They are found, however, in the Icelandic text masterfully interwoven throughout the original plot.[2] As shown in the collations below, except for the lacunae due to loss of manuscript material, the four interpolations are shared by all other manuscripts in the tradition. Moreover, there is reasonable evidence to suppose that the material lost also contained the interpolated text.

The First Textual Interpolation

A 52r/32–3 Þar var tvennt fyrer at þar var elldr brenna⟨n⟩di at banna manni hveriom at⟨gøngo paradisar⟩ enn englar at veria øllom dioflom oc øndom synðogra manna.[3]

B lacuna

C lacuna

D 4r/24–6 Þar var tvennt vardhald ad veria fiandanum inn ad ganga i hlid paradísar oc syndugum mǒnnum.[4]

E 1r/9–10 Eg sa elld brennanda sa er bannade hverium sem einum manne ingaungo ok einglar Guds vardveittu þessi hlid bædi firir dioflu⟨m⟩ ok syndugum monnum.[5]

The Second Textual Interpolation

A 52v/17–19 Satan iotunn helvitis hofðingi er stundom er meþ VII høfðom enn stundom meþ III enn stundom i drekalike þess er omorlegr er oc ogorlegr oc illilegr a allar lunder.[6]

B 10r/19–21 Sat\`h´an heims hofþingi er stundum er þar met VII hau\`f´þom ęþa III i hreþiligo drekaliki oc omorligo á allar lundir.[7]

C lacuna

D 4v/22–4 Satan helvítis hǒfdinge sá er stundum er med III hǒfdum enn stundum i drekalíke þess sem ofurlegr er oc illr á allar lundir.[8]

E 1r/23–5 Helvítis hofdígni leidtogi daudra i liking hrædilegs dreka ok miog auskurlegs sa er stundum syndiz þeim med VII hofdum enn stundum med III i manzliki.[9]

The Third Textual Interpolation

A 53r/20–7 Þat var mioc i þat mund døgra er himenenn opnaþisc. Þa com fram fyrst hestr hvitr enn hofðinge sa reiþ hesti þeim er morgom hlutom er gofgari enn gørvaster aller aþrer. Augo hans voro se⟨m⟩ elldz logi. Hann hafði corono a høfþi þa er morg sigrsmerki matte of syna. Hann hafði cleþi þat umb aunnor uta⟨n⟩ er bloþstocet var. A cleþi hans yfer mioþmenni voro orþ þessi riten. Rex regum et Dominus dominantium. Hann var solo biartare. Hann leidde eptir ser her mikinn oc aller þeir er honom fylgþo riþo hestom hvitom oc voro aller cleddir silki hvito oc voro liosir mioc.[10]

B 11r/8–18 Þat var mioc i þat mund dęgra at himinn opnaþisc. Þa rann fram hestr hvitr er reíþ higgiligr maþr sa er hveriom var vegligri oc tigologri. Augo hans voro sem logi a ęldi corono þa bar hann á hǫfþi er mǫrg sigrmerki matti syna. Hann \`h´afdi clęþi þat umb aunnor føtt utan er bloþstokit var. A cleþi hans yfir m\`i´oþminni voro orþ þessi ritin Rex regum et

Dominus dominancium. Hann var solu biartari oc fylgþi honom ovigr her riddara oc hofþu hvita hesta allir sniavi hv\`i´tari.[11]

C lacuna

D 5v/21–6r/5 Þad var miǫ́g i þad mund dægra er himininn opnadist oc kom þar framm hestr hvítr. Enn kongr sá er reid hesti þeim var mǫ́rgum hlutum vænne enn aller adrer oc gǫ́fuglegre enn allt annad. Enn augu h⟨a⟩ns vóru so sem loge. Hann hafde koronu á hǫ́fde sier þá er ytarleg var á syndum oc mǫ́rg sigrmerke mátti hann sína á sier. Hann hafde særdann fót sinn utan þad er blódstokid var. Yfir enni hans midiu var ritad. Kongur konga og Drottin drottna. Hann var sólu biartare. Hann hafde hinn megtugasta einglaher. Allir þeir er hǫ́num filgdu ridu hvítum hestum. Aller skríddir hvítu silke oc vóru lióser sem sól.[12]

E 1v/16–22 Þar var ok i þat mund dægra ok þennan tíma at himenn opnadiz. Þa kom fram fyrst hestur hvitur enn sa kongur er reid hesti þeim er maurgum hlutum er fridari ok fegri en allir adrir ok tilgolegri. Augu hans voru sem eldz loge hann hafdi koronu þa ǻǻ hofdi er morg sigurmerke synde. Hann hafdi þat klædi um onnur utan er blodstocket var. ǺǺ kledi hans yfir miodmenne voru þessi ord ritud. Kongur konga ok Drottín drottna. Hann leiddi med sier her hinn mesta. Þeir ⟨er⟩ honum fylgdu ridu hvitum hestum ok voru klæddir silke hvito liosir hardla.[13]

The Fourth Textual Interpolation

A 53v/12–19 Þa bra hann ser i drecalike oc gørdiz þa sva mikill at hann þottesc liggia mundo umb heimenn allan utan. Hann sa þau tiþende ⟨er gørdoz⟩ at Iorsolom at Iesus Christus var þa i andlati oc for ⟨hann⟩ þangat þegar oc ætlaþi at slita ondina þegar fra honom. Enn er hann com þar oc hugþez gløpa mundo hann oc hafa meþ ser þa beit øngullinn goddomens hann enn crossmarkit fell a hann ovann oc varþ hann þa sva veiddr se⟨m⟩ fiscr a øngle eþa mus under treketti eþa sem melraki i gilldro eptir þvi sem fyrer var spat. Þa for til Dominus Noster oc batt hann.[14]

B 11v/9–17 Oc bra ser í drekaliki oc gørdisc þa sva mikill at hann hugþisc liggia mondo umb allan heiminn utan. Hann sa þau tiþendi er þa gorþosc at Iorsaulom at Iesus Christus var þa í andlati oc flo hann þangat til þagar oc villdi slęgia aundina fra honom. Enn þa er hann villdi gleypa hann oc hafa meþ ser þa bęit hann aungul guþdoms hans enn crossmark fell á hann ofan oc varþ hann sva veiddr sem fiskr a aungli ęþa melracki í gilldro eptir þvi sem fyrir var spat. Þa for Drottinn oc batt hann.[15]

C 28ra/9–16 Þa bra hann ser i drekaliki oc hugdiz at vera sva mikill at hann mundi liggia i hríng um helviti. Hann sa þau tidindi er gerduz at Iorsolum at Iesus Christr var i líflati ok for þangat þagar hann matti ok hugdiz slita mundu aundina fra Iesu. Enn þa er hann kom ok hugdizst mundu gleypa Iesum ok hafa hann med ser þa beit aungull guddomsins hann en krossmarkit fell æ hann ofan ok vard hann sva veiddr sem fiskr æ aungli edr mus undir treketti edr melracki i gilldru eptir þvi sem fyrir var spád. Þa for til Várr Drottinn ok batt hann.[16]

D 6r/28–6v/12 Oc brást i drekalíke oc svo giördist hann mikill ad hann þóttist meiga liggia um allan heim utann. Þá sá hann þa atburde er giördust ad Jórsölom ad Jesus var þá i andláte sínu á krossenum helga. Þá for Satan þangad oc þótte hönum nu allt vel á horfast oc ætlade ad slíta öndina frá hönom. Þá com svo fyrer hönum ad hann þóttist ⟨hafa⟩ gleipt hana i kvid illsku sinnar oc hafa med sier. Enn þá beit aungullin guddómsins Satan of fiell krossmarkid á hann ofan oc vard Satan so veiddr sem fiskr á augle edr mús undir fellu enn þad vard epter þvi sem fyrir var sagt ad þessu næst fór Drottinn til helvítis oc batt þar óvin alls mannkyns fiandan.[17]

E 1v/34–6 Þa likti hann sik i mynd ogurligs dreka þeim er jafnat er at mikeleik vid Midgard⟨z⟩ orm sa er sagt ⟨er⟩ at ligi um allan heiminn. Hann sa þa takn þau er voru i Jorslalaborg ⟨at⟩ Drottinn Varn ⟨var⟩ i andlati ok jamskott. *explicit E.*[18]

Disagreement of Readings between the Two Redactions

Gabriel Turville-Petre was the first scholar to note that, except for their agreement in terms of content, the readings of E were considerably closer to those of the Latin text and that this vicinity may have resulted from a secondary learned revision of the original translation. To exemplify the closeness of E to the Latin text, he called to attention the fact that although the character of Inferus is depersonified in the older redaction – described as a host of devils, monsters, and evil beings, as for instance in A 52v/19–20: "viþ iotna oc viþ diofla oc viþ rikistroll ⟨oc⟩ gørvoll þau er i helvite voro" ("with the giants, the devils, and the mighty trolls, and all of those who were in Hell") – he is mentioned in E as a single character named "Helvíti" ("Hell").[19]

The following instances exemplify the evident discrepancies between the older redaction of *Niðrstigningar saga*, which is represented by manuscripts A, B, C, and D, against the newer revised redaction represented by E. In the first six instances, the readings of E are more accurate and adherent to the Latin text throughout, and in the last three cases, they preserve important sections of the text absent in the older redaction. These readings should be considered as secondary innovations and integrations typical of E, rather than relicts of the older translation subsequently lost in A, B, C and D. In fact, as suggested later, the high level of accuracy of E derives from a thorough revision of the text of the older redaction, whose readings were carefully corrected *ex libro* on the basis of another exemplar of the Latin *Evangelium Nicodemi.*

Furthermore, there is evidence that rather than using a Latin text of type T – which, as argued in chapter 4, was consulted and (at least partially) employed for the compilation of the older redaction of *Niðrstigningar saga* – the scribe of E seems to have used a Latin codex transmitting the Majority Text, K.[20] Evidence of this is seen in the very example proposed by Turville-Petre to support his theory of the two redactions. Interestingly, Inferus is personified in the Majority Text of the Latin tradition, but he is already depersonified in T.[21]

Nevertheless, K and T agree in all instances highlighted by the collations below, and references will consequently be made exclusively to the folios and lines of T.

Accuracy of the Younger Redaction Against the Older Redaction

A 52r/21–2	B	C	D 4r/8	E 1r/3	T 99r/25
i heliar myrcrom[22]	lacuna	lacuna	i heliar myrkrum[23]	i myrk⟨r⟩ um ok i skugga daudans[24]	in tenebris et umbra mortis[25]
A 52v/2–3	B 10r/1	C	D 4v/3–5	E 1r/12	T 99v/3
Ec em til þess setr at sia um hvers mans hag[26]	Ec emc til þess setr at lita hvers manz hag[27]	lacuna	Eg er settr til ad siá um þad ad syndugr eingin fari i paradísu[28]	Eg er skipadur yfir mannlegum likama[29]	Ego enim constitutus sum super corpus humanum[30]
A 52v/4–5	B 10r/4	C	D 4v/7	E 1r/14	T 99v/4–5
þo at hann se allsiucr[31]	þot hann se siucr[32]	lacuna	þó hann se siukr[33]	at betriz likams sott hans[34]	pro dolore corporis sui[35]
A 52v/5–6	B 10r/5	C	D 4v/8	E 1r/15	T 99v/5–6
fyrr enn liþner verþa heþan[36]	fyrr enn liþnir ero heþan[37]	lacuna	fyrr enn lidnir eru upp hedan[38]	nema æfstum dogum okomins tíma[39]	nisi in nouissimis diebus temporum[40]
A 53v/9–10	B 11v/7	C 28ra/6	D 6r/24	E 1v/31–2	T 101r/1–2
Þeir raco þa braut høfði⟨n⟩ gia sinn or helvite[41]	om.[42]	Þeir raku þa hofdingia sinn or helvíti[43]	Oc ráku hann edr dróu í burt úr helvíti[44]	Ok eptir þat rak þad Satan hofdíngia sinn ut af sætum sinum[45]	Et eiecit Inferus Sathan de sedibus suis[46]
A 52v/4	B 10r/3–4	C	D 4v/6–7	E 1r/13–14	T 99v/4
til handa føþur þinom[47]	til handa fauþor þinom[48]	lacuna	til handa fô⟨d⟩ ur þínum[49]	at þu smyrir fodur þinn Adam[50]	ut perungas patrem tuum Adam[51]

Accuracy of the Younger Redaction Against the Older Redaction

A 52v/27	B 10v/6	C	D 5r/8	E 1r/30–2	T 99v/21–2
om.	om.	lacuna	om.	þviat alla mattuga jardar hofdingia hefi eg halldit undir mino vallde þa er þu fluttir nu yndir orpna med þinum styrk[52]	omnes enim potentes in terra mea potestate subiecti tenentur quos tua potentia uinctos ad me perduxisti[53]
A 52v/22	B 10r/24	C	D 5r/2	E 1r/27	T 99v/16–17
om.	om.	lacuna	om.	Hrygg er aund min allt til dauda[54]	Tristis est anima mea usque ad mortem[55]
A 52v/28	B 10v/7	C	D 5r/8	E 1r/32–33	T 99v/23–24
om.	om.	lacuna	om.	Enn ef þu ert mattugur hverr er þessi`madur´Jesus er ottaz dauda ok stendur þo i moti þier ok þinu valldi[56]	Si ergo potens es tu qualis est homo ille Ihesus qui timens mortem potentiam tuam aduersatur[57]

Significant Errors within the Older Redaction

The following section examines the textual transmission of *Niðrstigningar saga* on the basis of the classic genealogical method of textual criticism first conceived by Karl Lachman and subsequently elaborated by Paul Maas.[58]

The errors below have already been identified in the thorough study on the stemmatics of *Niðrstigningar saga* undertaken by Odd Einar Haugen, who has highlighted all possible textual corruptions of the text in each single witness and has established a stemma codicum of the tradition on the basis of multivariate data analysis.[59] Nevertheless, in this discussion reference will be made exclusively to what can unequivocally be considered as indicative or significant textual corruptions, defined by Paul Maas as "conjunctive" and "separative errors." The first group includes errors shared by two or more witnesses, notably characterized by the improbability of being produced independently by two or more scribes during the time of transcription of the text, and therefore a monogenetic origin has to be postulated. On the other hand, the second group includes both monogenetic and polygenetic errors, which separate one or more witnesses from the rest of the tradition. By definition, they should conceivably be errors impossible to be emended conjecturally by their scribes during the time of their transcription.[60]

Significant Errors in A, B, and D

In contrast to C, there are two conjunctive and separative errors shared by manuscripts A, B, and D, indicating that they derive from a common ancestor.[61] Moreover, an important omission in A, B, and D, which might not have been conjectured during the time of composition of C, can be counted as a single, either monogenetic or polygenetic, separative error, which separates A, B, and D further from C.[62] All three cases indicate that manuscript C adheres more closely to the Latin text.

In chapter XXI.2, after Satan is cast out of Hell and the patriarchs sing the *Tollite portas* verses derived from Psalm 24(23):7–9[63] in chorus, exhorting Hell to open its large gates for the arrival of Christ, King David recalls to the patriarchs that when he was alive on earth, he pronounced the words commemorating the power of the Redeemer derived from the well-known Psalm 107(106):15–16. The reading of C 28r/26, "er ek var lifs æ iordu" ("when I was alive on earth"), is certainly the closest variant to that of the Latin text, which in this place reads T99r/7–8 "Nonne cum essem uiuus in terris predixi uobis" ("When I was alive on earth, did I not foretell you"), whereas the reading shared by A, B, and D, "þa er ec lifða" ("when I lived"), seems to transmit a considerable trivialization of the original reading.

A 53v/27–8	B 11v/25–6	D 6v/22	C 28ra/26	T 99r/7–8
þa er ec lifða[64]	þa er ec lifþa[65]	þá er eg lifda[66]	er ek var lifs æ iordu[67]	cum essem uiuus in terris[68]

In chapter XXVI, after the patriarchs have been freed from the bondage of sin and have been delivered to Paradise, they see the Good Thief Dismas walking towards them and bearing a cross on his shoulders. The *lectio difficilior* is again transmitted in C, where the present participle C 28vb/15 "hafandi" ("having, carrying") reflects the present participle of the Latin text T 103r/18 "portans" ("carrying"). On the other hand, A, B, and D share a considerably less learned relative clause, "sa hafði" ("who had, carried"), formed by the demonstrative pronoun "sá" and the praeteritum of the verb "hafa."

A 55r/27	B 14r/13	D 9r/9	C 28vb/15	T 103r/18
sa hafði[69]	sa hafði[70]	hann hafde[71]	hafandi[72]	portans[73]

In chapter XXVI, after the patriarchs' encounter with Dismas, A, B, and D omit a clause of the text which survives in C 28v/15–16, "Þa er Guds helgir sæ þenna man spurdu þeir" ("But when the saints of God saw that man, they asked"), translating the Latin T, 103r/11–12 "Uidentes autem sancti omnes dixerunt ad eum" ("Moreover, when all the saints saw [him], they told him").

A 55r/28	B 14r/14	D 9r/10	C 28vb/15–16	T 103r/11–12
om.	om.	om.	Þa er Guds helgir sa þenna man spurdu þeir[74]	Uidentes autem sancti omnes dixerunt ad eum[75]

Possible Significant Errors of A, C, and D

Manuscripts A, C, and D share three possible conjunctive and separative errors[76] and a single separative error[77] against the readings of B, whose text seems in all cases to be more accurate.[78]

Nevertheless, the accuracy of B cannot be conclusive evidence in determining its authority, as the first two readings belong to the fourth interpolation and are consequently absent in the Latin source text T.[79] However, they are also absent in the texts of Revelation 12:9 and Augustine's *Sermo* 265D, from where the interpolation ultimately derives.[80] As a matter of fact, it is more likely that the first three conjunctive errors presented here are in fact the original readings transmitted in the common ancestor of A, B, C, and D, and that the diverging readings of B are the result of a subsequent correction of its text, possibly *ex ingenio*, as suggested below.

In chapter XXI.1, within the fourth and last interpolation of the Icelandic text, which relates to the transformation of Satan into a terrifying dragon and to his travel to Jerusalem, where Christ had just been crucified, B 11v/12 reports that Satan "flo hann þangat" ("and he flew there"), whereas A, C, and D have "oc for þangat" ("and [he] travelled there"). Since Satan had just acquired the shape of a great dragon, it is plausible that the scribe of B may have decided to correct the original generic verb "for" ("travelled") with "flo" ("flew"), specifying that Satan's travel from Hell to Jerusalem was a flight rather than simple journey.

A 53v/14	C 28ra/11	D 6v/3–4	B 11v/12	T 101r
oc for þangat[81]	ok for þangat[82]	fór Satan þangad[83]	oc flo hann þangat[84]	–

Again, in the above-mentioned interpolation of chapter XXI.1, manuscripts A, C, and D may transmit a possible trivialization of the text. Their narratives describe how at the sight of Christ's dead body on the cross, Satan wanted to "tear away the soul" of Christ ("slita ondina"), whereas B 11v/12–13 reads "to steal the soul" ("slęgia ǫndina"). The verb "slægia," literally meaning "to clean out fish," found in B (here meaning "to steal") may be an embellishment of the verb "slita" ("to tear away") shared by the rest of the tradition. The latter verb may have been perceived as either erroneous or inappropriate with reference to the soul of Christ. Within this connection, it should be noted that the fourth interpolation was probably inspired by Augustine's *Sermo* 265D, which relates to the Devil being "greedy and avid for the death" of Christ ("Mortis avidus diabolus fuit, mortis avarus diabolus fuit"), and that rather than aiming to steal the soul of Christ, Satan was craving to "swallow" it ("devorare"/"gløpa") like a voracious animal.[85] Hence, the more dramatic verb "slita" ("to tear away") may have been the one present in the common ancestor of A, B, C, and D, which was subsequently revised in B with the considerably less incisive verb "slægia" ("to steal").

A 53v/14–15	C 28ra/12	D 6v/5	B 11v/12–13	T 101r
slita ondina þegar fra honom[86]	slita mundu aundina fra Ihesu[87]	slíta ȯndina frá hȯnum[88]	slęgia aundina fra honum[89]	–

In the above-mentioned chapter XXI, when the patriarchs encounter the Good Thief in Paradise carrying his heavy cross, B 14r/13 reads "otirligr maþr" ("wretched man"), which precisely renders the Latin T 103r/11 "vir miserrimus" ("most wretched/miserable man"). This adjective was employed in the Latin text to describe his physical appearance, as he is later asked by the patriarchs T 103r/12, "Quis es tu anime quia uisio tua latronis est?" ("Whoever are you, O soul, for your face is that of a thief?"). A, C, and D, on the other hand, seem to transmit a common error, "maþr allosęlligr" ("most joyless/ill-favored man"), that does not fit the context and could possibly have been an attempt of the first redactor to calque the Latin "miserrimus." As a matter of fact, at the moment of narration, Dismas is neither sorrowful nor ill-favoured, since he was granted entrance to Paradise before any other mortal soul (except for Enoch and Elijah), and being in Paradise, he has already reached a state of bliss. Nevertheless, "otirligr" ("inglorious") could possibly be a second intervention of the scribe of B, possibly unsatisfied with the less elegant adjective "allosæligr" ("most joyless") shared by the rest of the tradition.

A 55r/27	C 28vb/14–15	D 9r/9	B 14r/13	T 103r/11
maþr allosęlligr[90]	maþr allosælligr[91]	madr allsiálligr[92]	otirligr maþr[93]	vir miserrimus[94]

Although unstable in all three manuscripts, the reading below can be counted as a separative error of A, C, and D against B. In chapter XXV, the patriarchs encounter Enoch and Elijah, who had been already living in Paradise, and inform them of the prophecy foretelling their future death at the hands of the Antichrist. A, C, and D transmit a secondary reading, which specifies that before fighting the Antichrist, they shall first come down to earth from Paradise: A 55r/22–3 "Enn þa munom viþ ðanga⟨t⟩ coma" ("And then we shall come there"). Being a separative error, this omission may have aroused independently from that of the Latin source text T.

A 55r/22–3	C 28vb/10	D 9r/3	B 14r/9	T 103r/8
Enn þa munom viþ ðanga⟨t⟩ coma[95]	Enn þa skulum vid fara nídr i heiminn[96]	Vid fǫ́rum þa til ydar[97]	om.	om.

Possible Significant Errors of A and B

There is a single instance in which A may share with B a monogenetic, conjunctive, and separative error against D.

In chapter XXIV.3, Habakkuk recalls one of his canticles in praise of God, as related in Habakkuk 3:13: "existi in salutem populi tui ad liberandos electos tuos" ("you came out for the salvation of your people and set free your chosen ones").[98] The text of D in this case transmits the correct reading, "útvalda þina" ("your chosen ones"), using the past participle of the verb "útvelja" ("to choose / to select") reflecting the Latin "electos" ("chosen ones"). A and B, on the other hand, transmit a significantly different reading "valaþa ðina" ("your poor ones"), which differs considerably from the source, T 102v/21 "ad liberandos electos tuos" ("to set free your chosen ones"). However, being a section of text extracted from a renowned canticle, this reading may have been easily emended *ex ingenio* in D (or in its antigraph) during the time of their transcriptions.

A 55r/8	B 13v/14	D 8v/9	C	T 102v/21
at leysa valaþa ðina[99]	at leysa valaþa þina[100]	ad leisa útvalda þina[101]	lacuna	ad liberandos electos tuos

Possible Significant Errors of A and C

A single monogenetic, conjunctive, and separative error is shared by A and C against B in the Latin text of Psalm 107(106):15–16, transmitted in chapter XXI.2. The third person plural subjunctive of the original text, T 101r/8–9

"Confiteantur Domino" ("They would confess to the Lord"), is well preserved in B but corrupted into a second person plural, indicative as "Confitemini Domino" ("You confess to the Lord"), in both A and C. This reading, as in the previous case, being a section of a well-known psalm, may have been easily emended by the scribe of B during the time of its transcription.

A 53v/29	C 28r/27	B 12r/1	D 6v/23	T 101r/8–9
Confitemini Domino[102]	Confitemini Domino[103]	Confiteantur Domino[104]	om.	Confiteantur Domino[105]

Errors of A and D

In a single case, A and D share a monogenetic, conjunctive, and separative error,[106] which further highlights their filiation from a common ancestor and separates them from B and C. Moreover, there are two separative errors that separate them from B.[107]

In chapter XXVI, the Latin text relates that the Good Thief was accompanied in Paradise by the archangel Michael, who exhorts him to wait there for the arrival of the patriarchs, who will shortly thereafter be freed from Hell. Michael pronounces the words "modicum sustine" ("wait a while"), which are still well preserved in both B and C: "scalltu biþa litla stund" ("you shall wait a while"). On the other hand, A and D seem to share a trivialization in substituting the second person plural "scalltu" ("you shall"), with the first person plural of the modal "skulu" ("shall"): "scolom biþa litla stund" ("we [two] shall wait a while").

A 55v/9	D 9v/4–5	B 14v/5	C 28vb/27	T 103r/23
scolom biþa litla stund[108]	skulum vid bída litla stund[109]	scalltu biþa litla stund[110]	skaltu nu bida litla stund[111]	modicum sustine[112]

In chapter XVIII.1, A and D omit one of the five invectives pronounced by Hell against Satan, T 102r/1 "sputum iustorum" ("spittle of the just"), which is still preserved in B, where it is rendered more metaphorically as "hrøptr af monnom" ("defamed by men").[113]

A 54v/5	D 7v/12	B 12v/21	C	T 102r/1
om.	om.	hrøptr af monnom[114]	lacuna	sputum iustorum[115]

In chapter XXIV.3, A and D omit the conclusive line of the prophecy voiced by Micah after the deliverance of the patriarchs from Hell, T 102v/28 "sicut iurasti patribus nostris" ("as you promised to our fathers"), derived from Micah 7:18–20. The clause is fully extant in B: "sva sem sem þu svaraþir feþrom orom" ("as you promised to our fathers").

A	D	B 13v/21–2	C	T 102v/28
om.	om.	sva sem sem þu svaraþir feþrom orom[116]	lacuna	sicut iurasti patribus nostris[117]

Stemmata Codicum

Turville-Petre's Stemma

As mentioned above, Turville-Petre rightly believed that the four medieval manuscripts A, B, C, and E derived from a common original but that E must have been thoroughly emended and revised on the basis of the Latin text of *Evangelium Nicodemi.* He also maintained that although the "first" and the "second" interpolations (here referred to as the "third" and the "fourth") derived from the older redaction were intentionally maintained in E, the subsequent modifications of readings applied to E created a new textual *facies* considerably different from that of A, B, and C. These considerations led him to suspect contamination in the tradition of *Niðrstigningar saga.*[118] Taking his suggestions into account, his stemma could be similar to that proposed by Odd Einar Haugen, as illustrated in the following section.

Aho's Stemma

In his PhD dissertation, Gary L. Aho agrees with Turville-Petre in that the four medieval manuscripts A, B, C, and E derive from a common original translation X, but he also argues that it is not necessary to postulate a contamination in the tradition. He suggests instead that the text of X is more faithfully preserved in E, which stands alone in a single branch of the tradition, and concludes that this may be the reason why its readings are so remarkably close to the Latin text. He also maintains that A, B, C, and D all derive from a secondary, now lost, redaction of X (indicated as X^1), which has further separated them from the Latin text.[119] His stemma is implemented in Figure 2.

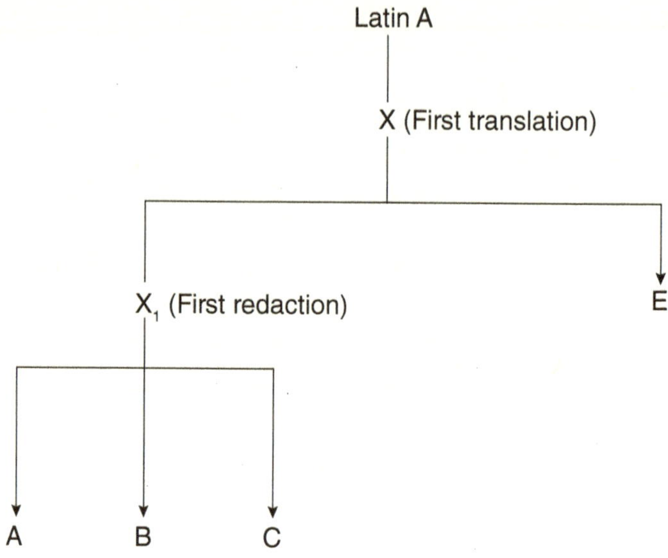

Figure 2. Gary L. Aho's stemma

Haugen's Stemma

Odd Einar Haugen, who has conducted the most thorough and comprehensive analysis of the *Niðrstigningar saga* stemmatics, also recognizes that E should be separated from A, B, C, and D and that it should be counted alone as a different translation. On the basis of the data discussed in his survey, Haugen concludes that both Aho's and Turville-Petre's stemmata are plausible filiations of the tradition of *Niðrstigningar saga* and that internal evidence is, in this case, insufficient to reach any conclusive decisions. He then resorts to external evidence, such as the high presence of archaisms in both A and B, and the dates of the four medieval manuscripts, which naturally indicate that the revision was made on E rather than on A and B, since A and B are the oldest manuscripts of the tradition. Moreover, he draws attention to the contexts into which the third and the fourth interpolations are interwoven and concludes that these passages of foreign text are remarkably more fitting in the narrative contexts of A, B, and C, rather than in E.[120] His stemma is shown in Figure 3.

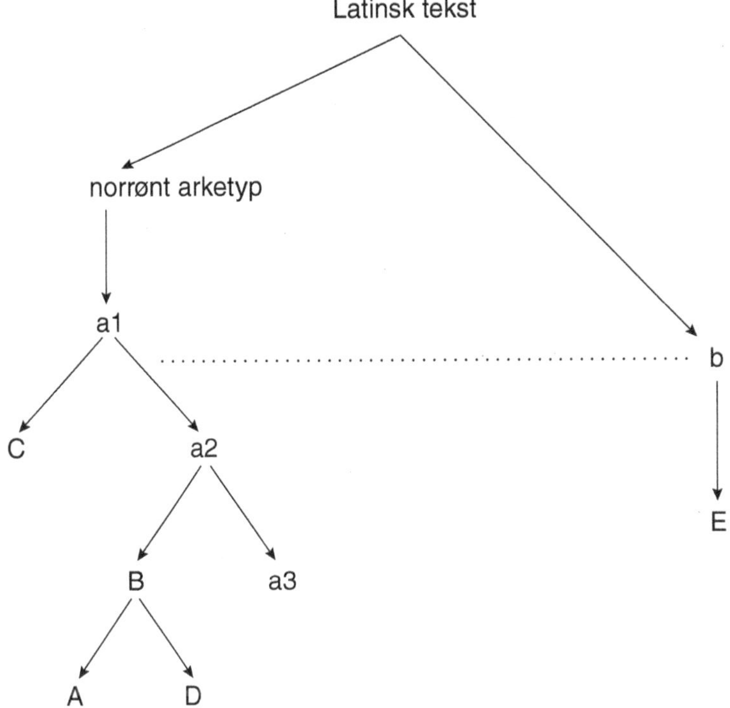

Figure 3. Odd Einar Haugen's stemma

The Present Stemma

As shown in Figure 4, A, B, C, D, and E share a common archetype α, which includes the four interpolations typical of *Niðrstigningar saga*. From α, a lost manuscript β was copied, and from this C is ultimately derived. C stands alone in a distinct branch of the stemma, separated from the rest of the tradition, and in view of its absence of errors must be considered a more reliable and stable text. C also seems to be the closest of all manuscripts to α. As a matter of fact, rather than the textual corruptions shared by A, C, and D, the three possible conjunctive errors – "oc for þangat" ("and [he] travelled there"), "slita ondina" ("[to] tear away the soul"), and "maþr allosęligr" ("a most joyless man") – seem more likely to be secondary innovations exclusive to B. They may simply have been readings already present in α, from which they were transmitted to

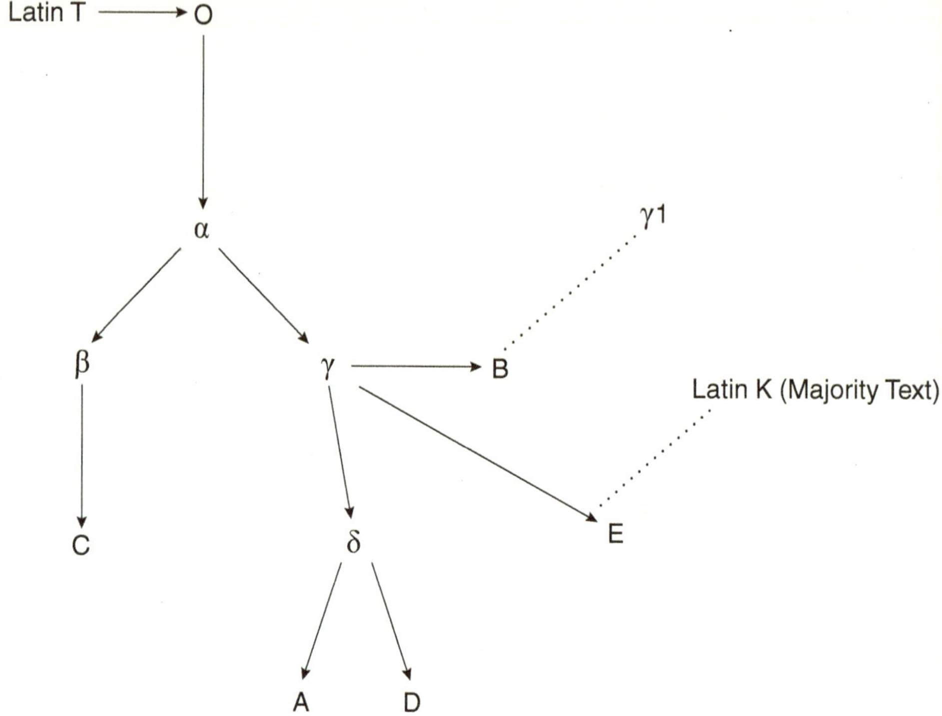

Figure 4. The present stemma

the two lost exemplars, β and γ, and from there to the daughter manuscripts. This evidence excludes Magnús Már Lárusson's hypothesis that held B to be the closest variant text to the archetype of *Niðrstigningar saga*.[121] The copy γ introduced two new errors – "þa er ec lifða" ("when I lived") and "sa hafði" ("who had") – which separates it from β. The errors typical of γ were then transmitted to one of its lost copies, δ, which along with another error introduced by δ alone – "scolom biþa" ("we shall wait") – was transmitted to the two sister manuscripts A and D.

This picture is then complicated by the vicissitudes of B and E, which are also derived from γ but, on the basis of the evidence discussed, seem to have undergone secondary revisions. B embellished some of the original readings of γ (possibly *ex ingenio*), harmonizing them to its taste and possibly conforming and adopting them to their literary context. This revision of γ is indicated below as γ^1. As shown in the collations above, it seems clear that text E also descends from γ on account of the vicinity of its readings to those of A and B within the interpolated portions of text. However, there are indications that the text of E was subsequently recorrected (this time *ex libro*) on the basis of another exemplar of the Latin *Evangelium Nicodemi*, which did not pertain to Latin T. The text of E seems instead to have been corrected on the basis of a codex displaying features of the Majority Text K, as deduced from their agreement of readings below.[122] It is therefore appropriate to refer to an older redaction of *Niðrstigningar saga*, represented by A, B, C and D, and a more recent fully-revised redaction of the text, represented by E alone.

The two possible conjunctive errors of A and B and A and C cannot be conclusive evidence of their close relationships, as the readings in question are parts of common canticles and psalms abundantly sung in a monastic environment and could therefore have been easily emended during the time of the transcription of C and D. From the evidence discussed, it is clear that C is the closest surviving codex to the archetype, which is evidently contaminated due to the secondary revisions of B and E, *ex ingenio* and *ex libro* respectively. Accordingly, the new stemma can be implemented as shown in Figure 4.

4 The Latin Source Text Underlying *Niðrstigningar saga*

The text of *Niðrstigningar saga* has hitherto been related and compared to the so-called A version of the apocryphon, representing the Majority Text (K) of the Latin tradition.[1] This version was by far most widely diffused in medieval Europe as, judging from their incipit, over 380 out of the 434 counted witnesses transmit the Majority Text either fully or in an abridged form.[2]

Despite the overall agreement of readings, lexicon, and style, the Majority Text does not fully represent the Old Icelandic rendition. Already after a first collation, it seemed clear that the older redaction of *Niðrstigningar saga* exhibited major and minor narrative details typical of the hybrid redaction (T) rather than the more conventional readings of K. Evidence of their dependence is confirmed by several textual and thematic correspondences, as illustrated by the collations of readings below. In addition to T and K, the collation also comprises the readings of the R text, the sole surviving Icelandic exemplar of the Latin *Evangelium Nicodemi*, Reykjavík, Þjóðminjasafn Íslands, 921, a fragment dating to the thirteenth century that also transmits readings typical of the Majority Text.

The Icelandic text is represented in the collations by the readings of A (AM 645 4to), which is the oldest surviving manuscript to transmit the older redaction of *Niðrstigningar saga* and the only medieval codex to preserve the text in its entirety. Its readings are collated and tested with those transmitted by the younger redaction E (AM 238 V fol.), a single fragment leaf copied during the fifteenth century. Its text ultimately derives from the same archetype as recension A but with subsequent corrections and revisions based on a Latin exemplar transmitting the Majority Text.[3] Aside from its distinctive textual divergences from the Latin source text – such as evident omissions, abridgements, and rearrangements of the plot – the older redaction reflects, to different extents, both major and minor textual features typical of T.

In contrast with the Majority Text type, the hybrid redaction rephrases and reformulates the original text several times and concurrently substantiates the plot with dramatic details and anecdotes. These new additions, all varyingly mirrored in the Icelandic translation, must have originated within the hybrid text as important logical threads, apt to integrate and develop the narrative of the original pseudo gospel when it was perceived as either limited or deficient. During the twelfth century, secondary revisers might have intervened to adjust and amplify certain passages of the Majority Text, enriching it with details of Christ's Descent and Harrowing of Hell derived from other popular religious narratives concerning the same catabasic theme (such as homilies and sermons) and also possibly adding realistic details from visual art pieces that depict this prominent scene.[4]

In general terms, the Majority Text is characterized by constant stateliness and sobriety in the treatment of the Christ figure and seems to avoid any detailed description of his Harrowing of Hell or of the military imagery traditionally associated with it. The hybrid redaction seems to compensate for this absence of action by adding more traditional iconographic details to the figure of Christ, hence giving a much more vivid and dramatic force to his arrival in Hell and his dealings with Satan.

Although highly elaborated and adapted to a new literary context, five major textual digressions of *Niðrstigningar saga* (confined in a short emphatic passage corresponding to the end of chapter XX1.3 and the beginning of chapter XXII.1), absent from the Latin Majority Text, find thematic and formal correspondences in T. In order of their appearance in the text, they involve Christ's physical shattering of the gates of Hell; a description of a host of angels attending him; his breaking of the infernal bonds that chained the patriarchs and prophets in Hell; the astonishment of the inhabitants of Hell at his sight in their realms; and his physical binding of Satan. As will be shown below, these details are either absent or highly elusive in the Majority Text. The other textual differences between the Majority Text and the hybrid redaction are minor and mostly concern a different choice of lexicon or alternative wording.

The Prologue

The prologue of the Majority Text lacks the assertion typical of T, which allegedly ascribes the commission of the first translation of the Hebrew apocryphon to the Emperor Theodosius the Great (†395). Its prologue simply ends by attributing the authorship of the text to Nicodemus: K "Mandauit ipse Nichodemus litteris ebraicis" ("This same Nicodemus wrote it himself in the Hebrew script").

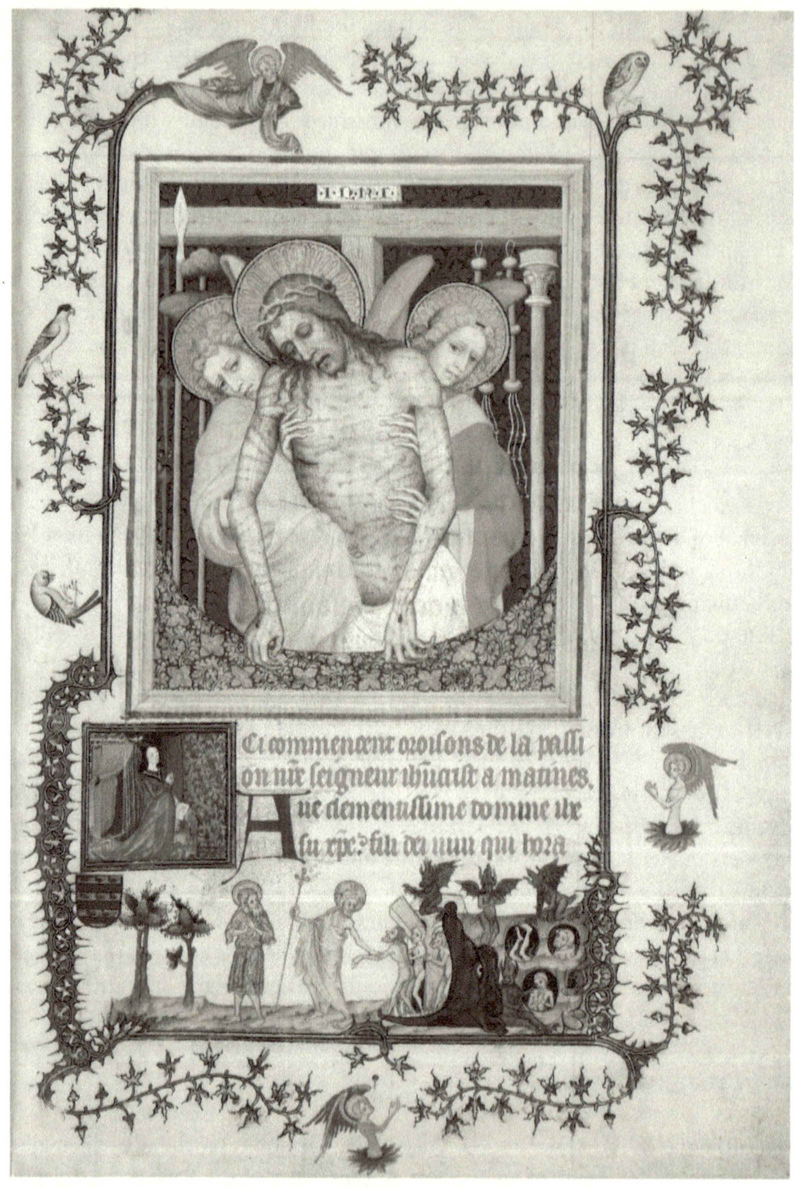

Figure 5. Illumination attributed to the Master of the Parement of Narbonne in the *Très belle Heures de Notre-Dame* (Paris, BnF, nuov. acq. lat. 3093), f. 155r, lower side (ca. 1375–1400) depicting the Harrowing of Hell as related in the *Gospel of Nicodemus*. Reproduced with permission of the BnF.

K Prologue 13/13–14	T 90r/9–11	A 54v/20–3 (Epilogue)
Mandavit ipse Nichodemus litteris ebraicis.[5]	Ipse Nichodemus scripsit in litteris hebraicis. Theodosius autem magnus imperator fecit ea transferri de hebreo in latinum.[6]	Enn morgom mannzøll⟨drom⟩ siþar comsc at boc þeire Theodosius keisere sonr Archadii. Hann hafði meþ sér i Miclagarþ oc let þar uppraþa oc varþ þar monnom alldat umb.[7]

The additional detail found in the prologue of the hybrid redaction could have originated as a secondary development of the prefatory rubric shared by the entire Latin tradition. Due to the swift assertion that the text was discovered in Jerusalem during the reign of Theodosius the Great, the compiler of the hybrid redaction must have made the consequent assumption that its translation into Latin was made at the personal instance of the Emperor: K Rubric 13/1–4 "IN NOMINE SANCTAE TRINITATIS INCIPIUNT GESTA SALUATORIS DOMINI NOSTRI IESU CHRISTI INUENTA THEODOSIO MAGNO IMPERATORE IN HIERUSALEM IN PRETORIO PONTII PILATI IN CODICIBUS PUBLICIS."[8]

Notwithstanding the unambiguous reference to the Emperor Theodosius I as the owner of the text and commissioner of some literary initiative to promote the circulation of the apocryphon – which clearly establishes a close relationship of the Icelandic text to T against the Majority Text – it is worth noting the unusual choice of the verb "uppráða" ("to read aloud"), which renders the Latin verb "transfero" ("translating, interpreting") of T.[9] The Icelandic compiler removes this information from the prologue and briefly recalls it in the epilogue of the narrative, which follows a considerably abridged version of chapter XXVII.5, a section describing how, after hearing the dramatic accounts of Carinus and Leucius, Joseph and Nicodemus reported to Pilate their accounts of Christ's Descent into Hell.

K XXVII.5 49/1–5	T 103v/27–8	A 55v/19–20
Haec omnia quae dicta et facta sunt a Iudaeis in sinagoga eorum statim Ioseph et Nichodemus adnunitiauerunt presidi.[10]	Hec omnia que dicta sunt et facta a Iudeis in synagoga eorum Ioseph et Nichodemus anuntiauerunt presidi Pylato.[11]	Nicodemo oc Iosep⟨h⟩ enn þeir reþo upp ⟨fyrer⟩ \`oðrom´.[12]

The semantic correspondence of the Icelandic verb "uppráða" ("to read aloud") with the verb "annuntiare" ("to announce") is considerably stronger in this context than in the previous case, as the Latin verb "annuntiare" also implies a public speech or exposition ("to reveal / to proclaim / to declare publicly"). The use of the verb "uppráða" in this passage, immediately preceding the reference to Theodosius, may have been at least partially influenced by its second employment in the following sentence. The Emperor's request to translate the Hebrew pseudo gospel is adopted into Joseph and Nicodemus's report of the previous sentence and is converted into a request for a simple public reading of the text. A second, more reasonable explanation of the divergence of the readings T "transferre" and A "uppráða" can also be seen as a deliberate attempt of the Icelandic compiler to conform the epilogue of *Niðrstigningar saga* to that of the *Jarteinabók Þorláks byskups in forna* ("The Ancient Miracle Collection of Bishop Þorlákr "). In the latter, the first and foremost item of AM 645 4to (ff. 1r–11v), the unusual verb "uppráða" – rather than the considerably more common synonym "upplesa" – is also employed for the public reading of Þorlákr's miracles at the Althing of 1199.[13]

The Shattering of the Gates of Hell

The Majority Text remains silent about Christ's physical shattering of the gates of Hell and mentions only briefly that Christ "broke the indestructible bonds" (K XXI.3 41/18–19 "insoluta uincula disrupit") of the souls of the righteous with the aid of his "unconquered power" (K XXI.3 41/19 "inuictae uirtutis").

The beginning of chapter XXII.1 is emblematic of this discretion and solicitousness in the treatment of the figure of Christ; here, it is clear that only at the sight of Christ in Hell do its inhabitants hurry to fully acknowledge his victory: K XXII.1 42/1–5 "Haec uidentes Inferus et Mors et impia officia eorum cum crudelibus ministris expauerunt in propriis regnis agnitam tanti luminis claritatem dum Christum repente in suis sedibus uiderunt, et exclamauerunt dicentes: 'Uicti sumus a te.'"[14] This brief description of Christ's effortless victory over the inhabitants of Hell does not seem to have convinced or amused the compiler of the hybrid text. He expanded and magnified this image in the following section, XXI.3, creating a much vivider and fiercer scenario that describes Christ's physical destruction of the gates of Hell in detail. At Christ's appearance in Hell, "all the infernal gates, bars, and locks were destroyed" ("omnes porte infernales et uectes et sere in accessu eius confracte sunt"), and "everything gave Him space and made room for Him" ("omnia locum illi et uiam dederunt").

This additional scene within the hybrid text concerning Christ's physical destruction of the gates of Hell was most probably influenced by the wording of Psalm 107(106):15–16, transmitted in chapter XXI.2. This section immediately precedes Christ's destruction of the gates of Hell and has King David recall in his own words one of the psalms commemorating the power of the Redeemer: "Let them confess to the Lord His mercy and His wonders to the sons of men, because He has shattered the gates of bronze and destroyed the bars of irons" (T 101r/8–10 "Confitaentur domino misericordie eius et mirabilia eius filius hominum quia contriuit portas ereas et uectes ferreos con⟨f⟩regit").

The Icelandic translator further emphasizes Christ's warfaring spirit and physical strength, especially in his peculiar choice of vocabulary describing the fortress-like architecture of Hell. Christ, it is said, "arrived to the stronghold of Hell" ("com at helvitis virki"); he abruptly "destroyed" ("braut") "the fortress of Hell" ("borg helvitis") and finally opened up "a large gate" ("hliþ miket"). The choice of the word "fortress" ("borg") in this passage prefigures the description of the innermost infernal fortified compound, the "inner fortress of the prison" (T 102r/4 "ima carceris claustra") of chapter XXIII.1, which Christ is doubtless able to destroy.[15]

K XXI.3 41/16–20	T 101r/26–9	A 54r/13–16
Superuenit Rex Gloriae in forma hominis, Dominus Maiestatis, aeternas tenebras inlustrauit, et insoluta uincula disrupit. Inuictae uirtutis auxilium uisitauit nos sedentes in tenebris delictorum et umbra mortis peccatorum.[16]	Filius Dei Christus Rex Glorie superuenit in forma hominis et eternas tenebras splendore uultus sui illustrauit et omnes porte infernales et uectes et sere in accessu eius confracte sunt et omnia locus illi et uiam dederunt.[17]	Þa com Konongr Dyrþar at helvitis virki. Hann braut þegar borg helvitis oc gørþi a hliþ miket. Hann hevir vitraz i manz asiono meþ liose miclo svat myrcr helvites hafa þa horfit.[18]

A Host of Angels Attending Christ

The Majority Text mentions no celestial being other than the archangel Michael, whose name occurs twice in the section derived from the Latin *Vita Adae et Evae*, where Michael prophesies the coming of the Messiah,[19] and once towards the end of the text, where he accompanies the souls of the righteous to Heaven.[20]

After Christ's destruction of the gates of Hell, the hybrid redaction asserts that the inhabitants of Hell saw him "coming with His angels" ("uenientem cum angelis suis"), a wording reminiscent of Matthew 16:27, describing Christ's Second Coming.[21] The Icelandic translator anticipates this detail in chapter XXI.1 and sets it out just before the second major textual interpolation.[22] When the inhabitants of Hell hear that Christ has descended into their realm and is about to enter, they promptly cast out Satan and hastily close the gates. The Icelandic text relates that once out of Hell, Satan saw that "a great host of angels had arrived to Hell" ("þa sa hann engla⟨liþ⟩ mikit vera comet til helvetis").

There are two more references to heavenly armies led by Christ in the Icelandic text: the first is interwoven into the third textual interpolation at the end of chapter XX.3, where "He led with Him a great army" (A 53r/27 "hann leide eptir ser her mikinn"), and the second is in chapter XXIV.2, where Christ triumphally ascends from Hell "with a great army" (A 55r/5 "meþ her miclom"). In both instances, it is easily inferred that Christ's heavenly forces are composed of angels. Consistent with the Majority Text, the text of R also altogether omits this reading.

K XXI.3 41/21	R 1rb/29	T 101r/29–30	A 53v/10–11
om.	om.	Uidentes autem omnes sancti Saluatorem Ihesum uenientem cum angelis suis.[23]	Þa sa hann engla⟨liþ⟩ mikit vera comet til helvetis.[24]

Destruction of the Bondage of Sin

The description of Christ's luminous arrival in Hell in the form of a humble man constitutes one of the great turning points of the narrative. Despite the relevance of this scene, the Majority Text condenses this event into one scanty sentence. To compensate for this sterility, the compiler of the hybrid redaction inserts the above-mentioned details describing Christ, attended by a host of angels, shattering the gates of Hell. The presence of these additions in the hybrid text and in the Icelandic translation is represented below by the ellipsis. They are absent in the Majority Text and in the Icelandic fragment, where the narrative continues regularly.

K XXI.3 41/16–19	R rb/24–6	T 101r/23–101v/3	A 54r/12–17
Haec dicente Dauid ad Inferum, superuenit Rex Gloriae in forma hominis, Dominus Maiestatis, aeternas tenebras inlustrauit et insoluta uincula disrupit.[25]	In forma hominis. Dominus maiestatis quis eternas tenebras illuminauit insolubilia uincula disrupit.[26]	Hec dicente Dauid ad Infernum. Ecce desideratus omnibus gentibus[27] Filius dei Christus Rex Glorie superuenit in forma hominis et eternas tenebras splendore uultus sui[28] illustrauit [...] Tunc introiens Christus ad eos uincula quibus erant colligati disrupit.[29]	Þa er David hafði þetta męlt þa com Konongr Dyrþar at helvitis virki [...] Hann hevir vitraz i manz asiono meþ liose miclo svat myrcr helvites hafa þa horfit. Hverr goðr maþr hevir þa losnat or þvi bandi sem bundinn var.[30]

The Majority Text, along with R (which begins deficiently in this very passage), is once again obscure in its formulation and in the presentation of the events. It is asserted that Christ "enlightened the eternal shadows" (K XXI.3 41/18 "aeternas tenebras inlustrauit") and "broke the indissolvable bonds" (K XXI.3 41/18–19 "insoluta uincula disrupit") without any further indication of whom the bonds were fastening. This vagueness in the description of Christ's actions could be misleading, as the second excerpt may also imply that the "indissolvable bonds" pertained to Hell (the object of the previous excerpt), which had just been illuminated by Christ's divine light. In order to clarify this passage, the hybrid redaction adds a clause specifying that the bonds were those that had fastened together the souls of the righteous and that these were shattered by Christ.

The Icelandic text omits the first reading and renders the second only partially, translating correctly the Latin ablative of means "with radiance" (T 101r/27 "splendore"), absent in the Majority Text, with "with a great light" (A 54r/15 "meþ liose miclo"), but it leaves out the reference to the face of Christ.

Amazement among the Inhabitants of Hell

The final sections of chapter XXII.1 preserve the first part of the pseudo-Augustian *Sermo* CLX *De Pascha* II, possibly the most authoritative medieval source, along with the *Evangelium Nicodemi*, to address Christ's Harrowing of Hell.

The hybrid redaction already anticipates the the devils' amazement and state of shock at the beginning of the chapter; it specifies that the legions, just before conclusively declaring Christ's absolute victory over them, were "terrified and confused" by the mere sight of Christ (T 101v/7 "perterriti et confusi"). The Icelandic text describes the infernal legions who, because of great fear, barely dared to "bend forward and stare in that direction" ("þa hafa þeir til kagat þangat").

K XXII.1 42/1–5	R rb/32–4	T 101v/6–8	A 54r/19–21
Haec uidentes [...] Christum repente in suis sedibus uiderunt, et exclamauerunt dicentes: "Uicti sumus a te."[31]	Christum repente in suis sedibus uiderunt et exclamauerunt dicentes. Uicti sumus a te.[32]	Et uidentes Christum repente in sedibus suis descendisse perterriti et confusi exclamauerunt. Victi sumus ad te o Ihesu.[33]	Er þeir sa Christum þar ganganda Guð þeira þa hafa þeir til kagat þangat aller oc męlto þetta. Yfer hevir þu nu oss stigit.[34]

The Physical Binding of Satan

The traditional imagery of the Harrowing of Hell culminates with Christ's binding of Satan, a scene that not only appears in a vast amount of religious narratives that deal with the same catabasic theme but is also abundantly portrayed in the visual arts.[35]

The high circulation of this popular motif can be justified by its dramatic efficacy and duality; appealing to the actual binding of Satan highlights the devil's physical strength, the potential risk of dealing with him in first person, and the danger of leaving him without constraints. At the same time, it denotes a certain faintness and paucity of his power compared to that of Christ. The Majority Text makes no reference to any bondage; it ends with Satan being "grasped" ("conprehendens") by Christ and "delivered" ("tradidit") to Hell. The hybrid redaction, on the other hand, makes clear that "through his power" ("sue potentia"), Christ was able to deliver Satan "bound" ("colligatum"). These readings are reflected in the Icelandic text, where it is said that the "bonds" ("bondom") binding Satan – here described as being "made of fire" ("elldigom")[36] – derive from Christ's "own powers" ("crapta sinna").

K XXII.2 43/1–3	R 1vb/1–4	T 101v/26–8	A 54v/1–2
Tunc Rex Gloriae Dominus maiestate sua conculcans Mortem, conprehendens Satan principem, tradidit Inferi potestati.[37]	Tunc Rex Glorie Dominus maiestate sua conculcans Mortem et conprehendensque Sathan principem atque Inferi potestatem.[38]	Tunc Rex Glorie Christus Dominus maiestatis sue potentia conculcans mortem et conprehendens Sathan principem tradidit eum Inferi potestate colligatum.[39]	Þa toc Dominus Rex Glorie at troþa niþr hofðingi⟨a⟩ dauþans oc batt hann meþ elldligom bondom ⟨crapta sinna⟩.[40]

Minor Variants of T Reflected in A against K

The text of *Niðrstigningar saga* also reflects minor but significant variants found in the hybrid redaction. These include a change of lexicon, rephrasing of sentences, evident omissions, and innovations of T in contrast with the Majority Text. Moreover, in three instances,[41] the ancient readings of the Majority Text that were ultimately derived from the *Vetus Latina* – possibly entered into the *Evangelium Nicodemi* via various ancient collections of psalters – were revised in the hybrid redaction on the basis of their counterparts in the Vulgate.

K XVIII.1 36/7–9	T 99r/3–4	A 51v/30–1
subito factus est aureus solis calor purpureaque regalis lux illustrans super nos.[42]	subito facta est in aureo solis lumine quedam regalis lux illustrans super nos.[43]	nęsta vaveifes scein þar lios fagrt oc biart sicut af solo iver oss alla.[44]

Both the hybrid redaction and the Icelandic translation omit the Majority Text reading of "purpurea" ("purple") to describe the nuances of the royal light generated by Christ in Hell and instead transmit the adjective "aureus" ("golden"). The latter is preserved in T in the ablative case "in aureo" ("in the golden") and rendered with a translation doublet of semi-synonyms "fagrt oc biart" ("fair and bright") in the Icelandic text.

K XVIII.1 36/9–11	T 99r/4–5	A 51v/31–3
Statim omnis generis humani pater Adam cum omnibus patriarchis et prophetis exultauerunt dicentes.[45]	Statimque generis humani pater Adam cum omnibus patriarchis et prophetis exultauerunt in gaudio dicentes.[46]	Þa toc Adam faþer allz mannkyns oc aller høfotfeðr oc spamenn at fagna miog oc męla sva.[47]

Throughout the translation, the Latin "exultare" ("rejoice") is punctually rendered with the Icelandic "fagna" ("rejoice"); for instance, T 101r/12–13 "exultabunt qui in terris sunt" ("those on earth shall rejoice") becomes A 54r/1 "enn fagna þeir er i grofom væri" ("and those who were in [their] graves would rejoice"). In the following example, the Latin ablative "in gaudio" ("with happiness") is rendered with the Icelandic adverb "miog" ("much/greatly").

K XVIII.1 36/16–18	T 99r/9–10	A 52r/2–3
Populus qui sedet in tenebris uidebit lucem magnam, et qui sunt in regione umbrae mortis lux fulgebit super eos.[48]	Populus qui sedebat in tenebris uidit lucem magnam et qui sunt in regione umbre mortis lux orta est eis.[49]	Populus qui sedebat in tenebris lucem uidit magnam habitantebus in regionibus umbre mortis lux orta est eis.[50]

These words are proclaimed by the prophet Isaiah in Hell, recalling what he himself reported in Isaiah 9:2 in order to describe the darkness in which the inhabitants of Galilee were abiding before the coming of the Messiah. The original reading of the Majority Text, "lux fulgebit super eos" ("a light shall shine over those"), is a combination of an ancient reading of Isaiah 9:2 derived from the *Vetus Latina*, "lux fulgebit super uos" ("a light shall shine over you"), as for instance transmitted in the European text E, and the common reading transmitted by the Vulgate, "lux orta est eis" ("a light has dawned on them").

In the hybrid recension and in the Icelandic translation, the reading appears corrected and conforms to the reading transmitted in the Vulgate.[51]

K XVIII.3 37/2–3	T 99r/16–17	A 52r/10–12
Et post haec supervenit quasi heremicola interrogatus ab omnibus, "Quis es tu?" Quibus respondens dixit.[52]	Et post hec superuenit quidam quasi heremicola et interrogatus ab omnibus quis esset respondit.[53]	Þa com þar at gangandi maþr sa er þeir kendo eigi. Sa maþr var gørvilegr oc a þann veg buenn sem af eyðimorc væri comenn. Þeir spurðo þann mann at namni eþa hvat hann cynni nytt at segia.[54]

The original direct speech of the Majority Text is transported into indirect speech in both the hybrid redaction and the Icelandic text.

K XVIII.3 37/11–12	T 99r/22–3	A 52r/18
Hic est Filius meus dilectus in quo bene conlpacui.[55]	Hic est Filius meus dilectus in quo mihi bene complacui.[56]	Hic est dilectus meus in quo mihi complaqui.[57]

John the Baptist states this verse in Hell and recalls the words of God during Christ's baptism in the river Jordan, as reported in Matthew 3:17. The Majority Text again preserves an ancient reading transmitted by several manuscripts of the *Vetus Latina*, where the personal pronoun in the dative case "mihi" ("to me") is omitted: "et ecce vox de caelis, dicens: Hic est Filius meus dilectus, in quo bene complacui" ("And behold, a voice from Heaven, saying: This is my beloved Son, in whom [I am] well pleased").[58]

The hybrid redaction makes reference instead to an analogue passage in Matthew 17:5, in which, with the same words used by God during the transfiguration of Christ on the mountain, the adverb "bene" ("well") is added: "Hic est Filius meus dilectus, in quo mihi bene conplacui" ("This is my beloved Son, in whom I am well pleased").

K XXIV.1 45/19–21	T 102v/11	A 55r/1–2
sicut per legem et prophetas tuos perdixisti, factis adimplesti. Redemisti uiuos per crucem tuam et per mortem crucis ad nos descendisti.[59]	sicut per legem et prophetas tuos predixisti. Re\`de´misti nos per crucem tuam et per mortem crucis ad nos descendisti.[60]	þu spaþer fyrer løg oc spamenn at leysa oss oc heim allan fyrer crossdauþan ⟨þinn⟩ oc niþrstignig til var.[61]

The trivialization of the reading "uiuos" ("living") into the personal pronoun "nos" ("us") in the hybrid redaction and in the Icelandic text, "oss" ("us") may be the result of a scribal error due to a paleographical change of the grapheme cluster *uiu* with the letter *n*. Indeed, the pronoun "us" does not fit the context of this passage, as this is a verse pronounced by the patriarchs and prophets, who at this point of the narrative are kneeling at Christ's feet and glorifying him for his final victory over Satan and Hell. With the word "uiuos," they are obviously not referring to themselves, who at the time of the narration have long been dead, but are rather addressing those who shall die after the death of Christ to inform them that one day, they shall also enjoy the same faith and redemption.

K XXIV 45/3	T 102r/16	A 54v/4–5
tenens dexteram Adae ascendit ab inferis.[62]	tenens manum dexteram Ade ascendit ab inferis.[63]	toc i hønd Adams oc ⟨ste⟩ upp or helvite.[64]

In this scene, Christ ascends from Hell grasping Adam's right hand , delivering him to Paradise along with the souls of the righteous, finally fulfilling their long-awaited redemption. The Majority Text differs from the hybrid redaction by omitting the object of the sentence, "manum" ("hand"), and exclusively transmitting the adjective "dexteram" ("right"). Although its absence does not compromise the logic and meaning of the passage, the word "manum" should nevertheless be restored, as it already occurred in this same chapter and in the very same context: K XXIV.1/6–7 "tenens autem Dominus manum dexteram Adae dixit ad eum" ("Moreover, the Lord, holding the right hand of Adam, said to him"). The Icelandic text is also deficient in this regard, omitting the adjective "right," which was also translated along with ("hand") in the above mentioned passage: A 54v/27–28 "þa toc Dominus i hønd ena høgri Adams oc mę̨lti sva" ("Then the Lord took Adam's right hand of and said this").

K XXV 46/13–14	T 103r/8–9	A 55r/23–4
diuinis signis et prodigiis preliaturi cum eo, et ab eo occisi in Hierusalem.[65]	preliari cum eo diuinis signis et prodigiis et ab eo occidemur in Iherusalem.[66]	oc beriaz a mot honom meþ Guþs iarteinom oc tacnom. Hann mon ocr lata vega ⟨i⟩ Iorsalaborg.[67]

Enoch states the above text in Paradise after Christ's deliverance of the souls of the righteous. It refers to the slaying of the two Christ-like witnesses – here identified as Enoch and Elijah – after their testimony as relayed in Revelation 11:7–8.[68] The hybrid redaction changes the past participle "ab eo occisi" ("they [shall be] slain by him") of the Majority Text with a first person plural passive, "ab eo occidemur" ("we shall be slain by him"), which is well reflected in the Icelandic text A 55r/24 "hann mon ocr lata vega" ("he shall slain us in Jerusalem").

Minor Variants of T Reflected in A against K and R

K XXI.2 40/1–2	R 1ra/22–4	T 101r/4–5	A 53v/25–6
Haec audiens omnis multitudo sanctorum cum uoce increpationis dixit ad Inferum.[69]	Hec audiens omnis multitudo cum uoce increpationis dixerunt ad Infernum.[70]	Hec audi'e'ns omnis multitudo sanctorum cum uoce increpationis dixerunt ad demones.[71]	Guþs helgir er þeir heyrðo þetta þa męlto þeir sva viþ ðær illar vættir.[72]

Whereas the Majority Text transmits the correct reading that refers to Hell with its name in the singular "Inferus," the hybrid recension, and consequently the Icelandic translation, depersonifies Inferus, who in the hybrid redaction is addressed in the plural as "demones" ("devils") and rendered in the Icelandic text with "illar vættir" ("evil spirits"). Turville-Petre noted this divergence, but traced it back to the inventiveness of the Icelandic translator and regarded it as one of his literary licenses, instead of postulating his consultation of a different Latin source text.[73]

The transportation of the figure of Hell into a plurality of devils might have been used in the hybrid text as a consequence of the three instances within the Majority Text, where Hell refers to his servants: K XX.3 40/13–16 "contremui perterritus pauore et omnia impia officia mea simul mecum conturbata sunt" ("I was afraid and terrified with fear and all my impious servants were also disturbed with me"); K XX1.1 40/8–9 "et dixit Inferus ad sua impia officia" ("and Hell said to his impious servants"); K XXII.1 42/1–2 "Hec uidentes Inferus et Mors et impia officia eorum cum crudelibus ministris expauerunt" ("seeing these things, Hell and Death and their impious servants with the cruel ministers were afraid").[74]

K XXI.3 41/3	R 1rb/8–9	T 101r/16–17	A 54r/4–5
Et facta est uox magna ut tonitruum.[75]	Et facta est uox magna ut tonitruum.[76]	Et facta est iterum uox magna ut tronitrui.[77]	Þa hafa þeir i annat sinn heyrþa rødd sva micla at scialfa þotte helvite allt.[78]

This is the second instance of Psalm 24(23):7–9 and the *Tollite portas* verses. The hybrid redaction and the Icelandic translation share the presence of the adverb of frequency "iterum" ("a second time") and "i annat sinn" ("a second time") while there is no trace of it in the Majority Text and in the Icelandic fragment R.

K XXI.3 41/12–14	R 1rb/19–22	T 101r/22–3	A 54r/11
Et ipse Dominus de caelo in terris prospexit ut audiret gemitum uinculorum et solueret filios interemptorum.[79]	Et ipse Dominus de celo in terris perspexit ut audiret gemitum uinculatorum et solueret filios interemptorum.[80]	Et ipse Dominus de celo in terris prospexit ut audiret gemitus compenditorum et solueret filios interemptorum.[81]	Dominus de celo in terram aspexit ut audiret gemitus compenditorum ut solueret filios interemptorum.[82]

These words, stated by King David in Hell, are directly quoted from Psalm 101(100):21. The genitive plural "uinculorum" ("of the chains") is clearly a scribal error transmitted by the Majority Text and should therefore be emended with the genitive plural of the past participle "uinculatorum" ("of those who had been bound in chains"), as found in the Icelandic fragment R. The Majority Text and consequently the Icelandic fragment R preserve again an older reading, "gemitum uinculatorum" ("the groan of those who had been bound in chains"), transmitted in numerous manuscripts of the *Vetus Latina*.[83] The reading extant in the hybrid redaction and in the Icelandic text "gemitus compeditorum" ("the groans of those who had been fettered") is derived from the Vulgate.

Agreement between K and E against T and A

K XX.3 39/1–2	E 1v/3	T 100r/3–4	A 53r/7–8
Tu mihi dixisti quia ipse est qui mortuos a me traxit.[84]	Þa sagdir mier at þessi er sa sialfur er dauda menn dro fra mer.[85]	Tu mihi dixisti ip⟨s⟩e est qui mortuos `a te´ tulit.[86]	Enn þat vitom ver at hann hevir menn marga dauþa af ðer teket.[87]

The above sentence is stated by Hell when he addresses Satan to express his perplexity towards the intrinsic nature of Christ. It suggests that despite his human appearance, the power of his divinity had in several instances proven to be almighty. Hell laments that even before his death on the cross, Christ had been able to resurrect men who were already dead, such as Lazarus.

Whereas the Majority Text preserves the correct reading "mortuos a me traxit" ("dragged away the dead from me") – implying that the souls were snatched out of Hell (Hell being the first person in this sentence) – the compiler of the hybrid text changes this perspective, suggesting that the dead were ultimately the property of Satan "mortuos 'a te' tulit" ("took away the dead from you"). The use of the verb "tulit" ("took away") in the hybrid recension was probably influenced by K XX.3/2–4, "Multi enim sunt qui a me hic detenti sunt qui dum uixerunt in terris a me mortuos tulerunt" ("There are many who are held captive here by me who when they lived on earth have taken away the dead from me"), and altogether omitted by the hybrid redaction. Also worthy of note are the correspondences of the verbs "trahere" ("drag") and "ferre" ("take"), respectively, with the Icelandic "draga" ("drag") and "taka" ("take"), respectively.

K XXIII.1 43/3	T 101v/30–102r/1	R 1vb/7–8	A 54v/4–5
dux exterminationis Beelzebub.[88]	dux exterminationis tricabite Beelzebub.[89]	dux exterminationis tricapita Beelzebub.[90]	dauþa ioforr þrihofða⟨ð⟩r Bee⟨l⟩zebub.[91]

Agreement between T, R, and A against K

The epithet "triceps" ("three-headed") has been given to Beelzebub in connection to Cerberus, the mythological hound guarding the underworld in Greek and Roman pagan traditions, and can be traced back to a Good Friday sermon by Eusebius of Alexandria.[92] However, it is more likely that the compiler of the hybrid redaction was acquainted with the "Cerberus triceps inferorum canis" ("Cerberus, the three-headed hound of Hell") mentioned by Augustine in his *De civitate Dei*.[93]

The Icelandic compiler is faithful to his source and recalls the image of a three-headed devil in chapter XX.1, where he juxtaposes it to the adjective which describes Satan as a "seven-headed" dragon, an interpolated reading derived from Revelation 12:3 absent in the Majority Text and in the hybrid redaction and peculiar only to the Icelandic translation.[94] The compiler specifies that Satan may at times also reveal himself with seven or three heads: A 52v/17–19 "Satan iotunn helvitis høfðingi er stundom er meþ VII høfðom enn stundom meþ III enn stundom i drekalike þess er omorlegr er oc ogorlegr oc illilegr a allar lunder."[95]

The noun "iotunn" ("giant") in connection to Satan is an innovation and peculiarity of AM 645 4to. It may have come about through a paleographical change and confusion of the grapheme clusters *-fvrr* and *-tvnn* from an original "iofurr" ("prince") translating the Latin "princeps" ("prince"). The changing of "iofurr"/"iotunn" in this passage may have influenced its subsequent employment in chapter XX.1, where Inferus is first introduced in the story and referred to with the appellative T 99v/15 "preparatorem inferorum" ("preparer of Hell"). In the Icelandic translation, Inferus is described as a "host" of evil beings, composed of creatures of Nordic mythology and of Christian devils of the Latin source: A 52v/19–20 "viþ iotna oc viþ diofla oc viþ rikistroll ⟨oc⟩ gørvoll þau er i helvite voro" ("with the giants, the devils, the mighty trolls, and all of those who were in Hell"). The original reading "prince," in place of the later variant "giant," is preserved in chapter XXIII.1, where the compiler of AM 645 4to twice translates the Latin "dux" ("prince, duke") and "princeps" ("prince") with the Icelandic "iofurr" ("prince"): T 101v/30 "dux exterminationis" ("Prince of destruction") is translated as A 54v/4–5 "dauþa ioforr" ("Prince of Death") and T 102r/9–10 "O princeps omnium malorum pater impiorum" ("O Prince of all evil and father of the wicked") as A 54v/13 "Satan ioførr helvitis oc allz illz" ("Satan, Prince of Hell and of all evil").

K XXIII.1 43/7–9	T 102r/3–4	R 1vb/12–15	A 54v/7–9
Ecce iam iste Iesus diuinitatis suae fulgore fugat omnes tenebras mortis, et firmum carcerum confregit.[96]	Ecce iam iste Ihesus diuinitatis sue fulgore fugauit omnes tenebras mortis et ima carceris claustra confregit.[97]	Etiam iste Iesus sue diuinitatis fulgore fugauit omnes tenebras mortis et ima claustra carceris confregit.[98]	Þat ma nu of sia at Christus fer her nu oc rekr a braut meþ liose guþdoms sins dauþa myrcr oc braut byrgi var øll.[99]

The reading "firmum carcerum confregit" ("He has broken the steadfast prisons") transmitted by the Majority Text seems to have caused a scribal error during one of its subsequent transcriptions. A second reviser of the Majority Text has substituted the adjective in the accusative form "firmum" ("steadfast"), which is clearly apposed to the noun "carcerum" ("prison"), also in the accusative form, with the less ambiguous noun "claustrum" ("enclosure"). The proximity of the two nouns "claustrum" and "carcerum" in the sentence might have generated further confusion, so at a certain point, the original object of the sentence "carcerum" ("prison") in the accusative case was perceived as incorrect and was transferred into the genitive case "carceris" ("of the prison"), referring to the object "claustra" ("the enclosures of the prison").

Subsequently, the noun phrase "claustra carceris" started to be understood with the stricter military acception of "claustra" ("defence, fortress, walls"). The adjective "ima" ("innermost, deepest") was added for further specification. The Icelandic text mirrors the hybrid text, rendering the Latin "claustrum" ("enclosure, fortress") with the Icelandic "byrgi" ("enclosure, fortress").

5 The Textual Interpolations of *Niðrstigningar saga*

As has been shown in chapter 4, the difficulty in assigning a particular source to certain passages of *Niðrstigningar saga* is mostly due to the fact that its text is not a translation sensu stricto but rather an adaptation and reformulation of the Latin apocryphon, involving profound elaboration of the original narrative fabric. Numerous textual variants and departures from the most plausible underlying sources must be ascribed to the translator's own editorial predilections and to no other particular source. Besides adjusting lexicon and sentence structure to his taste, the compiler felt compelled to integrate into the original plot substantial narrative details extraneous to the Latin apocryphon. These secondary additions are all biblical and patristic in nature, and some of them are so intricately woven into the primitive narrative framework that the task of identifying and sourcing them may at times feel overwhelming.

Throughout the narrative, the Icelandic compiler alters the regular course of the Latin text four times, introducing the description of the gates of Paradise as guarded by a cherub, substantially augmenting the antithetical description of Christ and then of Satan, and inserting a section relating to the epic and figurative victory of Christ over the Devil. All the interpolated sections, here surveyed in their order of appearance in the Icelandic text, are signalled by editorial notes or additional sentences, which introduce sudden changes or recovery of the narrative.

The Gates of Paradise

At the beginning of the *Descensus*, the original Latin text focuses on Seth's journey to Paradise in a quest for the Oil of Mercy to anoint the body of his father Adam, who had long lain infirm and in terrible pain as a consequence of his fall from Paradise.[1] At the news of Christ's baptism in the river Jordan, announced in Hell by John the Baptist himself, Adam asks his son Seth to relate to the patriarchs his quest to Paradise for the Oil of Mercy. At the beginning of Seth's narrative, after a mention of the gates of Paradise – "Þat var qvat Seth þa er ec for eyren⟨dis⟩ foþor mins at ec com of siþir til paradisar hliþs"[2] ("It occurred, said Seth, when I travelled on my father's errand, that I came at last to the gates of Paradise"), the Icelandic compiler inserts additional narrative material describing the fierce scenario at its entrance:

> Þar var tvennt fyrer at **þar var elldr brenna⟨n⟩di at banna manni hveriom at⟨gøngo paradisar⟩ enn englar at veria øllom dioflom oc øndom syndogra manna**.[3]

> (There were two things before me: there was burning fire to deny any man any entrance to Paradise and angels to guard it against all devils and the souls of sinful men.)

The very same description of the gates of Paradise is in fact extant in Peter Comestor's *Historia scholastica*, chapter 25. After quoting Genesis 3:24, relating the expulsion of Adam and Eve from the Garden of Eden and the placement of cherubims as guards of the gates of Paradise in order to protect the tree of life,[4] Comestor further specifies that God purposely deployed an angel or a rank of angels ("angelus," "ministero angelorum" / "englir") to guard ("arceret" / "veria") the threshold of Paradise against the advances of (the) devil(s) ("diabolum" / "øllom dioflom"), whereas fire ("ignis" / "elldr") would deny ("intercluderet" / "banna") entrance ("ingressum" / "hveriom atgøngo") to men ("hominem" / "øndom synðroga manna").[5]

> Et collocauit ante paradisum uoluptatis cherubim, flammeum gladium atque uersatilem, **ut angelus arceret diabolum, ignis hominem. Vel ministerio angelorum posuit ignem ibi, qui intercluderet paradisi ingressum**, qui nomine gladii non cuiuslibet, sed uersatilis dicitur, id est utrobique secantis, quia pena fuit homini in utraque parte sui puniri.[6]

> (And He placed before the Paradise of pleasure cherubims, and a flaming sword, turning every way, so that an angel would defend it against the Devil, and fire against men. He also placed a ministry of angels and fire, which obstructed the entrance to Paradise. The name of the sword does not exist, but it is said to be turning every way, that is, cutting on both sides, wherefore it was a punishment to man, who is to be punished on both sides.)

Peter Comestor (†1178) wrote his *Historia* in Paris around the year 1170, roughly the same year he retired from teaching to the Abbey of Saint Victor. He intended it as a biblical compendium and explanatory gloss for the students of theology at the cathedral school of Notre-Dame.[7] The *Historia* soon circulated widely throughout Europe, not least in Norway and Iceland, where, along with Vincent of Beauvais's *Speculum historiale* (compiled between 1244 and 1259), it was repeatedly employed for its interpretation and amplification of devotional literature, most notably in the redactions of the first extensive Old Norse biblical compilation known as *Stjórn*.[8]

As a matter of fact, the very same commentary on Genesis 3:24 figures in the section concerning the expulsion of Adam and Eve from the Garden of Eden in *Stjórn* I, the youngest of the three biblical compilations, written in Norway at the beginning of the fourteenth century, roughly a century after *Niðrstigningar saga*.[9]

> **genesis** Ok sem guð hafði adam oc eua*m* b*ro*tt rekit or p*ar*adiso þa skipaði h*an*n *þar fyrer* til v*er*ndar .ij. lutí. at eingi mętti lifs trenu namunda koma. Cherubín ein*n* engill af þui engla fẏlkí er cherub*i*m heit*er*. settí h*an*n motí fiandans a̋ laupum en*n* elldin*n* móti man*n*inu*m* hu*er*n er moẏses nefn*er* elldligt su*erð ok* snuanlegt eðr brott tękiligt. af þui s*ua* at þ*en*na sama elld let guð beði f*ra* snuaz þan*n* tíma s*em* enoch uar numin*n* i f*yrr* nefnda *ok sua* þa er helyas var numín*n*. Ef nǫkkuʀ spẏʀ huat sa elldr hafi ser t*il* nęringar þa má þi vel þartil suara at nǫkkur elldzens mẏnd er su er æ*igi* þarf nǫkkut efni ser t*il* nęring*ar* sem sa̋ er lesit er af i sǫgu heilags nícholai af hu*er*ium er maðren*n* kenner hita ef h*an*n rett*er* sína hǫnd at h*onu*m en*n* bren*n*r þo æ*igi*. En*n* þ*ers* hattar elldr brenn*er* andana ept*er* þi s*em* i skiluísum bokum fin*nz* skrifat.[10]

> (Genesis. And after God had expelled Adam and Eve from Paradise, He placed there two things for protection, so that no one could come near the tree of life: a cherub, who is an angel from that rank of angels called cherubim, whom He set against the leaps of the Devil, and fire against man. It is mentioned by Moses as a fiery and flexible sword or as removable, because God let that same fire turn sideways at that time when Enoch was taken up into the aforementioned [Heaven] and also when Elias was taken up. If anyone asks what this fire has for nourishment, it may be answered what is read in the history of Saint Nicolas [*Nikuláss saga erkibiskups*], that one feels the heat if one stretches his hand towards it and yet does not burn. In this way, the fire burns the souls, as it is found written in trustworthy books.)

However, the two passages show no evidence of direct textual filiation and seem to have been translated independently from the same Latin source.

Accordingly, the first interpolation in *Niðrstigningar saga* might represent one of the earliest examples of the employment of Comestor's *Historia* in Iceland. The year 1170 may, therefore, be considered a terminus post quem for the compilation of the Icelandic translation, or at least for the editorial interventions with which it has been transmitted up to the present.

Seven-Headed Satan

A second source for the interpolated passages was the text of Revelation as transmitted in the Bible (Vulgate) per se, which provided extensive details for the depictions of the figures of Christ and Satan. Except for the epithets, mostly concerning the role of Satan as the undisputed sovereign of Hell,[11] the Majority Text omits any detailed physical description of the Old Enemy. Nevertheless, when Satan is finally overcome by Christ and Hell addresses him with the name Beelzebub – "princeps perditionis et dux exterminationis Beelzebub"[12] ("Prince of perdition and Ruler of destruction Beelzebub") – the source T adds the adjective "tricabite"[13] ("three-headed").

The Icelandic compiler anticipates this reading and employs it when he first introduces the character of Satan; however, he also mentions the adjective "seven-headed," a reading extracted from Revelation 12:3, in which Satan is described as a terrifying seven-headed dragon:

> **Satan** iotunn helvitis høfðingi **er stundom er meþ VII høfðom** enn stundom meþ III enn stundom **i drekalike** þess er omorlegr er oc ogorlegr oc illilegr a allar lunder.[14]
>
> (The giant Satan, the Prince of Hell, who sometimes has seven heads and sometimes three, and sometimes is in the shape of a dragon, which is horrible, terrible, and awful in all respects.)
>
> et visum est aliud signum in caelo et ecce **draco magnus** rufus **habens capita septem** et cornua decem et in capitibus suis septem diademata.[15]
>
> (And there was seen another sign in Heaven: and behold a great dragon, having seven heads, and ten horns, and on his head seven diadems.)

By including the above, the compiler informs the reader of the existence of both variants and implicitly alludes to the disagreement of the sources he is consulting.

Christ as Warrior-King

Revelation is again the source for what has been, up to now, considered the first textual interpolation of *Niðrstigningar saga*.[16] With an eloquent speech occupying the entire chapter XX.2, Hell anxiously attempts to warn Satan of the potential danger of Christ's divine powers, which, as he rightly fears, are deceivingly hidden in his human appearance: "Vissom ⟨ver⟩ þat þa sem nu at inn Almakti Guþ er i manni þeim innan oc mun comenn til þess hingat i heim at leysa menn af syndom oc leyþa til lifs guþdoms sins"[17] ("As for now, we know that the Almighty God is within that man and will have to come here into the world to release men from sins and bring them to the life of His divinity").

Despite Hell's persistence, Satan is only convinced of Christ's power when, in the beginning of chapter XXI.1, a great voice from above orders Hell to open his large gates and allow Christ to enter. These commanding verses, known by their incipit as *Tollite portas*, are borrowed from the triumphal words of Psalm 24(23):7–9, a Davidic praise to God emphasizing his sovereignty as a glorious warrior-king.[18] Psalm 24(23):7–9 plays an essential role within the narrative frame of the original *Evangelium Nicodemi* and is already transmitted in the oldest Latin redaction (represented by the *Codex Vindobonensis*) and in the Greek translation. Being emphatically repeated three times throughout the text, once by Christ himself[19] and twice by the patriarchs,[20] Christ's military kingship is impressed upon the reader. Its inclusion and repetition in the *Evangelium Nicodemi* seems to derive from an oral recitation of the *Tollite portas* verses within a liturgical ceremony or procession representing the Passion and Resurrection of Christ.[21] At the utterance of this verse, Hell promptly casts Satan out from his realms and dismissively encourages him to confront Christ alone: "far a braut nu or sætum v\`or´arom ef þu mat þa berstu nu hart viþ Dyrðar Konong\`en´"[22] ("Depart now from our seats, if you may, and fight hard with the King of Glory").

Before Satan is cast out of Hell and before the acclamation of Psalm 24(23):7–9, the original plot of the apocryphon is augmented with a detailed description of Christ arriving in Hell as a triumphant warrior-king in a similar manner, yet in this version, he is riding a white horse and leading a host of angels as reported in Revelation 19:11–17. This warlike imagery of Christ might have at least partially arisen during the process of interpretation and translation of the Latin apocryphon in combination with the repetition in the text of Psalm 24(23):7–10, which depicts the fearsome God of the Old Testament with powerful military imagery.[23] The Icelandic compiler may have made a typological connection between the historical Harrowing of Hell (which took place between Good Friday and Easter Sunday) and Christ's ultimate dealing with Satan during his Second Coming. This shifting of the narrative timeline from the first century AD to the Last Days renders the Icelandic translation more topical and confers on it a more liturgical character: the Christian audience is compelled to consider the future prophetic implications of the story, hence becoming all the more engrossed in the narrative action of the pseudo gospel.[24]

To mark the beginning of a new narrative section, the Icelandic compiler explicitly reveals himself in the first person, interrupting the dialogue between Satan and Hell and presenting the interpolated passage with this introductory clause: "Þar hverf ec nu fra fyrst er þeir Satan røddoz viþ. Enn ec tec fra þvi at segia er þa gørþisc enn fleira til stormerkia"[25] ("Now I shall turn away from when Satan and Hell talked first and begin to relate the most wondrous events that occurred next").

> Þat var mioc i þat mund døgra er **himenenn opnaþisc**. Þa com fyrst **hestr hvitr** enn hofðinge **sa reiþ hesti þeim er morgom hlutom er gofgari enn gørvaster aller aþrer**. **Augo hans uoro se⟨m⟩ elldz logi**. **Hann hafði corono a høfþi þa er morg sigrsmerki matte of syna**. **Hann hafði cleþi** þat umb aunnor uta⟨n⟩ **er bloþstocet var a cleþi hans yfer mioþmenni** voro orþ þessi **riten Rex regum et Dominus dominantium**. Hann var **solo** biartare. Hann leidde eptir ser **her mikinn** oc aller þeir er **honom fylgþo riþo hestom hvitom oc voro** aller **cleddir silki hvito** oc voro **lioser mioc**.[26]

> (It was at that point of the day that Heaven opened, and there came forth first a white horse, and the Prince who rode that horse was in many respects more noble than the most accomplished of all others. His eyes were like blazing fire. He had a crown on His head where many tokens of victory could be seen. He had a vestment above the others that was spattered with blood. On His vestment, around the waist, these words were written: King of kings and Lord of lords. He was brighter than the sun. He led a great army, and all those who followed Him rode white horses, and all were dressed in white silk and were very bright.)

> et vidi **caelum apertum** et ecce **equus albus** et **qui sedebat super eum** vocabatur Fidelis et Verax vocatur et **iustitia iudicat et pugnat oculi** autem **eius sicut flamma ignis** et **in capite eius diademata multa habens nomen scriptum** quod nemo novit nisi ipse et vestitus erat **vestem aspersam sanguine** et vocatur nomine eius Verbum Dei et **exercitus** qui sunt in caelo **sequebantur eum in equis albis vestiti byssinum album mundum** [...] et **habet in vestimento** et **in femore** suo **scriptum rex regum et Dominus dominantium** et vidi unum angelum stantem in **sole**.[27]

(And I saw Heaven opened, and behold a white horse; and He that sat upon him was called faithful and true, and with justice doth He judge and fight. And His eyes were as a flame of fire, and on His head were many diadems, and He had a name written, which no man knoweth but Himself. And He was clothed with a garment sprinkled with blood; and His name is called, The Word of God. And the armies that are in Heaven followed Him on white horses, clothed in fine linen, white and clean [...] And He hath on His garment, on His thigh, written: King of kings, and Lord of lords. And I saw an angel standing in the sun.)

The translator anticipates Revelation 19:16 but altogether omits Revelation 19:15, a prominent passage that preserves a metaphorical image of a sharp sword coming out of Christ's mouth and symbolizes Christ's future penetrating evaluation of the sins of mankind.[28] This figurative description of Christ implies his final judgment of the souls on Doomsday and does not involve any physical description of his person or the heavenly army preparing to destroy Hell. It might, therefore, have been of little use to the compiler of *Niðrstigningar saga* intent on a coherent elaboration of the plot at this point of the narrative.

The Capture of Satan on the Cross

The following interpolated section can undoubtedly be considered one of the high points of the narrative, as it describes the rapid succession of events after Satan has been cast out of Hell. First, taking the shape of a gigantic dragon, Satan threatens the world, and at the news of Christ's crucifixion, he travels to Jerusalem, convinced that he is capable of slaying Christ. Just as he is about to swallow the soul of Christ, he belatedly and bitterly realizes that he has instead been entrapped on the cross, much like a fish caught on a fishhook, a mouse in a mousetrap, or a fox in a snare.

Þa bra hann ser i drecalike oc gørdiz þa sva mikill at hann þottesc liggia mundo umb heimenn allan utan. Hann sa þau tiþende ⟨er gørdoz⟩ at Iorsolom at **Iesus Christus** var þa **i andlati** oc **for** ⟨**hann**⟩ þangat þegar oc **ætlaþi** at slita ondina þegar fra honom. Enn er hann com þar oc hugþez **gløpa mundo** hann oc hafa meþ ser þa **beit øngullinn goddomens** hann enn **crossmarkit** fell a hann ovann oc varþ hann þa sva **veiddr se⟨m⟩ fiscr a øngle** eþa **mus under treketti** eþa sem **melracki i gilldro** eptir þvi sem fyrer var spat. Þa for til Dominus Noster oc bat hann.[29]

(Then he transformed himself into the shape of a dragon and grew to such a stature that it seemed he could lie around the whole world. He saw those events that occurred in Jerusalem, that Jesus Christ was breathing His last, and immediately travelled there and intended to tear away His soul at once from Him. But when he came there, and thought he could swallow Him and carry Him away, the hook of divinity bit him, and the sign of the cross fell down on him, and he was caught like a fish on a fishhook, a mouse in a mousetrap, or an arctic fox in a snare, according to what was previously prophesied. Then Our Lord went to him and bound him.)

Previous studies have interpreted this passage in various ways. One theory posits that it is derived from the famous passage in Job 41,[30] where Yahweh warns Job of the absurdity of any attempt to catch the Leviathan (the mythological monster of chaos) and ironically asks his interlocutor whether he is able to simply catch the beast and pierce it with a fishhook:

an extrahere poteris Leviathan hamo et fune ligabis linguam eius numquid pones circulum in naribus eius et armilla perforabis maxillam eius numquid multiplicabit ad te preces aut loquetur tibi mollia numquid feriet tecum pactum et accipies eum servum sempiternum numquid includes ei quasi avi aut ligabis illum ancillis tuis concident eum amici divident illum negotiatiores numquid implebis sagenas pelle eius et gurgustium piscium capite illius pone super eum manum tuam memento belli nec ultra addas loqui ecce spes eius frustabitur eum et videntibus cunctis praecipitabitur non quasi crudelis suscitabo eum quis enim resistere potest vultui meo quis ante dedit mihi ut reddam ei omnia quae sub caelo sunt mea sunt.[31]

(Canst thou draw out the Leviathan with a hook, or canst thou tie his tongue with a cord? Canst thou put a ring in his nose, or bore through his jaw with a buckle? Will he make many supplications to thee, or speak soft words to thee? Will he make a covenant to thee, and wilt thou take him to be a servant for ever? Shalt thou play with him as with a bird, or tie him up for thy handmaids? Shall friends cut him in pieces, shall merchants divide him? Wilt thou fill nets with his skin, and the cabins of fishes with his head? Lay thy hand upon him: remember the battle, and speak no more. Behold this hope shall fall him, and in the sight of all, he shall be cast down. I will not stir him up, like one that is cruel: for who can resist my countenance? Who hath given me before that I should repay him? All things that are under Heaven are mine.)

A second theory has considered the interpolation as native narrative material derived from the mythological fishing for the *Miðgarðsormr* (the World Serpent of Norse mythology), related most extensively in the poem *Hymiskviða* of the *Elder Edda*, and subsequently treated by Snorri Sturluson (†1241) in the *Snorra Edda*, in which Þórr, on his fishing expedition, attempts to catch the

Miðgarðsormr but eventually fails.[32] James W. Marchand has subsequently discarded this theory and has instead drawn attention to a homily by Pope Gregory the Great on the Resurrection of Christ, in which Job 41 is quoted and commented upon; this homily made its way into the *Icelandic Homily Book* (Stockholm, Kb Holm. Perg. 15 4to), in which the name "Leviathan" is glossed above the line with "Miðgarðsormr."

> oc ſté h*a*ɴ þa yv*er* eɴ forna fiánda eſ h*a*ɴ lét ofriþar m*e*ɴ b*er*iaſc i gegn ſér. þ*at* ſýnde d*ró*tteɴ þa eſ h*a*ɴ mælte viþ eɴ ſæla iób. ᴍᴏɴ e*ige* þu d*ra*ga leviaþan miþgarþ*ar* ormr a ǫngle eþa bora kiþr h*an*ſ meþ báuge. Sia gléypande hvalr m*er*k*er* gróþgan aɴſkota þaɴ eſ ſvelga vill ałt maɴkyn idauþa. Agn eſ lagt a ǫngol en hvas broddr léyneſc. þeɴa orm tók almáttegr g*o*þ a ǫngle. þa eſ h*a*ɴ ſende ſon ſɪɴ til dáuþa ſýnelegan at líka*m* en oſýnelegan at g*o*þdóme. Diaboluſ ſa agn lika*m*ſ h*an*ſ þ*at* eſ h*a*ɴ beit oc viłde fyrfara. En g*o*þdo*m*ſ b*ro*ddr ſtangaþe h*a*ɴ ſvaſe*m* ǫngoł. A ǫngle varþ h*a*ɴ tekeɴ. þ*uia*t h*a*ɴ beideſc at g*ri*pa líca*m*ſ agn þ*at* eſ h*a*ɴ ſa. en vas g*o*þdó*m*ſ b*ro*dr ſa eſ léyndr vaſ ſærþe h*a*ɴ. A ongle varþ h*a*ɴ tekeɴ. þ*uia*t h*a*ɴ fek ſcaþa afþui eſ h*a*ɴ béit. oc glataþe h*a*ɴ þei*m* eſ h*a*ɴ hafþe áþr vełde yv*er*. þ*uia*t \`h*a*ɴ´ tréyſteſc at g*ri*pa þaɴ eſ h*a*ɴ hafþe etke vełde igegn.[33]

> (And then He [Christ] overcame the Old Enemy, who had let hostile people go against Him. This was shown by the Lord when He spoke to the blessed Job: *You cannot drag out the Leviathan* \`the Miðgarðsormr´ *on a fishhook, or pierce its jaw with a ring* [Job 41:1–3(40:20–1)]. This devouring whale symbolizes the greedy enemy that wants to swallow mankind into Death. The bait is lain on the fishhook, and its sharp point remains hidden. That serpent was taken on a fishhook by the Almighty Lord when He sent His Son to death with a visible body but an invisible divinity. The Devil saw the bait of his body, which he bit and wanted to destroy, but the divinity picked him like a fishhook. He was taken on a fishhook because he was impelled to seize the bait of the body, which he could see, but the sharp point of the divinity, which was hidden, injured him. He was taken on the fishhook because he was hurt by what he had bitten and he lost what previously was under his power because he trusted himself in seizing the One upon whom he had no power.)

It should nevertheless be noted that the first line of the interpolation makes no explicit reference to the Leviathan itself; instead it describes the terrifying transformation of Satan into a great dragon after his expulsion from Hell. This description seems to be typologically and formally more suitable to the literary context of Revelation, Satan's rejection from Hell being reminiscent of his other epic expulsion, his fall from Paradise. In Revelation 12:9, when he is expelled from Heaven and cast down to earth, Satan is powerfully described as having the shape of a great dragon ("draco magnus" / "dreki mikill"), threatening or lying around ("sedurre" / "liggia umb") the entire world ("orbem universum" / "allan heima"): "Et proiectus est draco ille magnus, serpens antiquus, qui uocatur diabolus, et Satanas, qui seducit universum orbem et proiectus est in terram et angelis eius cum illi missi sunt" ("And that great dragon was cast out, that old serpent, who is called the devil and Satan, who seduceth the whole world; and he was cast unto the earth, and his angels were thrown down with him").

As I will show below, the second section concerning the defeat of Satan is not derived from the Bible itself, and the homily of Gregory the Great in the *Icelandic Homily Book*, albeit thematically and theologically suitable, cannot be considered the ultimate source of this passage, since it lacks the other two images: those of a mousetrap and a snare.

The analogy between the cross and a fishhook, subsequently adopted by Gregory the Great at the end of the sixth century, was first employed in the fourth century by Gregory of Nyssa (†ca. 395) in one of his sermons to illustrate the meaning and consequence of the death of Christ.[34] Gregory of Nyssa suggested that the death of Christ was a necessary ransom paid to the Devil by God himself, who sacrificed his only Son to deliver humanity from original sin. Satan accepted God's bargain, but he was eventually defeated as he failed to recognize the duality of Christ's nature: both human and divine. Gregory tells that when the Devil, hungry for death and blinded by his greed, saw Christ in his earthly body on the cross, he rushed to gulp down Christ's body but was instead entrapped on the Cross like a "ravenous fish" on a "fishhook."[35] This view of Redemption, which would later be labelled as the "ransom theory of atonement," would become the most widely disseminated theory of Redemption throughout Late Antiquity and the Early Middle Ages.[36]

In the fifth century, Augustine drew extensively on this theory and further developed it, suggesting that God consciously decided not to defeat the Devil by exercising his absolute power over him but instead preferred to conquer him through justice in order to provide a good example to humanity.[37] Accordingly, Gregory's fishhook metaphor seems to have at least partially inspired Augustine to adopt the image of a "muscipula" ("a mousetrap") for the capturing of Satan on the cross, a gloomy image that was normally reserved for the temptations of Satan.[38]

On two occasions, Augustine employs the two images – that is, "hamus" ("fishhook") and "muscipula" ("mousetrap") – together to symbolize the cross. In both contexts, a third hunting trap, a "laqueus" ("snare or trap for lions"), is also involved to further emphasize the beastly nature of the Devil and the danger of leaving him unbound.[39] Of particular interest to this discussion is *Sermo* 265D, *De Quadragesima Ascensione Domini*, a sermon delivered against the Manicheans and their heresies, which contemplated Christ as a pure emanation of the deity and neglected his human substance.[40] A section of the text commenting upon 1 Corinthians 15:54,[41] entitled *Crux Christi muscipula fuit diabolo*, displays important verbal and thematic affinities to the interpolated text of *Niðrstigningar saga*:[42]

> quid ergo miraris? certe uita est **christus**: quare mortua est uita? nec **anima mortua** est, nec **uerbum** mortuum est: caro mortua est, ut in ea mors moreretur. mortem passus, mortem occidit: ad **leonem escam in laqueo** posuit. **piscis** si nihil **uellet deuorare, in hamo** non caperetur. mortis auidus **diabolus** fuit, mortis auarus diabolus fuit. **crux christi muscipula** fuit: mors christi, immo caro mortalis christi **tamquam esca in muscipula fuit**. **uenit, hausit et captus est**. ecce resurrexit christus: mors ubi est? iam in illius carne dicitur, quod in nostra in fine dicetur: absorta est mors in uictoriam. caro erat, sed corruptio non erat. manente natura qualitas immutatur: ipsa substantia, sed nullus ibi iam defectus, nulla tarditas, nulla corruptio, nulla indigentia, nihil mortale, nihil quale solemus nosse terrenum. tangebatur, tractabatur, palpabatur, sed non occidebatur.[43]
>
> (The Cross of Christ was a mousetrap for the Devil. So why be surprised? Surely, Christ is life: so why did life die? The soul did not die, the Word did not die, but the flesh died, so that Death would die in it. Having suffered Death, He slew Death; He put the bait for the lion in the snare. If the fish did not want to devour anything, he would not be caught on the fishhook. The Devil was greedy for Death, the Devil coveted Death. The Cross of Christ was a mousetrap: the death of Christ, or rather the mortal flesh of Christ, was like a bait in the mousetrap. He came, he swallowed it, and was caught. And Behold, Christ rose up again. Where is Death now? Already for His flesh can be said what will be said for ours in the end: *Death is swallowed up in victory* [1 Corinthians 15:54]. It was flesh, but it was not corruptible. Its nature remains the same, its quality changes. The substance is the same, but there is no deficiency there, no tardiness, no corruption, no neediness, nothing mortal, nothing which we know to be earthly. He was touched, He was patted, but He was not slain.)

In the Icelandic text, these narrative elements are presented in a different order due to the necessary reformulation and adaptation of the sermon to the plot of the pseudo gospel. Nevertheless, the Icelandic compiler seems to be attentive by partly translating and partly accommodating all the above-mentioned similes. Accordingly, the interpolated passage states that upon the death of Christ in Jerusalem (i.e., before his cross at Golgotha, right above the entrance to Hell), Satan wanted to tear away the soul of Christ ("slita ondina"), which, as Augustine asserts, would never die ("nec anima mortua est").[44] The Old Enemy craved to swallow it ("gløpa"/"devorare"), but being unable to recognize the true nature of Christ – that is, his hidden divinity ("verbum"/"godomens") – he was instead captured ("veiddr"/"captus") on the Cross ("Crux Christi"/"crossmarkit") like a fish ("piscis"/"fiscr") on a fishhook ("hamo"/ "øngullinn"), like a mouse in a mousetrap ("musicpula"/"treketti"), or even caught in a snare ("laqueo"/"gilldro") like an artic fox ("melracki") – a necessary adaptation of an African lion ("leo") into a suitable Nordic equivalent – the prey most commonly caught in traps in medieval Iceland.[45]

The sentence describing Satan being physically bound by Christ – "Þa for til Dominus Noster oc batt hann enn qvade til engla sina at varþveita hann"[46] ("Then Our Lord went to him and bound him and ordered his angels to guard him") – is a repetition and an anticipation of his final binding before the deliverance of Adam to Paradise[47] and should therefore not be considered part of the interpolation.

Augustine's *Sermo* 265D seems to have enjoyed limited circulation in Europe and is today extant in only two twelfth-century codices: Vatican City, BAV, 4951, copied in Rochester in the first decade of the twelfth century, and Worcester, Cathedral Library, F 93.[48] Although BAV 4951 was copied in England, the collection it contains shows greater similarity with Roman than Carolingian homiliaries, it resembles English collections even less, as it gives much space to the texts of Augustine, pseudo-Augustine, and Caesarius of Arles. Furthermore, the excellent state of the texts might be proof that it is a copy of a continental collection of sermons only recently acquired by the Rochester Cathedral Library.[49] Like the two great twelfth-century Rochester Bibles, sharing both textual and paleographic features with the northern French Bibles revised at Saint-Germain-des-Prés, the Rochester homiliary may have been brought to Rochester from Paris (or a nearby region) via Canterbury, which maintained strong ties with northern France throughout the twelfth century.[50]

At this point, the question arises as to whether the Icelandic compiler had access to *Sermo* 265D at length or whether he had acquaintance with the fishhook/mousetrap/snare metaphors through intermediate sources such as commentaries reporting Augustine's similes, explicit quotations, or scattered or continuous glosses.

It appears that, after a long absence from theological sources, the metaphor of the mousetrap for the Cross of Christ surfaces again in the theological and exegetical writings of Peter Lombard (†1160), Bishop of Paris and one of the greatest exponents of the Paris school of theology.[51] Perhaps prompted by renewed interest in the theological writings of Augustine, the metaphor is used in the *Sententiae in IV libris distinctae*, a comprehensive collection of theological texts extracted from the Bible and from the relevant patristic commentaries composed by Lombard at Saint Victor Abbey between 1157 and 1158.[52] The excerpts were systematically collected in the form of a continuous gloss divided into four main books, partitioned according to the main theological themes summarized in the articles of the Creed: the Trinity, the Creation, the Incarnation, and the Sacraments.

The *Sententiae* enjoyed extensive circulation and, towards the end of the twelfth century, the completion of individual scholarly commentaries on it became a fundamental requirement for the successful completion of a bachelor's degree in theology, the so-called baccalarii Sententiarii, which normally lasted two years and later led to the full degree known as "baccalarius formatus."[53] In book 3, distinction 19, chapter 1, which draws extensively on Augustine's *Sermo* 130 (a) – in which Christ is described as the Good Merchant who ransomed humanity from the Devil – Lombard illustrates how the Cross functioned as a mousetrap, and Christ's blood as bait for the devil.[54]

> Per illum ergo redempti sumus, in quo princeps mundi nihil inuenit. Unde augustinus, causam et modum nostrae redemptionis insinuans, ait: Nihil inuenit diabolus in christo ut moreretur, sed pro uoluntate patris mori christus uoluit; non habens mortis causam de peccato, sed de obedientia et iustitia mortem gustauit; per quam nos redemit a seruitute diaboli. Incideramus enim in principem huius saeculi, qui seduxit adam et seruum fecit, coepit que nos quasi uernaculos possidere. Sed uenit redemptor, et uictus est deceptor. Et quid fecit redemptor captiuatori nostro? Tetendit ei muscipulam, crucem suam; posuit ibi quasi escam, sanguinem suum. Ille autem sanguinem fudit non debitoris, per quod recessit a debitoribus. Ille quippe ad hoc sanguinem suum fudit, ut peccata nostra deleret. Unde ergo diabolus nos tenebat, deletum est sanguine redemptoris: Non enim tenebat nos nisi uinculis peccatorum nostrorum. Istae erant catenae captiuorum. Venit ille, alligauit fortem uinculis passionis suae; intrauit in domum eius, id est in corda eorum ubi ipse habitabat, et uasa eius, scilicet nos, eripuit; quae ille impleuerat amaritudine sua. Deus autem noster, uasa eius eripiens et sua faciens, fudit amaritudinem et impleuit dulcedine, per mortem suam a peccatis redimens et adoptionem gloriae filiorum largiens.[55]

> (Then through Him we have been redeemed, as in Him the Prince of the World [Satan] has found nothing. Hence, Augustine, alluding to the reason and manner of our Redemption, said: *The Devil found nothing in Christ for which He should*

die. Christ wished to die because that was His Father's will. Having no reason of death on account of sin, He tasted death through obedience and justice; through it He redeemed us from the servitude of the devil. Indeed, we had fallen upon that Prince of the World, who seduced Adam and made him his servant and he began to possess us almost like slaves. But the Redeemer came and the Seducer was overcome. And what did the Redeemer do to our Capturer? He set a mousetrap for him with His Cross. He set there His blood almost like a bait. He has shed there His blood not because He was the debtor, therefore He receded from the debtors. He shed His blood to extinguish our sins. Therefore, what held us detained by the Devil was destroyed by the Redeemer; he detained us only through the bonds of our sins, which were the chains of the captives. He came and bound the strong one with the bonds of His Passion. He came into His house, that is, into the hearts of those where He was living, and rescued His vases, that is, us, which he had filled with his bitterness. But Our God, rescuing his vases and making them His own, poured out the bitterness and filled them with sweetness, redeeming the sins through His death and bestowing the adoption of the glory of the sons.)

Lombard again quotes Augustine's *Sermo* 130 (a) in one of his sermons on the Nativity of the Lord[56] and in his *Collectaneorum in Paulum continuatio*, citing Hebrews 2:14.[57] It is from this last commentary that the mousetrap simile entered the *Glossa ordinaria* (the standard glossed Bible), which was initiated in Laon in the early twelfth century and completed in Paris and Auxerre. Lombard was one of the Parisian exegetes who edited the *Glossa* in the middle of the twelfth century.[58]

As the Apocalypse-based physical descriptions of Christ and Satan, resembling the descriptions in the Book of Revelation, has shown, the Icelandic compiler turned to the Bible when he felt the original descriptions in the Latin *Evangelium Nicodemi* were insufficient. He must have found the cursory description of Christ's final victory over Satan, which can certainly be viewed as the focal point of the *Evangelium Nicodemi*, equally unsatisfying. For a remedy, he may have turned to a copy of the *Sententiae in IV libris distinctae* in search for pertinent passages (such as, for instance, 1 Corinthians 15:54, Colossians 1:13–14, Hebrews 2:14–15) alluding to Christ's victory over the Devil through the Cross. Given the high variance of the interlinear and marginal glosses of the *Sententiae* – each copy represented a unique attempt to assist the student with issues of language, syntax, and rhetorical techniques of the Scriptures – it is highly likely that, much as in the case of Augustine's *Sermo* 130 (a) explaining Hebrews 2:14, the very copy consulted by the Icelandic compiler included a marginal gloss invoking Augustine's *Sermo* 265D with its fishhook/mousetrap/snare metaphors for the Cross.

Et pedibus ſegnis, tumida & propendulus aluo,
Hac tamen inſidias effugit arte fiber.
Mordicus ipſe ſibi medicata uirilia uellit,
Atq; abijcit ſe ſe gnarus ob illa peti,
Huius ab exemplo diſces non parcere rebus,
Et uitam ut redimas hoſtibus æra dare.

CAPTIVVS OB GVLAM

Regnator pœnus, & menſæ corroſor herilis,
Oſtrea mus ſummis uidit hiulca labris.
Quîs teneram opponẽs barbam falſa oſſa momordit
Illa recluſerunt tacta repente domum.
Deprænſum & tetro tenuerunt carcere furem,
Se met in obſcurum qui dederat tumulum.

Figure 6. Engraving depicting a mouse entrapped in a wooden mousetrap in Glasgow, UL, Special Collections, SM 19, f. E3v. Andrea Alciato, *Emblematum liber*. Augsburg: Heinrich Steyner, 1531. Reproduced with permission of the Glasgow UL.

The evidence discussed above necessarily excludes Magnús Már Lárusson's hypothesis that Jón Ögmundarson of Hólar – the first bishop of the northern diocese between 1106 and 1121 – could have been the translator and compiler of the text.[59] Instead, the date of composition should be moved closer to the date of the first witness of *Niðrstigningar saga*, AM 645 4to, one of the earliest Icelandic codices to transmit lives of saints and apostles, compiled in Skálholt in the second quarter of the thirteenth century.

6 The Theological Context of *Niðrstigningar saga*

The nature of the editorial interventions in *Niðrstigningar saga* indicates that the translation and revision of *Evangelium Nicodemi* was undertaken by an Icelandic cleric well acquainted with the contemporary biblical glosses and commentaries produced by the exegetes of the Paris school of theology during the second half of the twelfth century. Accordingly, the textual references to Comestor's *Historia scholastica* (ca. 1170), the knowledge of the *Glossa ordinaria*, and the echoes of Lombard's *Sententiae in IV libris distinctae* (ca. 1158–9), along with the employment of the Latin redaction T of *Evangelium Nicodemi*, indicate that the composition of *Niðrstigningar saga* could not have started before the third quarter of the twelfth century.

The Latin Fragments of French Provenance

An almost immediate circulation of writings produced by the Paris school of theology in early-thirteenth-century Iceland is confirmed by the survival of two texts, produced at Saint Victor around 1200, among the remnants of 144 Latin manuscripts of devotional literature. These manuscripts are today scattered throughout almost 500 fragments housed at the Arnamagnæan Institute in Copenhagen and have been recently catalogued and surveyed by Merete Geert Andersen.[1]

If the eighteen fragments of English origin are almost exclusively of liturgical nature (missals, graduals, antiphonaries, psalters, sacramentaries, breviaries, and lectionaries) and five of them are among the oldest surviving material of the collection, predating the year 1200,[2] the French fragments are both exegetical works of the Paris school of theology, dating from the thirteenth century. They are, therefore, representative, if on a small scale, of the theological texts and biblical commentaries that must have circulated in Iceland during the time of composition of *Niðrstigningar saga* and may offer some insights into the corpus of exegetical material consulted by the Icelandic compiler before he undertook his task.

For instance, it is remarkable that already around the year 1200, Iceland owned one of the few copies of the *Eulogium ad Alexandrum papam tertium*, composed by John of Cornwall in Paris between 1177 and 1178.[3] This work greatly influenced the debate concerning the hypostatic union, which took place during the Third Lateran Council, convened by Pope Alexander III in March 1179. In his treatise, John of Cornwall criticizes Peter Lombard's Christological views, accusing him above all of nihilism in asserting that Christ had assumed a human nature only accidentally.[4] This view clashed with the classical Boethian view, which traditionally contemplated the nature of Christ as a single unit of humanity and divinity, inseparable from each other.[5]

This antinihilistic position that spread rapidly throughout Europe after the Third Lateran Council (and all the more radically in the early thirteenth century) might well underlie the theological conception and interpretation of *Niðrstigningar saga*. Its influence on the theology and exegesis in the Icelandic text seems to be especially evident in the fourth textual interpolation. It has been suggested that with its inclusion into the original text of the *Evangelium Nicodemi*, the Icelandic translator places great emphasis on Satan's inability to recognize Christ's inseparable natures, the human and the divine. Indeed, it is this failure to perceive the one hypostasis behind Christ's bipartite nature that eventually causes Satan's final defeat.

The second piece of evidence of the circulation of the scholastic exegetical texts in thirteenth-century Iceland is the impressive Parisian Bible dating from the thirteenth century and consisting of seventy leaves scattered in the bindings of several manuscripts.[6] The text of this *Glossa ordinaria* covers the entire Old and New Testaments and transmits Peter Lombard's prologue to 1 Corinthians (*Corinthii sunt Achaei*) and Gilbert of Poitiers's (†1154) prologue to Revelation (*Omnes qui pie*).[7] Both scholars had worked at the Abbey of Saint Victor to finalize the text of the *Glossa ordinaria* in the middle of the twelfth century.[8] It is plausible that this volume, or a similar manuscript, was the biblical source consulted by the Icelandic compiler for the insertion of the interpolations derived from Revelation, since it still transmits sections of it and might have included the entire text.[9]

Along with other biblical literature, these texts might have been brought to Iceland by students, who in the fourth half of the twelfth century studied theology in either northern France or Paris. The only Icelander known to have studied in Paris in those years is Þorlákr Þórhallson (†1193), the patron saint of

Iceland, who between the years of 1153 and1159 attended the cathedral schools of both Saint Victor and Lincoln.[10] He then returned to Iceland and was later ordained bishop by Eysteinn Erlendsson in Niðaróss in 1178 and held the see of Skálholt from that year until his death on 23 December 1193.[11] However, the years he spent in Paris do not match with the textual evidence of the sources employed for the composition of *Niðrstigningar saga*, and the compiler of the Icelandic text needs thereafter to be searched for in the subsequent generation of clerics. There is, in fact, evidence that the text was composed at Skálholt in the first decade of the thirteenth century, along with the *Jarteinabœkr Þorláks byskups*, the first two collections of Þorlákr's miracles.

The *Jarteinabœkr Þorláks byskups*

In the five years following Þorlákr's death in 1193, and during the episcopacy of his nephew and successor, Bishop Páll Jónsson (†1211), the miracles attributed to Þorlákr became so great in number that at the Althing (the general assembly) of 1198, permission was given for vows to Þorlákr, and in the same year his relics were translated to Skálholt. The following year, the oral accounts of his reported miracles were recorded at Skálholt into a great collection under the supervision of Bishop Páll Jónsson. Þorlákr's wonders and signs were read before a great crowd at the Althing of 1199, an unparalleled event that further expanded Þorlákr's fame among Icelanders. This collection, known as the *Jarteinabók Þorláks byskups in forna* ("The Ancient Miracle Collection of Bishop Þorlákr") and containing forty-six miracles, is indeed part of the first section of AM 645 4to, where it is transmitted as item 1 (ff. 1r–11v). After the transcription of the forty miracles that took place before the Althing of 1199 (the additional six miracles that took place at the very assembly were added later), a small epilogue states that "At that same Althing, Bishop Páll had the miracles of the blessed Bishop Þorlákr – which are here written in this book – read aloud at the request of people" ("Á alþingi þessu enu sama lét Páll byskup ráða upp at bœn manna jarteinir ens sæla Þorláks byskups, þær er hér ero skrifaðar á þessi bók").[12]

The epilogue of *Niðrstigningar saga*, transmitted in the second section of the same codex (ff. 51v–55v), seems to be modelled to the epilogue of the *Jarteinabók in forna*. As already seen, the statement typical of redaction T of *Evangelium Nicodemi* asserts that after the discovery of the original pseudo gospel in Jerusalem, the Emperor Theodosius the Great had commissioned the translation of its text from Hebrew into Latin.[13] The Icelandic compiler seems to modify this statement, adapting it to the epilogue of the *Jarteinabók*; in the

Icelandic translation, the Emperor Theodosius did not commission the written translation of the text but rather requested a public reading of it, which implies that his decision was made to make the text available for the illiterate as well as the literate.[14]

The Icelandic compiler accordingly draws a parallel between Emperor Theodosius's acquisition of the apocryphon in Constantinople and his subsequent efforts to disseminate the miracles performed by Christ in Hell, and Bishop Páll's efforts to collect Þorlákr's miracles among the Icelanders and make them available for the community that gathered at the Althing in 1199. This hypothesis is further corroborated by the unusual choice of the verb "uppráða" ("read aloud") for the public reading, instead of the more conventional synonym "upplesa" ("read aloud"). Outside *Niðrstigningar saga* and the *Jarteinabók in forna*, the verb "uppráða" is only found in the nearly contemporary *Sverris saga* and refers to the public reading of a papal letter dated 15 June 1194, in which Pope Celestine III confirmed the charges of Archbishop Erik Ivarsson against King Sverrir. The letter was read aloud the same year at Lund Cathedral by Archbishop Absalon.[15] Taking into account the evidence discussed, one could argue that the year 1199, with the production of the *Jarteinabók in forna*, is a reasonable terminus post quem date of the composition of the epilogue of *Niðrstigningar saga.*

It is also likely that *Niðrstigningar saga* was already completed by the year 1211 and that its text was already available at Skálholt. Significant evidence of this is provided by the epilogue (chapter CLXXVII) of the *Jarteinabók Þorláks byskups ǫnnur* ("Second Miracle Collection of the Bishop Þorlákr"), compiled by Bishop Páll himself at Skálholt some years before his death in 1211 for the public reading on occasion of the newly instituted *Þorláksmessa* ("Þorlákr's Mass"), a holy day of obligation, celebrated on 23 December.[16]

In a highly alliterative and learned style, Páll draws a further parallel between the miracles performed by Christ and those ascribed to Þorlákr. Referring to hagiographical texts similar to those transmitted in AM 645 4to, he asserts that while the *vitae* and *passiones* of saints and martyrs are filled with cruelties and misdeeds perpetrated by evil rulers against them, the life of Þorlákr is filled with joy throughout and is incomparable to that of any other saintly man:

> Eru þær sögur margar sagðar frá helgum mönnum, postolum Guðs ok píningarváttum, att trautt verðr hitalaust huggóðum mönnum at heyra illsku ok ódáðir, geysinga ⟨ok⟩ grimmleik greifa ok höfðingja, ok hvers kyns kvalir ok harmkvæli gjörðu þeir Guðs vinum ok létu þá deyja eptir alls kyns píslir, þær er þeim kom áðr í hug þeim á hendr færa. Nú þó at öllum góðum mönnum sé stórligr fögnuðr í þeim fagnaði er nú hafa helgir menn at umbun sinna meinlæta, þá fylgja þar þó

mikil atkvæði er þeir inir grimmu menn skulu eigi snúizk hafa til Guðs frá sínum illverkum ok vánzku. En þessi frásögn sem hér er nú sögð frá inum sæla Þorláki byskupi er öll full fagnaðar ok farsælu, ok fylgir hvergi þó hryggð né hörmúng, lífit sjálft allt eptirlits ólíkt annarra manna lífi.[17]

(In the many stories that relate to the holy men, the apostles of God and the martyrs, it has become difficult for charitable men to hear without feeling compassion, the cruelties, the misdeeds, and the savageness of impetuous earls and chieftains, and of all kinds of torments and agonies which they inflicted to the friends of God, who are left to die after all sorts of tortures, which soon come to mind to those who are charged. Now, even if among all good men there is great joy in rejoicing with them, because now these holy men have received a reward for their pains, there nevertheless follows a great decree of faith, because those evil men should not have turned to God from their evil deeds and wickedness. But this story, which here has related to the blessed Bishop Þorlákr, is all full of joy and prosperity, and although it does not come anywhere near either grief or affliction, [Þorlákr's] life of guidance itself is unlike the life of any other man.)

As noted by Ásdís Egilsdóttir, Þorlákr's miracles highlight his similarity to Christ himself and to no other particular saint.[18] Interestingly, in his epilogue to the *Jarteinabók ǫnnur*, Bishop Páll attributes to Þorlákr a set of prodigious miracles performed by Christ in curing mostly physical infirmities, namely, blindness, deafness, lameness, leprosy, and demonic possession – a merging of Matthew 10:8 and 11:5,[19] which are twice referred to in Latin T and once in *Niðrstigningar saga*:[20]

Nú megum vér þat gjöra at sýna oss nú á þessari hátíð með siðlætis yfirbragði ok biðja þess almáttigan Guð, þann hinn sama, er þá krapta gefr inum sæla Þorláki byskupi at gefa sjón blindum mönnum, en heyrn daufum, göngu höltum, en hreinsa líkþrá, ok reka djöfla frá óðum mönnum, lífga þá er áðr eru dauðir, stöðva vötn ok vinda.[21]

(Now we can appreciate what has been presented on this anniversary [*Þorláksmessa*] with the bearing of virtue and praying to God the Almighty, the same who has given the powers to the blessed Bishop Þorlákr to give sight to blind men, and hearing to the deaf, walk to the lame, and [the powers] to clean leprosy and to drive out the devils from mad people, to resuscitate those who had previously been dead, and to halt waters and winds.)

Once again, drawing a parallel between the sanctity of Christ and that of Þorlákr, Páll adopts the similes of "trap" ("gilldra"), "bait" ("ögn"), and "wild animals" ("dýr"), employing them eleven times throughout the text. These amount to another echo of *Niðrstigningar saga*. Accordingly, we are told by the author that in our earthly life we encounter two kind of traps: those set by God to bless us and those set by the Devil to lead us into temptation. Páll explains that God has set before us "manifold traps of mercy" ("margafalliga miskunnar gildrur") in granting us the teachings and miracles of Bishop Þorlákr, into which we are drawn, attracted by the "accessible baits" ("aðgengiligum ögnum") of divine "love and affection" ("ást ok elsku"):

> Hefir allmáttigr Guð í lífi ok kenningum, dýrlingum dæmum ok ítarligu andláti en ótalligum jareinum ins sæla Þorláks byskups sett fyrir oss margafaldliga miskunnar gildrur með atgengiligum ögnum ok teygiligum tillögum, at heimta oss með ást ok elsku í sinn einangr, þann hvervetna er hirt ok haldit er í þann kemr.[22]

> (With the life and teachings, the saintly proofs, the glorious death, and the innumerable miracles of the blessed Bishop Þorlákr, God the Almighty has set before us manifold traps of mercy, accessible baits and seductive counsels, to draw us with love and affection into His narrow passage, which is hidden everywhere and holds in it whoever comes in.)

In the same manner, the Devil sets a trap of misfortune ("ófarnaðar gildru"), laying in it as bait "all the corrupted desires" ("allar rangar fýsnir"). Once a man is caught, it is impossible for him to escape, just as if it were done to an "evil and noxious animal" ("skaðasöm dýr ok meinsöm") that dies miserably inside the trap. It is easily inferred that Páll is here referring to a typical medieval Icelandic trap for foxes made of stone ("gildran er gjör af grjóti").[23]

> En at teygja til þessarar gildru er þessi ögn: röng ást óskaplig ok ágirni, metnaðr ok mannráð, reiði ok ranglæti ok allar rangar fýsnir. En þeir menn sem í þessa ófarnaðar gildru ganga eptir teygingu þessara ódáða ok ógna ok megu eigi til snúask ór henni at ganga, þá eru svá hörmuliga staddir. Ok þá hleypr fyrir hana hurð, þat er dauðinn, endir þessa heims lífs, ok þá eru gefnir í vald þess er egndi gildruna, fjándans sjálfs, segi ek, er þá dregr til eilífs dauða ok óendanligra kvala at þeim hætti sem gjört er hér við skaðasöm dýr ok meinsöm at þá eru deydd er þau koma ór gildrunni.[24]

> (And to allure these traps, there is this bait: corrupted unnatural love and greed, haughtiness and conspiracy, wrath and injustice, and all the corrupted desires. And those men who walk into this unfortunate trap, after the temptation of these misdeeds and baits, may not turn and escape from it, and in this way they are sadly stopped. And before it there slides a door, that is Death, which ends this earthly

life. And they are trapped in that power which baited the trap, the Devil himself, I say, which drags them to eternal death and endless torments, in the same way it is done to an evil and noxious animal, so that those who come into the trap are dead.)

The Skálholt Scriptorium ca. 1200–1210

During the first decade of the thirteenth century, the scriptorium of Skálholt flourished in the production of hagiographical and historical literature. With the great public acclaim generated by the numerous testimonies of Þorlákr's miracles, witnessed both before and after his death, and especially after the translation of his relics to the Skálholt Cathedral in 1198, the Icelandic ecclesiastical authorities were urged to provide texts commemorating his *vita* and wondrous portents for the benefit of the Christian community. In order to be accessible to all Icelanders, literate and illiterate alike, the life and deeds of the first local saint had to be adapted into the vernacular. Moreover, to further legitimize and validate his memorable deeds and their venerable legacy, his biography had to be placed within the greater picture of the history of the Icelandic Church. In this manner, Þorlákr's saintly figure could be connected to Christianity's early history and its rise on the island, as the adoption of the new faith has been commonly contemplated as a sacred event.[25]

In the span of a decade or so, some of the greatest hagiographical and historical texts of the Icelandic Middle Ages were produced at the diocese of Skálholt. The *Jarteinabók Þorláks byskups in forna* was written around 1200, and around the same time, two biographies inspired by Þorlákr's saintly life were completed: the oldest redaction of *Þorláks saga byskups* in the vernacular and his *vita* in Latin, whose oldest witness dates to ca. 1200.[26] The first collection of his miracles was subsequently substantiated with more prodigious events and anecdotes ascribed to Þorlákr. Before the death of Bishop Páll Jónsson in 1211, the second redaction, the *Jarteinabók ǫnnur*, possibly compiled by Bishop Páll Jónsson himself, was also completed.

Before the death of Bishop Páll in 1211, and possibly after the death of the erudite lawspeaker and priest Gizurr Hallsson in 1206 (the great-grandson of Bishop Ísleifr Gizurarson, who is acknowledged in the preface of the *Hungrvaka* text as the greatest source consulted for its compilation), an epitome on the regencies of the first five bishops of that diocese, under the emblematic name of *Hungrvaka* ("hunger-waker or appetizer"),[27] was also completed in the Skálholt scriptorium. Accordingly, the vernacular chronicle had to "stimulate the appetite" of the lay people and clerics – that is, their curiosity to know more about the lives of the five Icelandic bishops who preceded Þorlákr

(†1193), namely, Ísleifr Gizurarson (†1080), Gizurr Ísleifsson (†1118), Þorlákr Rúnólfsson (†1133), Magnús Einarsson (†1148), and Klængr Þorsteinsson (†1176). Its text, in my view, also created an appetite for the very pièce de résistance of the scriptorium, the recently produced biography testifying Þorlákr's unparalleled sanctity, the first redaction of the *Þorláks saga byskups*, as implied in the concluding lines of the text:

> Nú er komit at frásǫgu þeiri er segja skal frá inum sæla Þorláki byskupi [...] er at réttu má segjask geisli eða gimsteinn heilagra, bædi á þessu landi ok svá annars staða um heiminn. Hann má at sǫnnu kallask postoli Íslands, sva sem inn helgi Patrekr byskup kallask postoli Írlands, því at þeir frǫmdu verk postola sjálfra í sínum kenningum ok þolinmœði, bæði við óhlýðna menn ok rangláta.[28]

> (Now, after their [the bishops'] story, the time has come to relate to the blessed Bishop Þorlákr, [...] who may justly be called the sunbeam and gemstone of [all] the saints, both on this land and also in other places in the world. He may truly be called the apostle of Iceland, much like the holy Bishop Patrick is called the apostle of Ireland, for they furthered the deeds of the apostles themselves in their teachings and with their endurance, both towards disobedient and unjust men.)

The bulk of information collected for the composition of the hagiographical texts concerning Þorlákr and his predecessors were naturally drawn from oral accounts – for instance, that of Gizurr Hallsson in the case of *Hungrvaka* – and from various written sources available at the scriptorium, most notably, annals and church registers. However, the basic literary framework for the constitution of the texts was borrowed from European hagiography. It has, for instance, been suggested how the *vitae* of the prominent continental bishops, especially Ambrose of Milan (†397), Martin of Tours (†397), and Nicolas of Myra (†343), must have represented primary literary models on which the Icelandic *gesta abbatum* were skillfully moulded, primarily on account of these bishops' political commitment and confrontation of powerful and potentially dangerous men.[29]

If the ethics, morality, and integrity attributed to the Skálholt bishops were partially modelled on those of their European predecessors, the greatest source for their sanctity and some of their most topical miracles and supernatural abilities were those of Christ himself. This connection is especially evident in the treatment of the miracles performed by the two most eminent bishops, Ísleifr and Þorlákr. Ásdís Egilsdóttir has for instance noted that some miracles attributed to the first bishop of Skálholt, Ísleifr, in *Hungrvaka*, recall those performed by Christ in his early career of thaumaturge. She draws attention to

Ísleifr's alleged restoration of deteriorated ale, which closely recalls Christ's transformation of water into wine at the wedding at Cana, mentioned as Christ's first miracle in the *Gospel of John*.[30] On the contrary, the list of healing properties attributed to Þorlákr in the *Jarteinabók Þorláks byskups ǫnnur*, namely, the healing of the blind, the deaf, the lame, the possessed, and the lepers, which are found in *Niðrstigningar saga*, in Latin T, and in the *Gospel of Matthew*, are significantly related to the miracles of a mature Christ. As a matter of fact, the texts of *Evangelium Nicodemi* and *Niðrstigningar saga* are filled with the supernatural and divine wonders performed by Christ, both during his lifetime and in the afterworld, when he confronted Satan alone.

There is reasonable evidence to support that the text of *Niðrstigningar saga* was already available in Skálholt by the time of composition of the *Jarteinabók ǫnnur* between 1200 and 1210, as Bishop Páll Jónsson seems to allude to it in his treatment of the sanctity of Þorlákr. Moreover, the fact that the oldest witness of *Niðrstigningar saga*, AM 645 4to, copied in Skálholt during the following decades (approximately in the years 1225–50), already transmits numerous textual corruptions and can actually be counted as evidence of the abundant scribal and editorial activity within the scriptorium during those years; one must postulate a considerable production of copies before the transcription of AM 645 4to.

With the advent of the first local saint and the great interest among Icelandic clerics and laypeople in the blessed life and miracles of Þorlákr, the scriptorium of Skálholt was urged to produce the first indigenous hagiographical material concerning Þorlákr and his predecessors. This cultural impetus was masterfully directed by Þorlákr's nephew and successor, Bishop Páll Jónsson, who commissioned, supervised, and even himself wrote new hagiographical texts, which would validate Þorlákr's sanctity and concurrently give prestige to the diocese. Moreover, Páll Jónsson seems to have encouraged readings in the vernacular among the young clerics, a cultural policy which necessarily involved the very composition of these texts, either *ex novo* or as translations of foreign Latin literature, as some of the introductory lines to *Hungrvaka* seem to indicate: "Þat berr ok annat til þessa rits at teygja til þess unga menn at kynnisk várt mál at ráða, þat er á norrœnu er ritat, lǫg, eða sǫgur eða mannfrœði"[31] ("And secondly, this writing is intended to allure young men to whom our tongue is known to read that which is written in Norse: laws or stories or genealogies").

The project of translating the Latin *Evangelium Nicodemi* may well have been initiated in the Skálholt scriptorium, favoured by this innovative and stimulating cultural context, which characterizes the first decade of the thirteenth century. Moreover, the young clerics addressed in *Hungrvaka* also seem to have profited greatly from the new cultural impetus, as many of them were able to study on the Continent for a considerable time. As a matter of fact, the number of clerics who were travelling abroad for education in those years – that is, around 1200 – was so high that Bishop Páll was urged to take a census of the priests who needed to perform services in his diocese, so that no parish church would remain uncovered.[32]

Some of these young clerics may well have decided to study in Paris in imitation of Þorlákr's own academic experience. It is consequently likely that upon the return of one of these young clerics from northern France, an exemplar of the T redaction of the Latin *Evangelium Nicodemi* was deposited in the Skálholt scriptorium, where its translation may have been initiated at the request of Bishop Páll. These years also saw the importation of the first biblical glosses and the great systematic exegetical treatises of the Paris school of theology, which were naturally consulted and interrogated by the compiler of *Niðrstigningar saga*, particularly in those cases in which the Latin *Evangelium Nicodemi* was perceived as scanty or uneventful.

7 Conclusion

The text of *Niðrstigningar saga* reflects a resourceful project of textual and biblical exegesis, especially in view of the editorial evaluation that must have preceded the translation work, such as choosing the version of the apocryphon to translate and determining how to supplement its core narrative with extra biblical material.

The Troyes redaction may have been chosen as the source because of its textual features for providing the scenes copiously attested both in sermons and in visual arts and mainly referring to the figure of Christ; most notably his arrival in Hell with a host of angels, the shattering of the gates of Hell, and the physical binding of Satan. The T text may consequently have been preferred to the Majority Text, which enjoyed enormous circulation in Europe and was also known in Iceland around the year 1200.

The textual matrix of the interpolations, on the other hand, reveals the availability in Iceland of the contemporary biblical glosses and commentaries of the Paris school of theology, especially the *Glossa ordinaria*, *Sententiae in IV libris distinctae*, and *Historia scholastica*. In all probability, the compiler consulted these texts for the interpolations into the original pseudo gospel and employed them to gloss, exemplify, and augment selected loci of his copy of *Evangelium Nicodemi*. Moreover, some allusions to the text of *Niðrstigningar saga* in contemporary devotional and hagiographical literature seem to suggest that its text was composed at Skálholt after Þórlakr's first collection of miracles had been written down and before the completion of the second collection. The work of translating and revising the Latin *Evangelium Nicodemi* might reasonably have been undertaken in Skálholt between the years 1199 and 1211 – roughly a century later than the date suggested by Magnús Már Lárusson.[1] The translation and adaptation of the Latin text may have initiated under the auspices of Bishop Páll Jónsson, a scholar of broad education, regarded as one of the most learned men of his time, under whom the bishopric of Skálholt flourished in the production of devotional texts.

Notes

Epigraph

1 ("And when this mortal hath put on immortality, then shall come to pass the saying that is written: Death is swallowed up in victory"). Paul proclaims the victory of Christ over Death, quoting the eschatological oracle of Isaiah 25:8 and Hosea 13:14.
Unless otherwise stated, all quotations of the Vulgate are taken from *Biblia sacra iuxta Vulgatam versionem*, ed. Robert Weber et al., revised by Roger Gryson. All English translations of the Latin Vulgate are taken from the Douay-Rheims Bible, accessed 18 December 2016, available at http://drbo.org.

Acknowledgments

1 *Heilagra manna sögur*, vol. 2, 1–20; Haugen, ed., *Stamtre og tekstlandskap*, vol. 2, *Tekster og tabellar*, 17–59; Haugen, ed., "Niðrstigningar saga," 250–6; Roughton, "AM 645 4to and AM 652/630 4to," 872–86.

Introduction

1 di Paolo Healey, "Anglo-Saxon Use of the Apocryphal Gospel," 98.
2 On the formation of the Latin text, see Izydorczyk, "The *Evangelium Nicodemi* in the Latin Middle Ages." Zbigniew Izydorczyk is currently preparing a critical edition of the Latin apocryphon for the CCSA.
3 A detailed census of the copious manuscript tradition of the *Evangelium Nicodemi* has been covered by Izydorczyk, *Manuscripts of Evangelium Nicodemi.*
4 The name *Niðrstigningar saga* is first attested in the rubric of Copenhagen, AM 645 4to (f. 51v), from around 1220. The title was first employed by Carl R. Unger in his edition of the text. See *Niðrstigningar saga* I and II.

5 See chapter 1, "The Latin *Evangelium Nicodemi* in Medieval Europe."
6 Karl Tamburr has recently discussed the use of the Harrowing of Hell in the *Evangelium Nicodemi*; see Tamburr, *The Harrowing of Hell*, 102–47.
7 As suggested in "The *Jarteinabœkr Þorláks byskups*" in chapter 6.

1 The Latin *Evangelium Nicodemi* in Medieval Europe

1 See the discussion in Izydorczyk, "The Unfamiliar *Evangelium Nicodemi*," 170–6. For a brief summary of the textual features of the *Gospel of Pseudo-Matthew* and the *Gospel of Nicodemus*, and for English translations, bibliographical references, and a useful index, see Elliott, *The Apocryphal New Testament*, 84–99, 164–204.
2 On the figure of Nicodemus in the *Gospel of John*, see Renz, "Nicodemus: An Ambiguous Disciple?" 255–83.
3 The title *Evangelium Nicodemi* is used in two of the most influential historical and hagiographical chronicles of the Middle Ages, Vincent of Beauvais's *Speculum historiale* and Jacobus de Voragine's *Legenda aurea*, both compiled during the second half of the twelfth century. On the different titles of the text, their history, and the misleadingly inconsistent use in previous research, see Izydorczyk, "Introduction," 2–3.
4 On the genesis and textual history of the oriental translations of the Greek *Acta Pilati*, see the useful summary in Hennecke, *Handbuch zu den Neutestamentlichen Apokryphen*, 143–52.
5 On the surviving Greek manuscripts of the *Acta Pilati*, see Izydorczyk and Dubois, "Nicodemus's Gospel," 28–9.
6 The oldest manuscript of the Greek tradition is in fact a text pertaining to Greek A, today Munich, BStB, cod. graec. 276, dating back to the twelfth century and transmitting chapters I–XVI. The two recensions are edited in von Tischendorf, *Evangelia Apocrypha*, 202–70, 270–300. A new edition of the Greek *Acta Pilati* is currently being prepared by Brigitte Tambrun-Krasker for the CCSA.
7 The second prologue of Greek A is transmitted exclusively in two manuscripts, today Paris, BnF, gr. 770 from 1315 and gr. 947 from 1574. Izydorczyk and Dubois, "Nicodemus's Gospel," 28.
8 A marginal note (f. 58r) refers to Abbot Meinhard as the commissioner of the manuscript in "loco novivillarensi" – that is, Neuwiller-lès-Saverne. See, for instance, Unterkircher, *Die datierten Handschriften*, 27.
9 The texts of section four of the Vienna palimpsest are edited by Philippart, "Fragments palimpsestes," 390–411.
10 Lowe, *Codices latini antiquiores*, vol. 10, no. 1485.
11 On this issue, see Campbell, "To Hell and Back," 129–32 and, more recently, Izydorczyk, "Two Newly Identified Manuscripts," 253–5.

12 Izydorczyk, *Manuscripts of Evangelium Nicodemi.*
13 See the discussion in Izydorczyk, "The Unfamiliar *Evangelium Nicodemi*," and Izydorczyk, "The *Evangelium Nicodemi* in the Latin Middle Ages," 43–102. Latin A corresponds to von Tischendorf's D^b and D^c, respectively, Einsiedeln, StB, 326 (ninth century) and Rome, Biblioteca dell'Accademia nazionale dei Lincei e Corsiniana, 1146 (fourteenth century), whose readings are available in the apparatus of the edited text in von Tischendorf, *Evangelia Apocrypha*, 312–95. These incongruences in Tischendorf's text were first noted by von Dobschütz, "Nicodemus, Gospel of," 545.
14 The term was first applied to Latin A in Bullitta "*Crux Christi muscipula fuit diabolo*."
15 Kim, ed.; *The Gospel of Nicodemus.*
16 K Prologue 13/5–14.
17 All translations are my own unless otherwise stated.
18 See the discussion in Izydorczyk, "The *Evangelium Nicodemi* in the Latin Middle Ages," 49–50.
19 Editions of the Latin *Vita Adae et Evae* have been prepared by Meyer, "Vita Adae et Evae," 185–250, and, more recently, by Pettorelli, ed., "La vie latine d'Adam et Ève," 18–104. On the development and circulation of the legend, see Quinn, *The Quest of Seth.*
20 K XIX.1 38/17–28.
21 Variant texts of *Sermo* CLX are available in the PL, where they are incorrectly attributed to Augustine in vol. 39, cols. 2059–61 and Martin of Léon (†1203) in vol. 208, cols. 925–32 with the title *Sermo vicesimus quintus. De Resurrectione Domini.* The pseudo-Augustinian *Sermo* CLX *De Pascha* II was well known in Anglo-Saxon England and has been recognized as one of the sources underlying the *Old English Martyrology*, which dates to the ninth century, and the Seventh Blickling homily for Easter, *Dominica Pascha*, which dates to the tenth. Respectively, see Cross, "The Use of Patristic Homilies," 107–28, and Dabley, "Patterns of Preaching," 478–92.
22 K XXII.1 42/22–43/3.
23 K XXIII.1 43/7–44/36.
24 K XXIV.1 45/19–20.
25 See Contreni, *The Cathedral School of Laon*, 36–8, 130–40.
26 See note 34 of this chapter.
27 See the discussion in Cross, "Saint-Omer 202," 82–104. The text of Saint-Omer 202 is edited in *Two Old English Apocrypha*, on the verso side of pp. 138–247. The Old English text is best represented by Cambridge, UL, Ii. 2. 11 (ff. 173r–193r), a manuscript copied in Exeter during the third quarter of the eleventh century. The readings of the other two manuscripts of the Old English *Evangelium*

Nicodemi – London, BL, Cotton Vitellius A XV (f. 60r–86v), that is, the first section of the *Nowell Codex* from the middle of the twelfth century, and London, BL, Cotton Vespasian D XIV (ff. 87v–100r), from the middle of the twelfth century – are available in the apparatus of *Two Old English Apocrypha*, on the recto side of pp. 139–247.

28 The manuscript was possibly chosen by the English copyist on account of the numerous homilies by Bede and Gregory the Great. See the discussion in Cross and Crick, "The Manuscript," especially pp. 31–5.

29 On its acquisition from the Continent, see, for instance, Rella, "Continental Manuscripts," 112. The text of London Royal 5 E. XIII is available as variant readings of Saint-Omer 202 in the apparatus of *Two Old English Apocrypha*, 138–247.

30 The manuscript is mentioned in Gijsel, *Die unmittelbare Textüberlieferung*, 137.

31 Whitman, nicknamed "Teutonicus," a native of what is today Germany, was the third Abbot of Ramsey between 1016 and 1020, as recorded in the cartulary of the abbey. See Hart and Lyons, *Cartularium monasterii de Rameseia*, 173.

32 See Bischoff, *Die südostdeutschen Schreibschulen*, vol. 1, *Die bayerische Diözesen*, 151.

33 See, respectively, Bischoff, *Die südostdeutschen Schreibschulen*, vol. 2, *Die vorwiegend Österreichischen Diözesen*, 230, 234.

34 See, for instance, Homburger, *Die illustrierten Handschriften*, 159–61.

35 Around the year 827, Hilduin of Saint Denis supervised the first Latin translation of a Greek manuscript containing the works of pseudo-Dionysius the Areopagite, granted by the Byzantine Emperor Michael the Stammerer (†829) to Louis the Pious (†840). However, the Latin translation turned out to be too literal and barely comprehensible, and around 860, a new translation and commentary of the same work was commissioned by Charles the Bald (†877) to Johannes Scotus Eriugena. Johannes Scotus was undoubtedly one of the most learned men of his time and a proficient translator of Greek texts, which included commentaries of Maximus the Confessor (†622) and Gregory of Nyssa (†ca. 395). On Hilduin and Johannes Scotus, see, for instance, Marenbon, "Carolingian Thought," 183–4. Sedulius Scotus, the eminent poet and Latin grammarian, was also much learned in Greek, and after his arrival in Liège from Ireland around 848, he is credited with the transcription of a voluminous Greek Psalter, today Paris, BdA, 8407, which also included the Canticles and the "Our Father" in Greek and Latin. See most recently McNamara, *The Psalms in the Early Irish Church*, 62–4. Martianus Hiberniensis is known for having produced an impressive Greek-Latin glossary at the cathedral school of Laon, today Laon, BM Suzanne Martinet, 444. See most recently Bonnet, "Survivance du grec au IX siècle," 263–78. Martianus was also accounted for the composition of the *Scholica graecum glossarum*, a list of mostly Greek words with their relative explanations extracted from the previous works

of eminent commentators such as Isidore of Seville and Martianus Capella. This attribution has been subsequently disregarded by Contreni, who instead suggested the Benedictine monastery of Ripoll in Catalonia as the possible place of composition. See the discussion in Contreni, "Three Carolingian Texts," 802–8.

36 David N. Dumville has proven that the Harrowing of Hell section in the early ninth-century English *Book of Cerne* is derived from a lost eighth-century Latin text of Irish provenance, which was later assembled with the pseudo-Augustinian *Sermo* CLX *De Pascha* II. See Dumville, "Liturgical Drama and Panegyric Responsory," 374–406. On the early knowledge and circulation of the Latin *Vita Adae et Evae* in Ireland, see Wright, "Apocryphal Lore and Insular Tradition," 130, and Wright, *The Irish Tradition*, 23.

37 See Bernhard Bischoff, *Katalog der festländischen*, vol. 1, *Aachen-Lambach*, 412n1985. The manuscript once belonged to the German scholar and philologist Friedrich Lindenbrog (†1648), who may have acquired it from a monastery during one of his visits to Paris. The codex was then deposited in the library of the Gottrop castle in Schleswig and was taken to Copenhagen only in 1735. See Jørgensen, *Catalogus codicum latinorum*, 15.

38 See Izydorczyk, *Manuscripts of Evangelium Nicodemi*, items 119, 215, 268, 255, and 425, respectively.

39 Ibid., items 75, 73, and 199, respectively.

40 See, for instance, von Dobschütz, "Nicodemus, Gospel of," 545. The manuscripts used by von Tischendorf in his edition, referred to as A (Vatican City, BAV, Vat. lat. 4578, from the fourteenth century), B (Vatican City, BAV, Vat. lat. 4363, from the twelfth century), and C (Venice, BNM, 4326, from the end of the fourteenth century), are in fact all manuscripts pertaining to Latin B. Their readings are available in von Tischendorf, *Evangelia Apocrypha*, 312–95.

41 As pointed out in Izydorczyk, "The *Evangelium Nicodemi* in the Latin Middle Ages," 51.

42 Respectively, Florence, Biblioteca Medicea Laurenziana, S. M. 599 (ff. 8r–25r), possibly from the Convent of San Marco in Florence; Vatican City, BAV, Vat. lat. 4363 (ff. 93ra–96va) and Vatican City, BAV, Vat. lat. 5094 (ff. 1r–18v), both from an unknown location; London, BL, Add. 29630 (ff. 93r–103rb); Paris, BnF, lat.14864 (ff. 109r–128r); and Salzburg, Bibliothek der Erzabtei St. Peter, a V 27 (ff. 111r–139r).

43 Cambridge, CCC, 288 (ff. 39r–54v) from Christ Church in Canterbury, and Oxford, Bodl, Rawlinson D. 1236 (ff. 60r–72r) from Saint Mary's Abbey in Dublin.

44 The manuscripts written in Italy are Paris, BnF, lat. 6041 A (ff. 178va–179vb); Vatican City, BAV, Vat lat. 4578 (ff. 35r–38rb); Venice, BNM, Marc. lat. II 65 (olim 2901) (ff. 59r–78r); and Venice, BNM, Marc. lat. XIV 43; It II 2 (olim 4326) (ff. 156r–171v). The manuscripts written in England are Cambridge, UL, Mm.

VI. 15 (ff. 87r–100v) and London, BL, Royal 8 B. XV (ff. 165r–175r). The manuscript written in Spain is Vallebona, Santa Maria de Vallebona, 3 (ff. 75rb–96v).

45 The three manuscripts from Italy are Florence, Biblioteca Nazionale Centrale, Fondo Nazionale II, II.453 (ff. 156–160); Paris, BnF, nuov. acq. lat. 1154 (ff. 10v–16r); and Vatican City, BAV, Reg. lat. 1037, 97–107. The four manuscripts from Czech Republic and England are respectively Cambridge, UL, Ff. VI. 54 (ff. 61r–111r); Oxford, Bodl, Canon. Pat. lat. 117 (ff. 9r–15r); Brno, Státní vědecká knihovna, Mk 99 (ff. 145r–154v); and Praha, Knihovna metropolitní kapituly, N. LIV (ff. 1r–21r). The French manuscript is Paris, BnF, lat.1652 (ff. 31rb–49vb).

46 Izydorczyk, "The Unfamiliar *Evangelium Nicodemi*," 169–91. Its text is hitherto unedited; a first critical edition is currently being prepared by Justin Haynes. See his introductory remarks on the problems and characteristics of the tradition in Haynes, "New Perspectives," 103–12.

47 The manuscript was subsequently transferred to the Girona Cathedral in the middle of the eleventh century. On the manuscript, see for instance Schapiro, "The Beatus Apocalypse of Gerona," 3:319–28. The last edition of the text is Romero-Posé, *Sancti Beati a Liébana Commentarius*.

48 As noted in Izydorczyk, "The *Evangelium Nicodemi* in the Latin Middle Ages," 52.

49 The standard text of the *Epistola Pilati* is available in K XXVIII 49/1–59/36.

50 The author of von Tischendorf's chapter XXVIII erroneously refers to "the first book of the Septuagint," alluding to the description of Noah's ark in Genesis 6:14–15 as the source of the quoted passage rather than Exodus 25:10, as the wording of the passage seems to indicate. Indeed, in his *Commentarii in Danielem*, 4.23–4, Hippolytus of Rome bases his calculation on Exodus 25:10. See Marcel, *Hippolytus Werke* vol. 1, *Kommentar zu Daniel*, 244–8.

51 On the influence of Fleury and Saint-Germain-des-Prés on the Ripoll scriptorium, see Beer, *Die Handschriften des Klosters*, 38–9, 92–5. On that of Laon, see Laistner, "*Rivipullensis* 74," 31–7.

52 Respectively, Paris, BnF, lat. 3214 (ff. 132vb–139vb) and Paris, BnF, lat. 4977 (ff. 227r–232va) from the fourteenth century; Paris, BnF, lat. 3628 (ff. 109r–122v) from the fifteenth century; Prague, Státní vědecká knihovna, III.C.18 (ff. 278ra–288rb) from the fourteenth century; and Milan, Biblioteca Ambrosiana, O 35 Sup. (ff. 65v–85r) from the fourteenth century.

53 Izydorczyk, "The Latin Source," 265–79. The only other text edited in the manuscript is the *Vita beatae Ame virginis* (ff. 79r–89r), immediately preceding the *Evangelium Nicodemi* (ff. 90r–104v) in the manuscript. See Dolbeau, "Vie latine de sainte Ame," 25–63. A first edition of Latin T is now available in Izydorczyk and Bullitta, "The Troyes Redaction." In the following discussion, I refer to the folios and lines of Troyes 1636.

54 T 90r/2–11.

55 The majority of the earliest manuscripts are of French origin: Troyes, Médiathèque du Grand Troyes, 1636 is from the twelfth century; Paris, BdA, 128 (39 A.T.L.); Cambridge (MA), Harvard University, Houghton Library, lat. 117; and Charleville-Mézières, BM, 61 were written in the fourteenth century; while Paris, BnF, nuov. acq. lat. 1755 was produced in the fifteenth century. Except Hannover, Niedersächsische Landesbibliothek, I 247, which dates to the fourteenth century, all other German manuscripts are from the fifteenth century: Berlin, SPK, Theol. lat. fol. 688; Berlin, SPK, Theol. lat. fol. 690; Stuttgart, Württembergische Landesbibliothek, HB I 119; Halle/Saale, Archiv der Franckeschen Stiftungen, P 7; Paderborn, Erzbischöfliche Akademische Bibliothek, Inc. 31; Wolfenbüttel, HAB, Cod. Guelf. 38.8 Aug. 2°; Wolfenbüttel, HAB, Cod. Guelf. 83 Gud. lat.2°; and Wolfenbüttel, HAB, Cod. Guelf. 279 Helmst. Only three manuscripts were produced outside this area: one in England, Cambridge, TC 0.9.10; one in Bohemia, Cambridge, CCC, 500 at the end of the fourteenth century; and one in Italy, Genoa, Biblioteca Universitaria, A.III.2, at the end of fifteenth.

56 For a detailed discussion of the all the vernacular renditions of Latin T, see Izydorczyk and Bullitta, "The Troyes Redaction," 577–86.

57 Paris, BnF, fr. 1850, from the thirteenth century; Oxford, Queen's College, 305, from the fifteenth; and Dijon, BM, 525. On this version and its relations to Latin T, see Izydorczyk, "The Latin Source," 265–79.

58 Barcelona, Biblioteca de la Universitat, 1029. See discussion in Izquierdo, "The *Gospel of Nicodemus* in Medieval Catalan," 145.

59 The manuscript is London, BL, Harley 149. The connections of the two Middle English versions to Latin T were first pointed out by Shields, "Bishop Turpin," 497–502.

60 London, BL, Cotton Galba E.IX; BL, Harley 4196; BL, Addit. 32578; Sion College, Arc. L. 40.2/E.25. Its text is edited in Hulme, *The Middle English Harrowing of Hell*.

61 The manuscripts were all written at Vadstena: Stockholm, Kb, A 110, in the last years of the fourteenth century; Stockholm, Riksarkivet, Skokloster 3 4to, in the fourth quarter of the fifteenth century; and Stockholm, Kb, A 3 in the beginning of the sixteenth. On the Old Swedish translation and its relations to Latin T, see the discussion in Bullitta, "The Old Swedish *Evangelium Nicodemi*," 282–99.

62 Lüneburg, Ratsbücherei, Theol. 2° 83, from the middle of the fifteenth century; Lübeck, Stadtbibliothek, theol. germ. fol. 9 and The Hague, Koninklijke Bibliotheek, 133 E6, from the fourth quarter of the fifteenth century; and Darmstadt, Hessische Landes- und Hochschulbibliothek, 1848, from the beginning of the sixteenth century. The text is edited as L in Masser, *Dat ewangelium Nicodemi*, 30–60.

63 Leiden, Bibliotheek der Rijksuniversiteit, B. P. L. 61, from the last decade of the fifteenth century and Linz, Bundesstaatliche Studienbibliothek, 194 (olim 244) (in Rhenish Franconian dialect, copied from a Dutch antigraph), from the second quarter of the sixteenth century. See Hoffmann, "The *Gospel of Nicodemus* in Dutch," 346–9.

64 The text is surveyed and edited in Masser and Siller, *Das Evangelium Nicodemi*, 468–92.

65 See Klausner, "The *Gospel of Nicodemus* in the Literature of Medieval Wales," 406–7.

66 A thorough diplomatic transcription of the five manuscripts containing *Niðrstigningar saga* is available in Haugen, *Stamtre og tekstlandskap*, vol. 2, *Tekster og tabellar*, 17–59. Modern English and Modern Norwegian translations of *Niðrstigningar saga* (AM 645 4to) are available respectively in Roughton, "AM 645 4to and AM 652/630 4to," 872–86, and Haugen, "Soga om nedstiginga i dødsriket," 250–6. The greatest survey on the vernacular legacy of the Latin *Evangelium Nicodemi* in medieval Scandinavia was undertaken by K. Wolf, "The Influence of the *Evangelium Nicodemi*." Preliminary results of the present research have been discussed in Bullitta, "*Crux Christi muscipula fuit diabolo*."

67 This view is also shared by Magnús Már Lárusson, "Um Niðrstigningar sögu," 161. For details, see the section titled "The Prologue" in chapter 4.

68 Mogk, *Geschichte der norwegisch-isländischen Literatur*, 890; Seip, *Nye studier i norsk språkhistorie*, 81, 135; Bekker-Nielsen, "Nikodemusevangeliet," cols. 308–9.

69 The second person plural imperative of the verb "láta" ("to let"), "latet er" ("you let") was misread with "later er," a form that developed in Norway during the Old Norse period. On the subject, see Mork, "Morphological Developments," 1144.

70 Archaisms are the sporadic use of the enclitic particle "of," the personal pronoun appended enclitically to the verb as in "vasc" ("I was") for "var ek," and the use of the grapheme *ð*, which first arrived in Iceland around 1200 under Norwegian influence. The use of *t* [t] for *d* [ð] in final position as "verit" ("you were") instead of the classic "verið" has also been interpreted as a Norwegian morphological mark and can instead be explained as a hyper-correctivism modelled on the Icelandic lenition of the final voiceless stops [t] and [k] into the respective voiced fricatives [ð] and [g], as in "blaðit" > "blaðið" ("leaf") and "ek" > "eg" ("I"). This change in Icelandic is already attested from the beginning of the thirteenth century. See, for instance, Stefán Karlsson, *The Icelandic Language*, 19. See the discussion in Haugen, "Soga om nedstiginga i dødsriket," 92n35.

71 See Magnús Már Lárusson, "Um Niðurstigningarsögu," 167.

72 Gschwantler, "Christus, Thor und die Midgardsschlange," 152; Kirby, *Bible Translation in Old Norse*, 35.

73 See Haugen, *Stamtre og tekstlandskap*, 1:46; K. Wolf, "The Influence of the *Evangelium Nicodemi*," 283; Roughton, "Stylistics and Sources," 45; and K. Wolf, *The Legends of the Saints*, 273.

74 Kirby has demonstrated that the earliest Old Norse translations of the Old Testament, the Psalter, and a yet undefined gospel harmony, which may well correspond to Tatian's *Diatessaron*, may have already been in existence by 1200. See Kirby, *Bible Translation in Old Norse*, 107. An overview of the evolution of the Icelandic language, surveyed on the basis of the increasingly more systematic and comprehensive medieval Icelandic biblical translations, has been recently conducted by Fabrizio D. Raschellà, "Le traduzioni bibliche."

75 The diplomatic transcription of the Latin text preserved in Þjóðminjasafn 921 was originally made by Ólafur Halldórsson for Odd Einar Haugen. See Haugen, *Stamtre og tekstlandskap*, vol. 2, *Tekster og tabellar*, 96–100. The history of the fragment remains unknown to the present.

76 Kim, *The Gospel of Nicodemus*.

77 Pelle, "Twelfth-Century Sources," 50n18. In his article, Stephen Pelle uses Hallgrímur J. Ámundason's transcription of AM 655 XXVII 4to, available in his unpublished BA thesis. See Hallgrímur J. Ámundason ed. *AM 655 XXVII 4to*. The translation is mentioned neither in the previous studies on *Niðrstigningar saga* nor in the new exhaustive catalogue of Old Norse hagiographical literature prepared by K. Wolf, *The Legends of the Saints in Old Norse-Icelandic Prose*. A first critical edition of the text is now available in Bullitta, "The Story of Joseph of Arimathea."

78 Corresponding to chapters XI.3–XVII.1 of the *Evangelium Nicodemi*.

79 Different, for instance, is the treatment of Simeon's presentation of Christ at the temple. Whereas *Niðrstigningar saga* translates "templum" ("temple") with the word AM 645 52r/8 "kirkio" ("church") and refers to Simeon with the appellative AM 645 51v/22 "ens gamla" ("the Old"), alluding to a certain tradition which addresses him as "Simeon senex" ("Simeon the Elder"), AM 655 XXVII 4to renders more precisely the first referent with the substantive 9r/18 "musteri" ("monastery, temple"), and it refers twice to Simeon with the proper appellative 9r/17 and 9v/17 "inn gaufgi" ("the Noble"), translating the Latin "iustus" ("the Just") of Luke 2:25.

80 See the discussion in Izydorczyk, "The *Evangelium Nicodemi* in the Latin Middle Ages," 99–100.

81 Besides Copenhagen, DKB, GkS 1335 4to (1ra–20rb), which was produced in France in the tenth century and transferred to Copenhagen only in 1735, three more manuscripts of the Latin *Evangelium Nicodemi* are found in Denmark. These are Copenhagen, DKB, GkS 1336 4to (ff. 1r–13), possibly written in Bordesholm, in the Holstein region, around 1400; Copenhagen, DKB, NkS 123 4to (ff. 39r–47r), written in Ribe in the Jutland region around the year 1454; and Copenhagen, DKB, Thott. 130 2° (ff. 18v–27r), written in the fifteenth century in an unknown

scriptorium of northern Germany. All these Latin manuscripts transmit a text of the Majority type. See Jørgensen, *Catalogus codicum latinorum medii aevii*, respectively 15–16, 163–5, and 175–6. The only Latin manuscript written in Sweden is Uppsala, UB, C 219 (16v–17r), a collection of *exempla* that first belonged to Carolus Andreae, a priest in Vist (Östergötland), who entered Vadstena Abbey in 1442 and donated the manuscript to its library. The abridged text *Evangelium Nicodemi* might be derived from its summary treatment in the *Legenda aurea*. See Andersson-Schmitt, Hallberg, and Hedlund, *Mittelalterliche Handschriften der Universitätsbibliothek Uppsala*, 68–9.

82 Stockholm, Kb, A 115. The text is edited in Brøndum-Nielsen, *Et gammeldansk digt*; see also K. Wolf, "The Influence of the *Evangelium Nicodemi* on Norse Literature," 280–3.

83 On the Swedish text, see Bullitta, "The Old Swedish *Evangelium Nicodemi*."

84 A single Latin manuscript preserving a text of the Majority type is of certain Norwegian provenance: Oslo, UB, Ms. 8° 2993 (ff. 91rb–93vb), a theological miscellany datable to the beginning of the fifteenth century. See Izydorczyk, *Manuscripts of Evangelium Nicodemi*: *A Census*, item 216.

85 The last critical edition of the *vísur* has been prepared by Jón Helgason, who distinguishes nine different redactions: A, B, C, D, E, F, G, H, and I. See Jón Helgason, *Íslenzk miðaldakvæði*, 1: 212–38.

86 Ibid., 231.

87 As summarized in K. Wolf, "The Influence of the *Evangelium Nicodemi* on Norse Literature," 274–7. See the section titled "The Capture of Satan on the Cross" in chapter 5.

88 Finnur Jónsson, ed., *Jón Arason religiøse digte*, 22–3.

89 See K. Wolf, "Om en 'tabt' islandsk oversættelse," 167–79.

2 The Manuscript Tradition of *Niðrstigningar saga*

1 For sake of consistency, in the following discussion I refer to the normalized Icelandic titles of hagiographical texts employed by the *ONP* and in K. Wolf, *The Legends of the Saints*, rather than to their older Latinate counterparts, even when these have an established tradition in previous scholarship (as, for instance, *Klements saga* for *Clemens saga*). In the transcriptions of the incipit and explicit of each text, I follow the same editorial conventions applied to the text of *Niðrstigningar saga*, as illustrated in "Editorial Procedure" in the "Texts" section of this book.

2 Respectively, items 7, 5, 4, 8, 2, and 10.

3 Items 3 and 6. See discussion in Turville-Petre, *Origins of Icelandic Literature*, 129–31, and Carron, *Clemens saga*, xiii, xxii. Philip Roughton has surveyed and

subgrouped the hagiographical texts transmitted in AM 645 4to on the basis of the presence or absence of supplementary homiletic material. See Roughton, "Stylistics and Sources."

4 *A Book of Miracles*, 13.

5 See *Postola sögur*, x, and Haugen, "Between Graphonomy and Phonology."

6 The influence of the insular script in Iceland was mediated by Norwegian scribal practices and therefore became especially substantial after the establishment of the diocese of Niðaróss (modern Trondheim) in 1153, to which the sees of Skálholt and Hólar depended. On the subject, see Haugen, "The Development of the Latin Script I," and Stefán Karlsson, "The Development of the Latin Script II."

7 Kålund, *Katalog*, 2:51–2.

8 Spehr, *Der Ursprung der isländischen Schrift*, 174; Hreinn Benediktsson, *Early Icelandic Script*, no. xx.

9 Seip, *Palæografi B*, 43.

10 *A Book of Miracles*, 9.

11 Ibid., 17.

12 *Jarteinabók Þorláks byskups in forna*, 135.

13 See the section titled "The *Jarteinabækr Þorláks byskups*" in chapter 6.

14 On Guðbrandur Björnsson, see *JÁM*, 10:274–5, and *ÍÆ*, 1, 235–6. On Björn Magnússon, see *JÁM*, 11:111.

15 The text of the slip is available from *Handrit.is*, accessed 18 December 2016, https://handrit.is/is/manuscript/view/en/AM04-0645.

16 AM 645 4to, ff. 51v/21–52v/2.

17 *Helgensagaer*, ii, and Hreinn Benediktsson, *Early Icelandic Script*, 44–5.

18 Kålund, *Katalog*, 2:37; *Postola Sögur*, xxi.

19 *Helgensagaer*, i.

20 Hreinn Benediktsson, *Early Icelandic Script*, xxxvii.

21 *ONP* Register, accessed 18 December 2016, http://dataonp.hum.ku.dk/ms/ms000861.htm.

22 A second recension of the Old Norse *Septem dormientes* survives in Stockholm, Kb, Holm. Perg. 3 fol. (ff. 93r–94v), dating from the sixteenth century. The original text of AM 623 4to was possibly substantiated here with material from the Low German *Passionael*. See Widding, Bekker-Nielsen, and Shook, "The Lives of the Saints," 331.

23 *DI*, vol. 5, *1330–1476*, 289.

24 At the time of the 1703 census, Bishop Björn Þorleifsson was 40; Ari Guðmundsson was 71. See "Bishop Björn Þorleifsson," accessed 18 December 2016, http://manntal.is/.

25 AM 645 4to, ff. 53r/6–54r/11 and 55r/16–55v/23.

26 See the discussion in Van Deusen, "The Old Norse-Icelandic Legend," 88.
27 Ibid., 83. Carl R. Unger had previously argued that one hand wrote folios 1v–12v and the second wrote folios 15–29. See *MS*, xxii.
28 See Stefán Karlsson, *Sagas of Icelandic Bishops*, 21; Ólafur Halldórsson, *Helgafēllsbækur fornar*, 10.
29 Ólafur Halldórsson, *Helgafēllsbækur fornar*, 41.
30 *DI*, vol. 2, *1253–1350*, 427.
31 On the church of Garður, see Cormack, *The Saints of Iceland*, 187.
32 AM 645 4to, ff. 52r/18–53v/14.
33 As shown in the section titled "Agreement between K and E against T and A" in chapter 4.
34 Kålund, *Katalog*, 1:200.
35 On the subject, see, most recently, Bullitta, ed. and trans., *Páls leizla* (forthcoming).
36 On Ólafur Jónsson, see *ÍÆ*, 4:62.
37 Þorvaldur Sívertsen was sixty-three during the census of 1860. See "Þorvaldur Sívertsen," accessed 18 December 2016, http://manntal.is/.
38 Magnús Jónsson is renowned for having commissioned the compilation of AM 148 8vo, a remarkable miscellany of poetry and prose written between 1676 and1677. The manuscript has been edited in facsimile by Jón Helgason, ed., *Kvæðabók úr Vigur*. See *JÁM*, 7:67, 147.
39 Magnús Ketilsson was twenty-eight during the census of 1703. See "Magnús Ketilsson," accessed 18 December 2016, http://manntal.is/.
40 Jón Helgason, "Bækur og handrit," 9.
41 Ibid., 18.
42 On the subject, see Henningham, *An Early Latin*, 43–9.
43 On the scholarly activity of Hans Hanssen Skonning, see Gyllerup, "Skonning, Hans Hanssen." A first synoptic edition of Skonning's *Collegium philosophorum* and the Icelandic translation transmitted as item 11in JS 405 is currently being prepared by Kirsten Wolf and me.

3 The Manuscript Filiation of *Niðrstigningar saga*

1 See Turville-Petre, *Origins of Icelandic Literature*, 127.
2 In terms of length and weight of the supplementary material they provide to the original text, the first and second interpolations, surveyed in the sections titled "The Gates of Paradise" and "Seven-Headed Satan" in chapter 5, represent minor suggestive details added to the descriptions of the fortress of Paradise and to the antithetical portrayal of Satan. On the other hand, the third and fourth interpolations (which coincide with Turville-Petre's "first" and "second" interpolations), surveyed in chapter 5 as "Christ as Warrior-King" and "The Capture of Satan on

the Cross," supplement the original plot with additional events and anecdotes that allegedly occurred during Christ's Harrowing of Hell.

3 A ("There were two things before me: there was burning fire to deny any man entrance to Paradise, and angels to guard it against all the devils and the souls of the sinful men").

4 D ("There were two things holding guard and denying the Devil and sinful men entrance through the gates of Paradise").

5 E ("I saw burning fire that denied any man entrance, and God's angels guarded these gates against both devils and sinful men").

6 A ("The giant Satan, the Prince of Hell, who sometimes has seven heads and sometimes three, and is in the shape of a dragon, which is horrible, terrible, and awful in all respects").

7 B ("Satan, the Prince of the World, who sometimes has seven heads or three, in the dreadful shape of a dragon and horrible in all respects").

8 D ("Satan, Prince of Hell, who sometimes has three heads, and sometimes is in the shape of a dragon, which is supreme and evil in all respects").

9 E ("The Prince of Hell and commander of the dead, in the likeness of a dreadful and roaring dragon, which sometimes reveals himself to them with seven heads, and sometimes with three in the shape of a man").

10 A ("It was at that point of the day that Heaven opened, and there came forth first a white horse and the Prince who rode that horse was in many respects more noble than the most accomplished of all others. His eyes were like blazing fire. He had a crown on his head where many tokens of victory could be seen. He had a vestment above the others that was spattered in blood. On His vestment, around the waist, these words were written: King of kings and Lord of lords. He was brighter than the sun. He led a great army, and all those who followed Him rode white horses, and all were dressed in white silk and were very bright").

11 B ("It was at that point of the day that Heaven opened, and there ran forth a white horse, which was ridden by a thoughtful man, who was more glorious and princely than anyone else. His eyes were like blaze on fire. He wore a crown on his head where many tokens of victory could be seen. He had a vestment above the other garments that was spattered in blood. On His vestment, around the waist, these words were written: King of kings and Lord of lords. He was brighter than the sun and an unarmed army of knights followed Him. They had white horses, all whiter than snow").

12 D ("It was at that point of the day that Heaven opened, and there came forth first a white horse and the King who rode that horse was in many respects more excellent than all others and more accomplished than anything else. But His eyes were like blaze. He had a crown on his head which could be seen in detail and displayed many tokens of victory. He had a wounded foot out [of the vestment] that was

spattered in blood. On his forehead, in the middle, there was written: King of kings and Lord of lords. He was brighter than the sun. He had the mightiest army of angels and all those who followed Him rode white horses. They were all sliding in white silk and were as light as the sun").

13 E ("It was at that point and hour of the day that Heaven opened, and there came forth first a white horse, and the King who rode that horse was in many respects more handsome, fair, and princely than all others. His eyes were like blazing fire. He had a crown on his head that displayed many tokens of victory. He had a vestment above the others that was spattered in blood. On His vestment, around the waist, these words were written: King of kings and Lord of lords. He led a great army, and all those who were followed Him rode white horses and were clothed with white silk and were very bright").

14 A ("Then he transformed himself into the shape of a dragon and grew to such a stature that it seemed he could lie around the whole world. He saw those events that occurred in Jerusalem, that Jesus Christ was breathing His last, and immediately travelled there and intended to tear away His soul from Him. But when he came there and thought he could swallow Him and carry Him away, the hook of divinity bit him and the sign of the cross fell down on him, and he was caught like a fish on a fishhook, a mouse in a mousetrap, or an arctic fox in a snare, according to what was previously prophesied. Then Our Lord went to him and bound him").

15 B ("And he transformed himself into the shape of a dragon and grew to such a stature that it seemed he could lie around the whole world. He saw those events that occurred in Jerusalem, that Jesus Christ was breathing His last, and immediately flew there and wanted to steal His soul from Him. But when he wanted to swallow Him and have Him for himself, he bit the hook of His divinity, and the sign of the cross fell down on him, and he was caught like a fish on a fishhook, or like an arctic fox in a snare, according to what was previously prophesied. Then Our Lord went there and bound him").

16 C ("Then he transformed himself into the shape of a dragon and thought he could lie in circle around Hell. He saw those events that occurred in Jerusalem, that Jesus Christ was breathing His last, and immediately travelled there as fast as he could and thought he would be able to swallow the soul of Jesus. But when he arrived and thought he could swallow Jesus and have Him for himself, the hook of divinity bit him and the sign of the cross fell down on him, and he was caught like a fish on a fishhook, a mouse in a mousetrap, or an arctic fox in a snare, according to what was previously prophesied. Then Our Lord went to him and bound him").

17 D ("And he transformed himself into the shape of a dragon and grew to such a stature that it seemed he could lie around the whole world. Then he saw the event that occurred in Jerusalem, that Jesus Christ was breathing His last on the Holy Cross. Then Satan travelled there immediately and thought that all would turn well

and intended to tear His soul away from Him. And then it occurred to him that he thought that he had swallowed it into his cruel stomach and that he had it with him, but then Satan bit the hook of the divinity, and the sign of the cross fell down on him, and he was caught like a fish on a fishhook or a mouse under a trap. Then it happened, as it was previously prophesied, that the Lord went to Hell, and there He bound the enemy of all mankind, the Devil").

18 E ("Then he made himself in the shape of an enormous dragon, whose largeness is compared to the Midgard Serpent, and about whom it is said that he lies around the whole world. He then saw those signs that were in Jerusalem, that Our Lord was breathing His last and immediately").

19 Turville-Petre, *Origins of Icelandic Literature*, 127.

20 See the section titled "Agreement between K and E against T and A" in chapter 4.

21 See the section titled "Minor Variants of T Reflected in A against K and R" in chapter 4.

22 A ("In the darkness of Hell").

23 D ("In the darkness of Hell").

24 E ("In the darkness and in the shadow of Death").

25 T ("In the darkness and shadow of Death").

26 A ("I am set up to see to each man's condition").

27 B ("I am set up to behold each man's condition").

28 D ("I am set up to see to it that no sinful [man] travels to Paradise").

29 E ("I am appointed over the human body").

30 T ("Truly, I am appointed over the human body").

31 A ("Although he is very sick").

32 B ("Although he is sick").

33 D ("Although he is sick").

34 E ("To improve the sickness of his body").

35 T ("For the pain of his body").

36 A ("Before [five thousand four hundred years] shall be completed from now").

37 B ("Before [five hundred thousand and thirty years] are completed from now").

38 D ("Before [five thousand and three years] are completed from now").

39 E ("Until the everlasting days of indefinite time").

40 T ("Until the latest days of times").

41 A ("Then they expelled their Prince out of Hell").

42 Like in the edited text, om. stands for "omissit" and signals scribal omissions.

43 C ("Then they expelled their Prince out of Hell").

44 D ("And they expelled him or drew [him] away from Hell").

45 E ("And thereafter he expelled Satan, his Prince, out of his seats").

46 T ("And Inferus ejected Satan from his seats").

47 A ("To give [it] to your father").

48 B ("To give [it] to your father").
49 D ("To give [it] to your father").
50 E ("So that you [may] anoint your father Adam").
51 T ("So that you [may] anoint the body of your father Adam").
52 E ("For I have held under my power all the mighty princes of the earth, whom you now carry subject with your strength").
53 T ("For in my land and through my power are held all the mighty ones, whom you have carried subject to me with your strength").
54 E ("My soul is afflicted all unto death"); cf. Matthew 26:38.
55 T ("My soul is sorrowful unto death"); cf. Matthew 26:38.
56 E ("But if you are mighty, who is this man Jesus, who fears death and yet opposes you and your power?").
57 T ("If, therefore, you are powerful, what sort of man is that Jesus who, fearing death, opposes your power?").
58 Maas, *Textual Criticism*. On the formation and legacy of the genealogical method, see Timpanaro, *The Genesis of Lachmann's Method*, and, more recently, Trovato, *Everything You Always Wanted to Know*.
59 All the textual corruptions of *Niðrstigningar saga* are listed and discussed in Haugen, *Stamtre og tekstlandskap*, 105–52. His stemma codicum is discussed in "Haugen's Stemma" and drawn in Figure 3.
60 Separation and conjunction of errors within the tradition are treated in Paul Maas's *Textual Criticism*, 42–9.
61 A, B, D "þa er ec lifða" / C "er ek var lifs aa iordu"; A, B, D "sa hafði" / C "hafandi."
62 A, B, D om. / C "En Guds helgir saa þenna man."
63 In Psalm references, the first number (24 in this example) is the psalm number given in Hebrew (Mesoretic) tradition, and the second number in parentheses (23) is the number given in the Greek Septuaginta and Latin Vulgate.
64 A ("When I lived").
65 B ("When I lived").
66 D ("When I lived").
67 C ("When I was alive on earth").
68 T ("When I was alive on earth").
69 A ("Who had").
70 B ("Who had").
71 D ("He had").
72 C ("Having, carrying").
73 T ("Carrying").
74 C ("When the saints of God saw that man, they asked [him]").
75 T ("When all the saints of God saw him, they said to him").

76 A, C, D "for þangat" / B "flo hann þangat"; A, C, D "slita ondina" / B "slęgia ǫndina"; A, C, D "maþr allosęligr" / B "otirligr maþr."
77 A, C, D "enn þa munom viþ ðangat coma" / B om.
78 They are treated as errors common to A, C, and D also in Haugen, *Stamtre og tekstlandskap*, vol. 1, *Teori og analyse*, 140n1, 140n2, 140n4, and 140n6.
79 A, C, D "for þangat" / B "flo hann þangat" and A, C, D "slita ondina" / B "slęgia ǫndina."
80 See the section titled "The Capture of Satan on the Cross" in chapter 5.
81 A ("And [he] travelled there").
82 C ("And [he] travelled there").
83 D ("Satan travelled there").
84 B ("And he flew there").
85 As suggested in the section "The Capture of Satan on the Cross" in chapter 5.
86 A ("[To] tear away the soul at once from Him").
87 C ("[He] would tear away the soul from Jesus").
88 D ("[To] tear away the soul from Him").
89 B ("[To] steal the soul from Him").
90 A ("A most joyless man").
91 C ("A most joyless man").
92 D ("A most prudent man").
93 B ("A wretched man").
94 T ("A most wretched man").
95 A ("And then we shall come there").
96 C ("And then we shall travel down to the world").
97 D ("Then we travel to you").
98 The reading "existi in salutem populi tui" is not derived from the Vulgate, which in this place reads "egressus es in salutem populi tui," but from the *Vetus Latina* "existi in salutem populi tui." This accordance may be due to the fact that the song of Habakkuk was one of the seven songs incorporated in the Roman series of canticles and that this, rather than the text of the Vulgate, was possibly used for the insertion of the above-mentioned songs into the composition of the *Evangelium Nicodemi*. The first known manuscript of the Roman canticles is the so-called *Vespasian Psalter*, copied in Canterbury at the beginning of the eighth century and containing the first interlinear translation of the Bible in Old English. Its text is available in Wright, ed., *The Vespasian Psalter*. On the alternative usage of its readings and those of the Vulgate in medieval England, see Marsden, *The Text of the Old Testament in Anglo-Saxon England*, 61, 214, and 228.
99 A ("To free your poor ones").

100 B ("To free your poor ones").
101 D ("To free your chosen ones").
102 A ("You confess to the Lord").
103 C ("You confess to the Lord").
104 B ("They would confess to the Lord").
105 T ("They would confess to the Lord").
106 A, D "scolom biþa" / B, C "scalltu biþa."
107 A, D om. / B "sputum iustorum"; A, D om. / B "sva sem sem þu svaraþir feþrom orom."
108 A ("We shall wait a little while").
109 D ("We two shall wait a little while").
110 B ("You shall wait a little while").
111 C ("Now you shall wait a while").
112 T ("Wait a little while").
113 On the different epithets addressed to Satan by Hell, see "Seven-Headed Satan" section in chapter 5.
114 B ("Defamed by men").
115 T ("Spittle of the just").
116 B ("As you promised to our fathers").
117 T ("As you promised to our fathers").
118 See Turville-Petre, *Origins of Icelandic Literature*, 127.
119 Aho, "A Comparison of Old English," 156. Aho's main positions have been recently presented in a brief uncritical summary by Langley, "The *Niðrstigningarsaga.*"
120 Haugen, *Stamtre og tekstlandskap*, vol. 1, *Teori og analyse*, 125–52.
121 See Magnús Már Lárusson, "Um Niðrstigningar sögu," 159.
122 See in the sections titled "Agreement between K and E against T and A" and "Minor Variants of T Reflected in A against K and R" in chapter 4.

4 The Latin Source Text Underlying *Niðrstigningar saga*

1 See Haugen, *Stamtre og tekstlandskap*, vol. 1, *Teori og analyse*, 46; K. Wolf, "The Influence of the *Evangelium Nicodemi*," 238; Roughton, "Stylistics and Sources of the *Postola Sögur*," 45; and K. Wolf, *The Legends of the Saints*, 273.
2 As can be gathered from Izydorczyk, *Manuscripts of Evangelium Nicodemi.*
3 As illustrated in the "Agreement between K and E against T and A" section in this chapter.
4 On the different themes and doctrines connected to Christ's Descent and Harrowing of Hell, see MacCulloch, *The Harrowing of Hell*, and, more recently, Tamburr, *The Harrowing of Hell*. On the iconography in the visual arts of the Middle Ages, see Schiller, *Ikonographie der christlichen Kunst*, 3:43 and

the introductory pages to its development in modern times by Böhm, "Von der Höllenfahrt Christi." One of the most exquisite rappresentations of the Harrowing of Hell as described in the *Evangelium Nicodemi* is an illumination attributed to the Master of the Parement of Narbonne in the *Très belle Heures de Notre-Dame* (Paris, BnF, nuov. acq. lat. 3093), f. 155r (ca. 1375–1400), which belonged to John, Duke of Berry (†1416). The narrative starts with John the Baptist announcing the coming of the Messiah in the wilderness of Judea (trees on the left side) and in Hell (chapter XVIII.3) and ends (right side) with Christ delivering the souls of the righteous and taking Adam by his hand (chapter XXIV.2). Also worthy of note are the details of the entrance to Hell (right side): the wood of the cross is stuck outside of the gates of Jerusalem and close to Adam, on whose grave (at Golgotha) the seed from which the wood of the cross was made was believed to have grown, and the Mouth of Hell, placed beneath Jerusalem, populated by host of devils dispersed outside its gates after the Harrowing. See Figure 5.

5 K ("This same Nicodemus wrote it in the Hebrew script").

6 T ("This same Nicodemus wrote it in the Hebrew script, then the Emperor Theodosius the Great had it translated from Hebrew into Latin").

7 A ("And many generations later their book came to the Emperor Theodosius, son of Arcadius. He had it with him in Constantinople and had it read aloud and people were very impressed by it").

8 K ("In the name of the Holy Trinity begin the 'Deeds of the Saviour' of Our Lord, Jesus Christ, which were found in Jerusalem among public documents, during the reign of the Emperor Theodosius the Great in the Praetorium of Pontius Pilate").

9 The preposition "upp" ("up") conveys the nuance of "declaiming, reciting" to the broader meaning of the base verb "ráða" ("explaining, reading") in the description of the Emperor's dealings with the apocryphon. On the particular usage of this verb in AM 645, see the section titled "The *Jarteinabœkr Þorláks byskups*" in chapter 6.

10 K ("All these things which were said and done by the Jews in their synagogue, Joseph and Nicodemus immediately reported to the Prefect").

11 ("All these things which were said and done by the Jews in their synagogue, Joseph and Nicodemus immediately reported to the Prefect Pilatus").

12 A ("And they, Nicodemus and Joseph, read [it] aloud before others").

13 See "The *Jarteinabœkr Þorláks byskups*" section in chapter 6.

14 K ("Seeing this, Hell, Death, and their impious servants with their cruel ministers were frightened in their own reigns. When the brightness of such a light had been recognized, they suddenly saw Christ in their dwellings, and exclaimed, saying: 'We have been conquered by You'").

15 A reading typical of the hybrid redaction, and again well reflected in the Icelandic translation; see the section "Agreement between T, R, and A against K" in this chapter.

16 K ("The King of Glory came up in the form of a man. The Lord of Majesty illuminated the eternal shadows and broke the indestructible bonds with the aid of His unconquered power. He visited us sitting in the darkness of our failures and in the shadows of our death").
17 T ("The Son of God, Christ, the King of Glory, came up in the form of a man; He illuminated the eternal shadows with the splendor of His face and all the infernal gates, bars, and locks were destroyed at His entrance and everything gave Him space and made Him room").
18 A ("Then the King of Glory came to the stronghold of Hell, destroyed at once the fortress of Hell and opened a large gate. He revealed Himself in the shape of a man with such a great light that the darkness of Hell vanished").
19 K XIX.1 37/4–5 and K XIX.1 38/11–12.
20 K XXV 46/1–4.
21 "Filius enim hominis venturus est in gloria Patris sui cum angelis suis et tunc reddet unicuique secundum upus eius." ("For the Son of man shall come in the glory of His Father with His angels, and then He shall reward every man according to his work.")
22 Surveyed in the section "Christ as Warrior-King" in chapter 5.
23 T ("Then, when all the saints saw Jesus the Saviour coming with His angels").
24 A ("Then he saw that a great host of angels had arrived to Hell").
25 K ("While David was saying this to Hell, the King of Glory, the Lord of Majesty, came up in the form of a man, enlightened the eternal shadows and broke the insolvable bonds").
26 R ("In the form of a man, the Lord of Majesty, who enlightened the eternal shadows and broke the indissoluble bonds").
27 The additional messianic epithet concerning Christ, "Ecce desideratus omnibus gentibus filius Dei Christus" ("Behold, the One Desired by all nations"), transmitted solely by the hybrid text, is reminiscent of the words spoken by God in Haggai 2:8 concerning the future splendor and glory of the Jewish temple: "Et mouebo omnes gentes et veniet desideratus cuntis gentibus et implebo domum ista gloria, dicit Dominus exercitus" ("And I will move all nations: and the Desired of all nations shall come").
28 With "splendore uultus sui" ("the radiance of His face"), the compiler of the hybrid redaction seems to draw a parallel between the radiance of Christ's face with that of Moses during his descent from Mount Sinai with the Ten Commandments as reported in Exodus 34:29 and possibly 2 Corinthians 3:13.
29 T ("While David was saying this to Hell, Behold, the One Desired by all nations, the King of Glory, the Son of God, Christ, came up in the form of a man who enlightened the eternal shadows with the radiance of His face and broke the

indissolvable bonds [...] Then Christ entered and shattered the bonds in which they were fastened together").

30 A ("When David had said this, the King of Glory came to the stronghold of Hell [...] He revealed Himself in the shape of a man with such a great light that the darkness of Hell vanished, and every good man then was freed from the bond binding him").

31 K ("When they suddenly saw Christ in their dwellings, they exclaimed, saying: 'We have been conquered by you'").

32 R ("They suddenly saw Christ in their dwellings and exclaimed saying: 'We have been conquered by you'").

33 T ("And when they suddenly saw Christ descending in their dwellings, terrified and confused, they exclaimed: 'We have been conquered by you'").

34 A ("When they saw Christ their God walking there, they all bent forward and stared in that direction, and said this: 'Now you have overcome us'").

35 For a general discussion of this motif and its specific treatment in the literature of medieval England, see Dendle, *Satan Unbound*, and, more recently, Lynch, "Satan Bound."

36 In Icelandic sources, an explicit reference to the devils being bound with "blazing bonds" is found in *Jakobs saga postola* (*ins eldra*), in which a group of devils, just before the binding of Hermogenes, explains to James the Elder: "þa batt oss engill goþs elldligom bǫndom oc iarnrekondom oc brennom vér," ("Then the angel of Christ [Michael] bound us with blazing bonds and iron chains, and we burnt"), *Jakobs saga postola*, 525/5–7. Another instance occurs in *Maríu Saga* II, in Theophilus of Adana's penitential prayer to the Virgin, in connection with the damnation of the human soul in Hell: "Nu þa huerr er sa er mina sal man freilsa or fiandans bondom, þa er hon leiðiz til heluitis brend ok bundin elligom bondom?" ("Now who is the one who shall free my soul from the bonds of the Devil when it shall be led to the fire of Hell and shall be bound with firing bonds?"), *MS*, 412/16–18.

37 K ("Then the King of Glory, the Lord, trampling down Death in His majesty, grasped Prince Satan and delivered him to the power of Hell").

38 R ("Then the King of Glory, the Lord, trampling down Death in His majesty, grasped Prince Satan and the power of Hell").

39 T ("Then the King of Glory, Christ, the Lord of Majesty, trampling down, grasped Prince Satan through His power and delivered him bound to the power of Hell").

40 A ("Then the Lord, the King of Glory, began to trample down the Prince of Death and bound him with blazing bonds of His powers").

41 K "lux fulgebit super eos" / T "lux orta est eis"; K "in quo bene conplacui" / T "in quo mihi bene complacui"; K "gemitum uinculatorum" / T "gemitum compeditorum."

42 K ("Suddenly, there occurred a golden glow of the sun and a purple and royal light shone over us").
43 T ("Suddenly, there occurred in the golden light of the sun a certain royal light, which shone over us").
44 A ("Suddenly, there shone over us all a fair and bright light as if from the sun").
45 K ("At once Adam, father of all human race, with all the patriarchs and prophets rejoiced saying").
46 T ("And at once Adam, father of all human race, with happiness with all the patriarchs and prophets rejoiced saying").
47 A ("Then Adam, father of all mankind, and all the patriarchs and prophets began to rejoice greatly and said this").
48 K ("The people who sit in darkness shall see a great light, and a light shall shine over those who are in the region of the shadow of death").
49 T ("The people who sat in the darkness have seen a great light, and a light has downed on those living in the region of the shadow of death").
50 A ("The people who sat in the darkness have seen a great light, and a light has downed on those living in the region of the shadow of death").
51 See Gryson, *Vetus Latina*, vol. 12/1, *Esaias*, 281.
52 K ("And thereafter, there came [a man] as if he were a hermit. Questioned by all: 'Who are you?' To them, he replied and said").
53 T ("And thereafter, there came [a man] as if he were a hermit. Questioned by all who he was, he replied").
54 A ("Then there came a walking man, whom they did not recognize. This man was accomplished and dressed in such a manner as if he had come from the desert. They asked that man his name and if he had anything new to say").
55 K ("This is my beloved Son in whom [I am] well pleased").
56 T ("This is my beloved Son in whom I am well pleased").
57 A ("This is my Beloved in whom I am pleased").
58 The reading is extant in the following manuscripts: *Codex Bezae d* (Cambridge, UL, Nn. II 41) from the fifth century (see Scrivener, *Bezae Codex Cantabrigiensis*, 7); *Codex Palatinus e* (Vienna, ÖNB, Cod. Lat. 1185; Dublin, TC, N. 4. 18; London, BL, Addit. 40107), also from the fifth century(see Belsheim, *Evangelium Palatinum*, 3); *Codex Brixianus f* (Brescia, Biblioteca Civica Queriniana, s.n) from the sixth century (see Wordsworth and Whithe, *Novum Testamentum Domini nostri*, 1:50); and *Codex Sangermansis* g^1 (Paris, BnF, lat. 11553) from the ninth century (see Wordsworth, *The Gospel According to Matthew*, 8). This ancient reading is still found in manuscripts younger than the *Codex Einsidlensis*, such as Saint-Omer, Bibliothèque de l'Agglomération de Saint-Omer, 202 and London, BL, Royal 5. E. XIII, both from the ninth century. See *Two Old English Apocrypha*, ed. Cross, 204.

59 K ("Just as You predicted through Your law and prophets, You have fulfilled your deeds. You have redeemed the living through your Cross and through Your death on the cross You have descended to us").

60 T ("Just as You predicted through Your law and prophets, You have redeemed us through Your Cross and through Your death on the cross You have descended to us").

61 A ("You prophesied through the law and the prophets, to free us and the entire world through Your death on the cross and Your descent to us").

62 K ("Holding Adam to the right side, He ascended from Hell").

63 T ("Holding Adam's right hand, He ascended from Hell").

64 A ("[He] took Adam by the hand and ascended from Hell").

65 K ("To fight against him with the divine signs and wonders, and they shall be slain by him in Jerusalem").

66 T ("They fight against him with the divine signs and wonders, and we shall be slain by him in Jerusalem").

67 A ("And fight against him with the miracles and signs of God. He shall slay us in Jerusalem").

68 "Et cum finierint testimonium suum, bestia, quæ ascendit de abysso, faciet adversum eos bellum, et vincet illos, et occidet eos. Et corpora eorum iacebunt in plateis civitatis magnæ, quæ vocatur spiritualiter Sodoma, et Ægyptus, ubi et Dominus eorum crucifixus est." ("And when they shall have finished their testimony, the beast that ascendeth out of the abyss shall make war against them, and shall overcome them, and kill them. And their bodies shall lie in the streets of the great city, which is called spiritually, Sodom and Egypt, where their Lord also was crucified.")

69 K ("Hearing these things, the entire multitude of saints said to Hell with a voice of rebuke").

70 R ("Hearing these things, the entire multitude said to Hell with a voice of rebuke").

71 T ("Hearing these things, the entire multitude said to the devils with a voice of rebuke").

72 A ("When the saints of God heard this, they said to those evil spirits").

73 Turville-Petre, *Origins of Icelandic Literature*, 127.

74 Some representations of the Harrowing of Hell depict a group of devils rather than a personified Inferus, as does, for instance, a particularly fine illumination in the *Très belle Heures de Notre-Dame* (f. 155r), a French manuscript compiled towards the end of the fourteenth century, which seems to be specifically indebted to the narrative of the *Gospel of Nicodemus* and to no other particular text describing Christ's Descent into Hell. See details in Figure 5.

75 K ("And there was a great voice like a thunder").

76 R ("And there was a great voice like a thunder").

77 T ("And there was a second time a great voice like [that] of a thunder").
78 A ("Then they heard a second time such a great voice that all of Hell seemed to quake").
79 K ("And the Lord Himself from Heaven has looked upon earth to hear the groan of those who had been bound in chains and free the sons of those who had been afflicted").
80 R ("And the Lord Himself from Heaven has looked upon earth to hear the groan of those who had been bound in chains and free the sons of those who had been afflicted").
81 T ("And the Lord Himself from Heaven has looked upon earth to hear the groans of those who had been fettered and free the sons of those who had been afflicted").
82 A ("The Lord Himself from Heaven has looked upon earth to hear the groans of those who had been fettered and free the sons of those who had been afflicted").
83 See for instance Thorpe, *Libri Psalmorum*, 277, and Gilson, *The Mozarabic Psalter*, 90.
84 K ("You told me that He is the one who dragged away the dead from me").
85 E ("You told me that He is the one who dragged away dead men from me").
86 T ("You told me [that] He is the one who took away the dead from you").
87 A ("And we know that He has taken many dead men from you").
88 K ("Leader of destruction, Beelzebub").
89 T ("Leader of destruction, three-headed Beelzebub").
90 R ("Leader of destruction, three-headed Beelzebub").
91 A ("Prince of Death, three-headed Beelzebub").
92 Thilo, ed., *Codex apocryphus Novi Testamenti*, 1:729.
93 Book 18, chapter 13, CCSL 48.4. For a discussion on the figure of Cerberus in the Middle Ages, see Savage, "The Medieval Tradition of Cerberus."
94 See the section "Seven-Headed Satan" in chapter 5.
95 A ("The giant Satan, the Prince of Hell, who sometimes has seven heads and sometimes three, and sometimes is in the shape of a dragon, which is horrible, terrible, and awful in all respects").
96 K ("For now, through the splendor of His divinity, Jesus chases away all the shadows of death and has broken the steadfast prisons").
97 T ("For now, through the splendor of His divinity, Jesus chased away all the shadows of death and has broken the inner enclosures of the prison").
98 R ("For now, through the splendor of divinity, Jesus chased away all the shadows of death and has broken the inner enclosures of the prison").
99 A ("It can now be seen that Christ comes here and, with the light of His divinity, drives away the darkness of death and broke all our enclosures").

5 The Textual Interpolations of *Niðrstigningar saga*

1 Seth's quest for the Oil of Mercy, derived from the Latin *Vita Adae et Evae*, was known also in Iceland through a translation of the so-called *Origo Crucis* ("Origin of the True Cross"). The text transmitted in Copenhagen AM 544 4to or *Hauksbók* (ff. 17r–18v) is edited in Overgaard, *The History of the Cross-Tree*, 1–18, and *Heilagra manna sögur*, vol. 1:298–301. The underlying Latin text has been edited in Meyer, "Die Geschichte des Kreuzholzes," 101–66. On the development and circulation of the legend, see Quinn, *The Quest of Seth*.

2 A 52r/31–2.

3 A 52r/32–3.

4 "eiecitque Adam et conlocavit ante paradisum voluptatis cherubin et flammeum gladium atque versatilem ad custodiendam viam ligni vitæ" ("And he cast out Adam, and placed before the Paradise of pleasure Cherubims, and a flaming sword, turning every way, to keep the way to the tree of life").

5 The end of the interpolation is clearly highlighted by an additional sentence in which Seth takes up again the narration of his travel, 645 52r/34 "Enn þa er viðtoc at nema of for mina þa nam ec staþar" ("When my passage was obstructed, I halted"), resuming the regular course of the translation and following afresh the Latin source text with his encounter with the archangel Michael: "oc baþc til Drottens oc syndisc mer þa þar Michael hofuðengill" ("And I prayed to the Lord, and then the archangel Michael appeared to me"); T 99v/1–2 "Ego cum orarem Dominum ad portas paradysi ecce angelus Dei Michael apparuit michi" ("When I was praying to the Lord, Behold, the angel of God, Michael, appeared to me").

6 Sylwan, *Petri Comestoris*, 47/37–9. See also *PL* 198/1075B–1075C.

7 On the circulation and reception of the *Historia scholastica* in medieval France and England, see Morey, "Peter Commestor, Biblical Paraphrase," 6–35.

8 On the composition of *Stjórn* I, see Kirby, *Bible Translation in Old Norse*, 52–6.

9 On the employment of *Historia scholastica* and *Speculum historiale* in *Stjórn* I, see Astås, *Et bibelverk fra middelalderen*, 140–6 and 146–8, respectively.

10 Astås, ed., *Stjórn*, 60/20–61/6.

11 Such as "princeps et dux mortis" in K XX.1 38/1 ("Prince and ruler of Death") or phrases that emphasize his low position in cosmogonical order as a consequence of his disastrous fall, such as "sputio iustorum, derisio angelorum Dei" in K XXIII 43/4–5 ("spittle of the just and scorn of the angels of God").

12 K XXIII.1 43/2–3.

13 T 101v/30.

14 A 52v/17–19.

15 Revelation 12:3.

16 Turville-Petre, *Origins of Icelandic Literature*, 126–8; Aho, "*Niðrstigningarsaga*," 150–9; Magnús Már Lárusson, "Um Niðrstigningarsögu," 159–68; Gschwantler, "Christus, Thor und die Midgardschlange," 152–3; Marchand, "Leviathan and the Mousetrap," 328; Haugen, "Soga om nedstiginga i dødsriket," 99; K. Wolf, "The Influence of the *Evangelium Nicodemi*," 269.

17 A 53r/16–18.

18 "Tollites portas principes vestras et elevamini porte eternales et introibit Rex Glorie." ("Lift up your gates, O princes, and lift up your eternal gates, so that the King of Glory may come in.")

19 In K XXI.1/3–4.

20 In K XXI.2/2–3 and K XXI.3/4–5.

21 See Dubois, "La représentation de la Passion," 77–89.

22 A 53v/7–8.

23 T 110v/7–8 and T 101r/17–18. The Icelandic compiler might have associated the sentences preceding and following the *Tollite portas*, verses 24(23):7 and 24(23):10, which describe God as "strong and mighty in battle" ("Dominus fortis et potens, Dominus potens in proelio") and as a "Lord of hosts" ("Dominus virtutum") with the images of Revelation 19:11–21, which portray the returning and avenging Christ as a victorious Roman emperor riding a white horse and wearing a scarlet robe. For a detailed historical, mythological, and literary analysis of Revelation 19, see Thomas, *Revelation 19*. Christ is depicted as riding a horse into Hell in the *Descent into Hell* poem of the *Exeter Book* (Exeter, Cathedral Library, 3501) from the second half of the tenth century. It has been suggested that this imagery in the Old English poem may have been inspired by the hymn *Gloria, laus et honor*. The hymn, first composed by Theodulf of Orléans (†821) and subsequently included in the *Roman Missal*, played a key role in the Palm Sunday ritual. See Ruggerini, "A Just and Riding God," 206–24.

24 For a discussion on the literary genre of Revelation, see Mazzaferri, *The Genre of the Book of Revelation*. On its imagery and reception in the Middle Ages, see Matter, "The Apocalypse in Early Medieval Exegesis," 38–50.

25 A 53r/18–20.

26 A 53r/20–7.

27 Revelation 19:11–17.

28 "et de ore ipsius procedit gladius acutus ut in ipso percutiat gentes et ipse reget eos in virga ferrea et ipse calcat torcular vini furoris irae Dei omnipotentis." ("And out of His mouth procedeth a sharp [two edged] sword; that with it He may strike the nations. And He shall rule them with a rod of iron; and He treadeth the winepress of the fierceness of the wrath of God the Almighty.")

29 A 53v/12–19.

30 Turville-Petre, *Origins of Icelandic Literature*, 126–8, and Magnús Már Lárusson, "Um Niðrstigningarsögu," 159–68. On the interpretation of Job 41, see Pelham, *Contested Creations*, 134–7.

31 Job 41:1–9(40:20–8).

32 Aho, "*Niðrstigningarsaga*," 151–9. The myth is addressed in Meulengracht Sørensen, "Thor's fishing expedition," 257–78. Snorri's treatment of the poem is discussed in A. Wolf, "Sehweisen und Darstellungsfragen," 1–27.

33 de Leeuw van Weenen, *The Icelandic Homily Book*, 35v/9–20. The Latin text was edited under the name *Homilia XXV in Evangelia*. See Gregory the Great, *Homiliae in evangelia*, CCSL 213/226 and PL vol. 76, cols. 1188–96, at col. 1194. See also Marchand, "Leviathan and the Mousetrap," 329.

34 Gregory of Nyssa, *Oratio Catechetica magna*, PG vol. 45, col. 65.

35 "For since, as has been said before it was not in the nature of the opposing power to come in contact with the undiluted presence of God and to undergo His enclouded manifestation, therefore, in order to secure that the ransom in our behalf might be easily accepted by him who required it, the Deity was hidden under the veil of our nature, so that, as with ravenous fish, the hook of the Deity might be gulped down along with the bait of flesh, and thus life being introduced into the house of death and light shining in darkness that which is diametrically opposed to light and life must vanish; for it is not in the nature of darkness to remain when light is present, or of death to exist when life is active." Schaff and Wallace, *Gregory of Nyssa*, 927–73. On Gregory of Nyssa's employment of the fishhook metaphor, see Satran, "Deceiving the Deceiver," 357–64.

36 For a historical overview of the different theories of atonement, see Rashdall, *The Idea of Atonement*, and Aulén, *Christus Victor*.

37 It is implicit then that Christ's victory over the Devil was the result of the Devil's own abuse of power: he tried to exercise over Christ the power that he possessed over earthly sinners only. The Devil's rights of possession are exposed in Augustine's *De Trinitate*, book 13, chapter 12, *Propter Adae peccatum iusto Dei iudicio in potestatem diaboli est genus humanum*, in PL vol. 42, col. 1026.

38 David Scott-Macnab has recently advanced that in his writings, Augustine might have intended "muscipula" simply as a synonym to the more common "laqueus" ("snare/trap for animals and birds") and not as a specific "mousetrap"; cf. Scott-Macnab "St Augustine and the Devil's 'Mousetrap,'" However, throughout the Middle Ages and modern times, "muscipula" has been consistently interpreted as a specific "mousetrap." For a survey of the mousetrap metaphor in the writings of Augustine, see Berchtold, *Des rats et des ratières*, 21–52. On this interpolation of the Icelandic text, see Bullitta, "*Crux Christi muscipula fuit diabolo*," especially 141–8.

39 In *Sermo* 265D, edited in *PLS*, 2:707, and in his *Enarrationes in Psalmos LI-C*, edited by Dekkers and Fraipont, 1414.
40 See, for instance, the discussion in BeDuhn, *Augustine's Manichaean Dilemma*, vol. 2, *Making a "Catholic" Self*, 129–37.
41 "cum autem mortale hoc induerit inmortalitatem tunc fiet sermo qui scriptus est absorta est mors in victoria." ("And when this mortal hath put on immortality, then shall come to pass the saying that is written: Death is swallowed up in victory.")
42 For a review of the imageries associated with the Devil in the New Testament, see Russell, *The Devil*, 221–49.
43 The text was first discovered and edited by Morin, "Un sermon," 134–43, and later included in *PLS*, 2:707. The edition followed here is *MiAg*, 1:662/8–19.
44 The entrance to Hell was held to be on Golgotha, which besides being the place of Christ's murder was also held to be the very place where Adam was born and died. Moreover, the tree used to make Christ's cross was believed to have grown from a seed taken from Eden and later planted on Adam's grave on the Golgotha; see Lima, "The Mouth of Hell," 36n2 and references there. See also details in Figure 5 in chapter 4.
45 The referent for "lion," the dangerous wild beast trapped in a snare, which in the New Testament (and in commentaries deriving from it) represents Satan, has in this instance been replaced with its Icelandic equivalent, a "melrakki" ("arctic fox"). One of the most prominent passages showing Satan in the shape of a lion is 1 Peter 5:8: "sobrii estote et vigilate quia adversarius vester diabolus tamquam leo rugiens circuit quaerens quem devoret" ("Be sober and watch: because our adversary the Devil, as a roaring lion, goeth about seeking whom he may devour"). On the hunting of arctic foxes in the Icelandic Middle Ages, see, for instance, Durrenberger and Gísli Pálsson, *The Anthropology of Iceland*, 39.
46 A 53v/19–20.
47 645 54v/1–2 "Þa toc Dominus Rex Glorie at troþa niþr hofðingi⟨a⟩ dauþans oc batt hann meþ elldligom bondom." ("Then the Lord, the King of Glory, began to trample down the Prince of Death and bound him with blazing bonds.")
48 On Worcester F 93, see for instance Floyer and Hamilton, *Catalogue of Manuscripts*, 46–7.
49 None of the 221 sermons is from Bede or Gregory the Great; only fifty-seven of them are connected to Paul the Deacon's reconstructed homiliary, while in the Roman homiliaries, seventy-eight are from Alan of Farfa and fifteen from Agimundus. See the discussion in Richards, *Texts and Their Traditions*, 112–20.
50 On the medieval Vulgate tradition at the Rochester Cathedral Library, see ibid., 61–84.
51 The most extensive study on Peter Lombard is Colish, *Peter Lombard*. A translation of all four books of the *Sententiae* is available in Lombard, *The Sentences*.

52 The familiarity of the author of *Niðrstigningar saga* with this passage of Lombard's *Sententiae* and the mousetrap metaphor was postulated by Otto Gschwantler, who suggested that the translation must therefore have been compiled in the second half of the twelfth century. See Gschwantler, "Christus, Thor," 155.
53 See the discussions in Wawrykow, "Peter Lombard," 650, and Edward, *The Foundations of Modern Science*, 48.
54 Augustine's *Sermo* 130 (a) is available in *Sermones ad populum, De verbis Evangelii Joannis, ubi narratur miraculum de quinque panibus et duobus piscibus*, PL vol. 38: cols. 725–8.
55 Lombard, *Sententiae*, par. 5/1–15. See also PL vol. 192, cols. 795–6.
56 The sermon has previously been wrongly attributed to Hildebert of Lavardin, archbishop of Tours (†1133). See Hildebert of Lavardin, *Sermones de tempore, IX in Nativitate Domini, Sermo primus, De Nativitate Domini*, in PL vol. 171: cols. 381–8, at 385A–385B. On Peter Lombard's sermons being mistakenly attributed to Hildebert, see Rosemann, *Peter Lombard*, 353.
57 Lombard, *Collectaneorum in Paulum continuatio* in PL, vol. 192: cols. 421B–421D. Hebrews 2:14: "quia ergo pueri communicaverunt sanguini et carni et ispe similiter participavit hisdem ut per mortem destrueret eum qui habeat mortis imperium id est diabolum." ("Therefore, because the children are partakers of flesh and blood, He also Himself in like manner hath been partaker of the same: that, through Death, He might destroy him who had the Empire of Death, that is to say, the Devil.")
58 The mousetrap simile occurs in Nicholas of Lyra's version of the *Glossa ordinaria*; see Nicholas of Lyra, *Textus Biblie cum glossa ordinaria*, f. 138r. The same topos, in a similar cautionary tale describing a mouse blinded by its greed and consequently caught in a mortal trap, would become extremely popular in the early modern times through Emblem 95 of Andrea Alciato's *Emblematum liber*, first published in 1531. The poem, entitled *Captivus ob gulam* ("Caught by Gluttony"), has been inspired by Antiphilus of Byzantium's epigram 86 in book 9 of the *Anthologia graeca*. See, for instance, Marsh, *Renaissance Fables*, 311. Alciato's Emblem 95 is available in Figure 6.
59 Magnús Már Lárusson gives no reasonable evidence for his suggestion other than Jón Ögmundarson's well-known erudition and his stature as one of the first translators of hagiographical literature into Icelandic. See Magnús Már Lárusson, "Um Niðrstigningarsögu," 167. He is later followed by Gschwantler, "Christus, Thor," 152, and Kirby, *Bible Translation in Old Norse*, 35.

6 The Theological Context of *Niðrstigningar saga*

1 Andersen, *Katalog over AM Accessoria 7*. The parchment fragments were already severely damaged when they were collected in Iceland and transferred to

Copenhagen by Árni Magnússon (†1730) in the early eighteenth century. It was on account of their apparently irreversible state of despair that they were subsequently used by him and his team to bind together scattered leaves or quires of mostly paper manuscripts transmitting secular literature. See discussion in Andersen, xviii–xix.

2 A leaf from a gradual (Andersen, *Katalog over AM Accessoria 7*, item 27), a leaf of a sacramentary (item 72), a leaf of a missal (item 78), and two psalters (items 108 and 113).

3 Ibid., item 103. Five manuscripts of the *Eulogium* are known today. Curley, "John of Cornwall," 1038.

4 Its text has been edited by Häring, ed., "The *Eulogium ad Alexandrum Papam*," 253–300. On the criticism advanced against Peter Lombard's *Sententiae*, see, most recently, Monagle, *Christological Nihilism*.

5 On Boethius's *hypostasis*, see Bradshaw, "The *Opuscula Sacra*," 123–4.

6 Andersen, *Katalog over AM Accessoria 7*, item 122.

7 See ibid., item 122. Guy Lobrichon rejects Gilbert of Poitiers's authorship of the prologue. See Lobrichon, "Une nouveauté," 113.

8 For an overview of the great exegetical work around the *Glossa ordinaria*, see van Liere, "Biblical Exegesis," 167–70.

9 Revelation 1–4:2 and 10:10–16:16 (ff. 69r–70v).

10 Several Scandinavian clerics are known to have studied at the influential Abbey of Saint Victor in Paris during the last decades of the twelfth century. These include the Danish Archbishops Eskil (†1181) and Absalon (†1201) of Lund. Norwegian Archbishops Eysteinn Erlendsson (†1188), Erik Ivarsson (†1213), and Þórir Gudmunsson (†1214) of Niðaróss, and Bishop Þórir (†1196) of Hamar, all believed to have studied theology in Paris. See Bekker-Nielsen, "The Victorines and Their Influence," 32–3.

11 The first to suggest that Þorlákr studied at Saint Victor Abbey was Paasche, *Norges og Islands*, 281. See also K. Wolf, "Pride and Politics," 244.

12 *Jarteinabók Þorláks byskups in forna*, 135/1–3.

13 See "The Prologue" section in chapter 4.

14 A 55v/20–23 "Enn morgom mannzøll⟨drom⟩ siþar comsc at boc þeire Theodosius keisere sonr Archadii. Hann hafði meþ sér i Miclagarþ oc let þar uppraþa oc varþ þar monnom alldat umb." ("And many generations later their book came to the Emperor Theodosius, son of Arcadius. He had it with him in Constantinople and had it read aloud and people were very impressed by it.")

15 Even within the manuscripts of *Niðrstigningar saga*, the reading "uppráða" is unstable. B 14v/23 reads "uppráða," while C 28v/43 and D 10r/5 both transmit "upplesa." The only manuscript of *Sverris saga* transmitting the reading "uppráða" is the so-called *Skálholtsbók yngsta* (AM 81 A fol.), dated to the years 1450–75.

AM 324 4to, possibly written in Norway by an Icelandic scribe around 1300 (on which the edition is based), transmits the synonym "upplesa." See Karl Jónsson, *Saga Sverris konungs*, 293. This piece of evidence may corroborate Anne Holtsmark's hypothesis that AM 645 4to was indeed written at Skálholt.

16 *Jarteinabók Þorláks byskups ǫnnur*, ci. The *Jarteinabók Þórlaks byskups ǫnnur* is appended to recension C of *Þórlaks saga byskups*. The text is transmitted along with *Hungrvaka* in AM 379 4to, copied in 1645. The *Jarteinabækr Þorláks byskups* are extensively surveyed in Kuhn, "The Emergence of a Saint's Cult," 240–54.

17 *Jarteinabók Þorláks byskups ǫnnur*, 249/6–19.

18 Ásdís Egilsdóttir, "St. Þorlákr in Iceland," 130.

19 Matthew 10:8 "infirmos curate mortuos sucitate leprosos mundate daemones eicite gratis accepistis gratis date" ("Heal the sick, raise the dead, cleanse the lepers, cast out devils: freely you have received, freely give"); Matthew 11:5 "caeci vident claudi ambulant leprosi mundatur surdi audiunt mortui resurgunt pauperes evangelizantur" ("The blind see, the lame walk, the lepers are cleansed, the deaf hear, the dead rise again, the poor have the gospel preached to them").

20 A 52v/23–25 "oc marga menn er ec hafða blinda gørva ⟨oc hallta⟩ oc biuga oc licþra oc oþa þa grøddi hann med orði sino" ("And many men, whom I have made blind, lame, leper and mad, He healed with His word"). The set of Christ's miracles is referred to once in the *Acta Pilati* – T 92r/20–21 "Iste autem claudos et surdos curuos et paraliticos cecos et leprosos et demoniacos curauit" ("He has cured the lame, the deaf, the crippled, the paralytics, the blind, the lepers and the possessed") – and once in the *Descenus Christi ad inferos* – T 99v/17–19 "Et multos quos ego cecos claudos curuos leprosos et uexatos feci ipse uerbo suo sanauit" ("And many, whom I have made blind, lame, crippled, leprous, and mad, He healed with His word").

21 *Jarteinabók Þorláks byskups ǫnnur*, 249/30–250/5.

22 Ibid., 247/23–8.

23 For a detailed description of medieval stone traps for foxes in Iceland and Greenland, see especially Þór Magnússon, "Hrafnahrekkurinn."

24 Ibid., 247/32–248/10.

25 On the legendary adoption of Christianity in Iceland, see Jón Hnefill Aðalsteinsson, *Under the Cloak*. For a historical overview of the event, see Strömback, *The Conversion of Iceland*.

26 Extant in Reykjavík AM 386 4to I, consisting of three leaves. See *Þórlaks saga byskups in elzta* and *Latínubrót um Þórlaks byskups*.

27 On the composition of the text, see, most recently, Wellendorf, "Whetting the Appetite," 123–42.

28 *Hungrvaka*, 42/5–43/4.

29 See the discussion in K. Wolf, "Pride and Politics," 249–50.

30 John 2:1–11. See Ásdís Egilsdóttir, "The Beginnings of Local Hagiography," 129.

31 *Hungrvaka*, 2/12–15.

32 *Páls saga byskups* relates that 220 churches and 190 priests were counted; see *Páls saga byskups*, 313. The affluence of Icelandic students at foreign universities in the Middle Ages is surveyed in Jónas Gíslason, "Island (til 1700)."

7 Conclusion

1 Magnús Már Lárusson, "Um Niðrstigningarsögu," 167.

Texts and Translations

Texts

Editorial Procedure

ICELANDIC TEXTS*: *SIGLA

A Copenhagen, Den Arnamagnæanske Samling, AM 645 4to, 51v–55v (s. $XIII^{2/4}$)
B Copenhagen, Den Arnamagnæanske Samling, AM 623 4to, 10r–14v (s. $XIV^{1/4}$)
C Copenhagen, Den Arnamagnæanske Samling, AM 233 a fol., 28r–v (s. $XIV^{3/4}$)
D Reykjavík, Landsbókasafn Íslands, JS 405 8vo, 2r–10v (1780–91)
E Copenhagen, Den Arnamagnæanske Samling, AM 238 fol. V (s. XV)

The base texts of the two redactions of *Niðrstigningar saga* are those of A, representing the oldest surviving witness and the only complete medieval manuscript transmitting the older redaction, and that of E, the sole surviving witness of the younger redaction. In the *apparatus criticus* to the text of A, all the variant readings of the other three manuscripts pertaining to the older redaction, B, C and D, are provided. The text of A and E, presented here in a semi-diplomatic transcription, are divided into chapters and paragraphs used by Hack C. Kim for his edition of the *Codex Einsidlensis*.

Lost or corrupted readings of A, either through physical damage of the manuscript or through obvious scribal errors, are restored and conjectured on the basis of C, identified in chapter 3 as the closest surviving manuscript to the archetype. In those cases in which A transmits ostensibly corrupted readings and the readings of C are missing, the errors of A are conjectured on the basis of B and D when these are in agreement and when its Latin counterpart is attested in T. Text supplied by the editor is indicated with open angle brackets ⟨ ⟩. Barely legible words due to wear of the parchment are placed in square brackets [ ]. Secondary scribal insertions, superscripted, subscripted, or added in the margins of the manuscripts, are all indicated with insertion characters ` ´. Abbreviations are expanded according to the spelling of the respective scribes. Geminates indicated in the manuscript with single majuscule letters are transcribed as digraphs in the edited text, as in "Terra" for A 52r/1 "TeRa". Geminates are indicated in the transcription also when they are found as single consonants in the manuscripts, as in "upp" for A 51v/24 "vp". Broken *ł* has been transcribed as a digraph *ll* as in "alla" for 51v/24 "ała" or "upphalldit" for 51/24–5 "vp hałdit". The letter *v* has been replaced with *u* when it has a syllabic value, as in "Guþi" for A 51v/34 "gvþi". Consequently, *u* has been transcribed as *v* when it represents a consonant, as in "vorum" for A 51v/27 "uorum". In B, C, D, and E, the acute accent denoting vowel length is kept only when etymological, as in B 12r/21 "góþr". It is omitted when it simply constitutes a paleographical variant of the same letter, as in "englom" for B 12v/22 "énglom". Compound words are set together when they are found disjointed in the manuscript, as in "þocusamt" for A 51v/29 "þocv samt". All place names, proper names, titles of texts, and the first word of each sentence have been capitalized according to modern practice. Manuscript punctuation has been normalized. Full stops have been preserved at the end of each sentence, omitted when redundant, and supplied where necessary. All editorial interventions are highlighted in the apparatus in the first person (*conieci*, *expunxi*, etc.) Direct literal quotations from the Scriptures are highlighted in italics; echoes or allusions to scriptural passages are noted in the footnotes. For sake of consistency, the orthographic conventions of the variant readings of B, C, and D in the apparatus and the text of E have been partially adapted and conformed to those of A.

LIST OF ABBREVIATIONS

ante corr. = *ante correctionem*; *add.* = *addidit*; *bis scr.* = *bis scripsit*; *cod.* = *codex*; *corr.* = *correxit*; *lect. dub.* = *lectio dubita*; *em.* = *emendauit*; *eras.* = *erasit*; *ex. grat.* = *exempli gratia*; *exp.* = *expunxit*; *in marg.* = *in margine*; *iter.* = *iterauit*; *praem.* = *praemisit*; *sub l.* = *sub linea*; *sup l.* = *supra linea*.

Niðrstigningar saga

The Older Redaction

(A Copenhagen, Den Arnamagnæanske Samling, AM 645 4to)

PROLOGUE

51v [51v] Niþrstigningar saga.[1] Karinus[2] oc[3] Leutius[4] fratres[5] syner Simeonis ens
Gamla[6] [7] segia sva[8] fra niþrstigningo Crisz[9] til helvitis a[10] boc þeire er ⟨þeir⟩
gørðo[11] of[12] þat hverso[13] Cristr[14] hafði[15] þa Adam ⟨leyst[16] oc⟩[17] alla saman fra[18]
helviti.[19] Enn þo at þvi se[20] varla[21] sva upphalldit er[22] of[23] þetta er gørt[24] sem
øþrom[25] helgom ritningom þa[26] er[27] ecki[28] þess[29] sact[30] fra[31] þvisa[32] er of[33] tor-
tryggva megi.[34] Boc[35] su er cøllot[36] Verk Grøðarans.[37] Segia menn[38] samsett
hava[39] Nichodemus[40] lerisveinn[41] Drottens.[42]

1 *rubrica om. D* **2** *post* Karinus *add.* er madr nefndr annar *D* **3** oc] *om. D* **4** Leutius *pro* Leucius **5** fratres] *om. D* **6** ens Gamla] *om. D* **7** Simeonis ens Gamla] Simeon senex cf. *ex. grat.* Aug. *In Ioh. Ev. tract. CXXIV* (CCSL 36, 449) *trans. post cap.* XVI.1, magnus sacerdos Symeon *T K* cf. Lc. 2:25 **8** sva] er *D* **9** Crisz] Drottins *D post* Drottins *add.* Vors Jesu Kristi *D* **10** a] i *D* **11** gørðo] *eras. et corr.* þørðo **12** of] um *D* **13** hversu] hvad *D* **14** Crists] Kristus **15** hafði] gjòrde *D* **16** leyst] leyste *D* **17** *post* oc *add.* þa *D* **18** fra] úr *D* **19** hverso Cristr hafði þa Adam ⟨leyst oc⟩ alla saman fra helviti] *praem. cap.* XXIV.2 tenens manum dextram Ade ascendit ab inferis ad superos et omnes sancti secuti sunt eum *T* **20** *post* se *add.* nu *D* **21** varla] ei *D* **22** er] þa *D* **23** of] *om. D* **24** gørt] rædt *D* **25** sem øþrom] i *D* **26** þa] þar *D* **27** er] ad *D* **28** ekki] ei *D* **29** þess] þessu *D ante* þessu *add.* so i *D* **30** sact] mále *D* **31** fra] oc *D* **32** þvisa] meþ *D* **33** er of] *om. D* **34** megi] má *D* **35** *ante* boc *add.* Þvi ad *D* **36** cøllot] heitir *D* **37** Verk Grøðarans] Gesta Salvatoris *D* **38** menn] þeir *D ante* þeir *add.* er *D* **39** *post* hava *add.* verit *D* **40** Nichodemus] *emendavi* Nichodemum *post* Nichodemus *add.* oc Ioseph *D* **41** lerisveinn] lærisveinar *D* **42** *post* Drottens *add.* Vors er grófu lík Drottins hverk hans ⟨…⟩ Af þeim verkum munum vier fá hlute *D*

XVIII.1

Ver vorom þar stadder sogdo[1] þeir[2] er sva þotti[3] sem væll⟨r⟩[4] vere. Þar var Adam
oc aller hofuðfeþr oc spamenn. Þaðra[5] var þocusamt[6] oc myrcr[7] vant at vera. Þa
gørþisc þat[8] minnilict[9] oc merkilict[10] at nęsta vaveifes[11] s[cei]n þar[12] lios[13] fagrt
oc biart sicut[14] af solo[15] iver oss[16] alla. Þa toc[17] Adam f[aþer] allz mannkyns[18] oc
aller høfotfeðr[19] oc spamenn[20] at fagna miog[21] [oc] męla[22] sva.[23] Lios þetta mon
scina af Guþi[24] er oss hefir heitet at senda[25] lios[26] sitt. Þa callaþi[27] Ysaias spamaþr
oc męlti sva.[28] Þetta lios er af Guþi sicut ec sagda þa er ec var lifs a iorþo oc
52r męlta ec sva.[29] [52r] *Terra Zabulon et Terra Neptalim trans Iordanis via maris* Mt.
Galilee ge[ntium].[30] *Populus*[31] *qui sedebat in tenebris lucem uidit magnam.*[32] 4:15–16

Habitantebus in regionibus umbre mortis lux orta est eis.[33] Nu er lios þat[34] comet iver oss er ec spaða þa[35] at coma mundi þviat sønno sitiom ver i heliar myrcrom. Enn nu megom ⟨ver sia oc⟩ mioc of[36] fagna aller[37] liose þvisa.

1 sogdo] segia *D* **2** *post* þeir *add.* Karinus oc Leusius *D* **3** þotti] var *D* **4** *post* vœll⟨r⟩ *add.* nockr *D* **5** Þaðra] Þar *D* **6** þocusamt] þocusamlegt *D* **7** myrcr] myrkt *D* **8** þat] þar *D* **9** minnilict] minnilegir *D* **10** merkilict] merkeligir *ante* merkeligir *add.* miög *post* merkeligir *add.* hluter *D* **11** nęsta vaveifes] ofarlega *D* **12** þar] *om. D* **13** *post* lios *add.* mikit *D* **14** sicut] sem *D* **15** *post* solo *add.* kunne ad verda *D* **16** oss] þá *D post* þá *add.* er þar voru inne *D* **17** toc] *om. D* **18** faþer allz mannkyns] *om. D* **19** høfotfeðr] forfedur *D* **20** oc spamenn] *om. D* **21** at fagna miog] fagnade *D* **22** męla] mælte *D* **23** sva] *om. D* **24** *post* Guþi *add.* Almáttugum *D* **25** senda] bod *D* **26** lios] *om. D* **27** *post* calladi *add.* upp *D* **28** sva] *om. D* **29** Þetta lios er af Guþi sicut ec sagda þa er ec var lifs a iorþo oc męlta ec sva] *om. D* **30** Terra Zabulon et Terra Neptalim trans Iordanis via maris Galilee gentium] *om. D* **31** Populus] *emendavi* Populis **32** Populis qui sedebat in tenebris lucem vidit magnam] Lydr sá er sat í myrkrunum sá liós mikid þar inne *D* **33** Habitantebus in regionibus umbre mortis lux orta est eis] Heriade hann i daudans skugga. Liós þad rann upp fyrir þeim *D* **34** er lios þat] *om. D* **35** þa] *om. D* **36** of] *om. D* **37** aller] *om. D* **38** þvisa] þessu *D*

XVIII.2

Þa com þar at[1] gangande[2] faþer ockar Simeon er fiolþinn[3] var allr[4] saman comenn oc męlti þa[5] allglaþliga[6] við Guþs vine.[7] Gøret[8] dyrð Domino Nostro[9] Ieso Christo[10] af þvi at ec toc hann i faþm mer þa er[11] ⟨hann⟩ var barn oc barc[12] hann[13]
i kirkio oc var ec þa kvøcþr[14] af Helgo⟨m⟩ Anda oc søng[15] ec þetta.[16] [17] *Nunc* Lc. 2:29
dimittis[18] usque in finem.[19] Þvisa[20] ørendi[21] føgnuþo miog[22] aller Guþs helgir.[23]

1 þar at] þángad *D post* þángad *add.* at segia þeim Karinus oc Leusius *D* **2** gangande] *om. D* **3** fiolþinn] mannfiöldinn *D post* mannfiöldinn *add.* sat oc *D* **4** allr] mestr *D* **5** þa] *om. D* **6** allglaþliga] glaþliga *D* **7** vine] líd *D* **8** Gøret] Giöre *D post* Giöre *add.* þier *D* **9** Domino Nostro] Drottne Varum *D* **10** *post* Christo *add.* seger hann *D* **11** er] ad *D* **12** barc] bar eg *D* **13** hann] *om. D* **14** kvøcþr] knúdr *D* **15** søng] mælti *D* **16** þetta] einn lofsöng *D post* lofsöng *add.* vid Drottin *D* **17** ec toc hann … / … søng ec þetta] cf. Lc. 2:25-28 **18** Nunc dimittis] dimitis *in cod., om. D* **19** usque in finem] allt til enda *D* cf. Lc. 2:29-32 **20** Þvisa] Af þessu *D* **21** ørendi] mále *D* **22** miog] *om. D* **23** *post* helgir *add.* menn *D*

XVIII.3

Þa com þar at gangandi maþr[1] sa er þeir kendo eigi.[2] Sa maþr var[3] gørvilegr[4] oc[5] a þann veg buenn[6] sem af[7] eyðimorc[8] væri comenn.[9] [10] Þeir[11] spurðo þann mann at namni[12] eþa[13] hvat hann cynni nytt at segia. Hann lezt[14] Iohannes heita[15] oc vasc[16] rodd[17] callandi av[18] ayþimorc oc fyrerrennere Sunar Guþs a iarþriki[19] oc[20] at segia monnom deili a þvi at[21] sa er[22] Sonr[23] Guþs er þa var þangat comenn at høndom þeim til þess at hialpa þeim er þat villdo þiggia.[24] Oc[25] þa er[26] ec sa hann coma at[27] finna mic þa[28] knuþi mic enn Helgi Andi oc[29] męlta[30] ⟨ec⟩[31]

þetta. *Ecce Agnus Dei*[32] usque in finem.[33] Ec[34] scirþac[35] hann þa[36] i onne Iordon Io. 1:29
enn þa[37] sa ec[38] *Anda Helgan coma*[39] *iver ⟨hann⟩*[40] *i dufolike oc heyrða ec þa*[41] Mt.
rødd af hi⟨m⟩nom[42] *męla.*[43] *Hic est Dilectus Meus in quo mihi complaqui.*[44] 3:16–17
Enn nu kann ec þetta[45] yðr at segia[46] at ec ⟨hevi⟩[47] nu[48] fyrer honom faret[49] hingat þess eyrendis at boþa yðr sva[50] at nu mun vera[51] allscamt[52] til ⟨þess⟩ unz[53]
I[ps]e[54] Filius Dei[55] mun her coma[56] ovan af himnom at vitia var[57] þeirra[58] manna er her sitia[59] i heliar myrcrom.[60]

1 *ante* maþr *add.* einn *D* **2** sa er þeir kendo eigi] *om. D* **3** Sa maþr var] *om. D* **4** gørvilegr] almennelegr *D* **5** oc] *om. D* **6** veg buenn] hátt *D* **7** af] *om. D* **8** eyðimorc] eydemarkar *D* **9** væri comenn] svín oc uxe *D* **10** sem af eyðimorc væri comenn] cf. Mt. 3:1 **11** Þeir] Aller menn *D* **12** namni] *emendavi* nanmi **13** þann mann at namni eþa] *om. D* **14** lezt] svarade *D* **15** heita] heiti *D* post heiti *add.* eg ad nafne *D* **16** vasc] var eg *D* **17** *ante* rodd *add.* einn *D* **18** av] in *D* **19** Sunar Guþs a iarþriki] *om. D* **20** *post* oc *add.* kallande *D* **21** deili a þvi at] *om. D* **22** sa er] *om. D* **23** Sunar] miskunn *D* **24** oc fyrerrennere Sunar Guþs … / … villdo þiggia] cf. Lc. 1:76-77. **25** Oc] *om. D* **26** er] *om. D* **27** at] oc *D* **28** *ante* þa *add.* oc *D* **29** oc] ad *D* **30** męlta] mæla *D* **31** ⟨ec⟩] *om. D* **32** Ecce Agnus Dei] Sie her Lamb Guds *D* **33** usque in finem] er burttekr syndir heimsins *D* **34** Ec] Ecc *in cod.*, *ante* ec *add* Oc *D* **35** scirþac] skírdi *D* **36** þa] *om. D* **37** þa] oc *D* **38** ec] *om. D* **39** *ante* coma *add.* ovan *D* **40** coma iver ⟨hann⟩] *conieci* descendentem super eum *T* **41** þa] *om. D* **42** *post* hi⟨m⟩nom *add.* ofann til hans *D* **43** męla] so mælande *D post* mælande *add.* á þessa lund *D* **44** Hic est Dilectus Meus in quo mihi complaqui] Sá er Sonur Minn Kiæraste vid hann líkar mier vel *D* **45** þetta] *om. D* **46** *post* segia *add.* óllum *D* **47** ⟨hefi⟩] em *D* **48** nu] *om. D* **49** faret] komin *D post* komin *add.* framm *D* **50** sva] siá *D ante* siá *add.* ad *D* **51** mun vera] er *D* **52** allscamt] skamt *D* **53** unz] *om. D* **54** Ipse] *eras.* **55** Ipse Filius Dei] Siálfr Guds Son *D* **56** *post* coma *add.* stigin *D* **57** *post* var *add.* oc *D* **58** *post* þeirra *add.* allra *D* **59** *post* sitia *add.* nú *D* **60** ec ⟨hevi⟩ nu … / … i heliar myrcrom] cf. Lc. 1:76–9

XIX.1

Þa var þa[1] er[2] Adam[3] fyrstscapaðr[4] faþer varr[5] heyrþi[6] sact fra þvisa[7] at Iesus
var[8] scirþr i Iordon er[9] sa maþr[10] Iohannes[11] for[12] af heimenum at[13] hann[14] varþ
allcatr viþ[15] oc hallaþiz ða[16] at[17] syni[18] sinom[19] oc męlti sva viþ hann. Seth
sunr[20] segðu[21] fra þvi patriarchis oc prophetis[22] er þu ⟨heirþir⟩[23] Michaele⟨m⟩
hofuðengil[24] [25] þer segia[26] þa er ec senda þic til paradisar at leita oc at qveðia[27]
Drotten Varn[28] þess[29] ef hann[30] myndi vilia[31] engil sinn senda[32] at føra þer[33]
þaðan viþsmior þat er þar[34] getr af[35] viþsmiorstre[36] miscunnar[37] at mætti með
ðvi[38] smyria licam minn[39] þa er ec var[40] siúcr at ec[41] of finga[42] heilso. Þa[43] hefir
Seth þangat til gengit[44] er[45] høfutfeþr oc spamenn voro.[46] Þa spurþi hann[47] [oc
toc sva[48] at] męla. Þat var qvat[49] Seth[50] þa[51] er ec for eyren⟨dis⟩ foþor mins at ec
com [of[52] siþir][53] til paradisar hliþs. Þar var tvennt fyrer[54] at þar var elldr
brenna⟨n⟩di [at banna] manni[55] hveriom at⟨gøngo paradisar⟩[56] [57] [58] enn englar[59]
at veria øllom[60] dioflom[61] oc øndom[62] synðogra[63] [manna].[64] [65] Enn þa er viðtoc
52v at nema of[66] for[67] mina[68] þa[69] nam ec staþar oc baþc[70] [til Drottens[71] [52v] oc[72]

syndisc[73] mer þa þar][74] Michael hofuðengill [oc męlti sva viþ mic.[75] Ec emc sendr til þin[76] af Drottni].[77] [78] Ec em[79] til þess[80] setr at sia[81] um[82] hvers mans [hag[83] [84] enn[85] sva[86] er þer at] segia Seth.[87] Eigi[88] þarftu meþ tarom[89] viþsmiors[90] [þess at biþia er] getr[91] i paradis⟨o⟩ til handa føþur þinom þo at[92] [hann] se allsiucr[93] af[94] þvi at viþsmior[95] mun hann[96] ⟨allz⟩ ecki[97] þaþan hava[98] fyrr [enn] liþner verþa[99] heþan[100] VMCCCC[101] ara. Þa[102] mun coma a iarþriki ynnelegr Guþs Sunr[103] sialfr Cristr oc mun þa gøra heila[104] marga siuca menn[105] enn suma reisa af dauþa[106] oc[107] þa mun sialfr[108] Christus[109] verþa scirþr i onne[110] Iordon.[111] Oc þa er hann stigr[112] or vatneno þa[113] mon hann meþ viþsmiorve miscunnar ⟨sinnar⟩[114] smyrva lata[115] þa[116] alla er a hann trua oc man[117] þat miscunnarsmior[118] þeim er endrgetasc[119] af vatne oc Helgom[120] Anda verþa[121] endrgetnaðr[122] [123] at[124] eilifre[125] sælo. Þat mon oc þa verþa at enn astsame[126] Guþs Sonr Iesus Christus mon stiga niþr vilia[127] under iarþrike[128] oc mon hann[129] þa[130] leiþa Adam[131] [føþor][132] þinn[133] i[134] parad⟨is⟩[135] til miscunnar tre⟨s⟩.[136]

1 *post* þa *add.* fyrst *D* **2** *post* er *add.* þeir spurdu *D* **3** *post* Adam *add.* oc mæltu svo *D* **4** fyrstscapaðr] *om. D* **5** *post* varr *add.* sógdu þeir *D* **6** heyrþi] hefr þu heyrt *D* **7** þvisa] því *D* **8** var] være *D* **9** er] sem *D* **10** sa maþr] *om. D* **11** Iohannes] Jon *D post* Jon *add.* seger **12** for] mundi coma *D* **13** at] *om. D* **14** hann] Adam *D* **15** *post* viþ *add.* þetta mál *D* **16** ða] *om. D* **17** *post* at *add.* Seth *D* **18** syni] *om. D* **19** *post* sinom *add.* oc ad hófudfedrunum *D* **20** sunr] son *post* son *add.* minn sagde hann *D* **21** *post* segðu *add.* mier nú oc so *D* **22** patriarchis oc prophetis] hófudfedrunum oc spámónnum *D* **23** þu ⟨heirþir⟩] *om. D* **24** *emendavi* hofuðengils *post* hofuðengil *add.* Drottins *D* **25** er þu ⟨heirþir⟩ Michaele⟨m⟩ hofuðengil] *conieci* que a Michele archangelo audisti *T* **26** segia] sagde *D* **27** at leita oc at qveðia] eptir *D post* eptir *add.* vidsmiórre ad rída á likama minn er eg lá siúkr ok vita *D bis scr.* sá likama minn *D* **28** Varn] Minn *D* **29** þess] oc vita *D* **30** hann] *om. D* **31** myndi vilia] vilde *D* **32** *post* senda *add.* mer *D* **33** þer] mer *D* **34** þar] eg *D* **35** getr af] giæta nád gótu *D* **36** viþsmiorstre] vidsmiórsins *D* **37** *post* miscunnar *add.* til Guds *D* **38** at mætti með ðvi] *om. D* **39** licam minn] *emendavi* lica minum, mig *D* **40** var] lá *D* **41** þa er ec var siúcr at ec] *om. D* **42** of finga] til *D* **43** Þa] Sídan *D post* Sídan *add.* reis upp oc *D* **44** hefir ⟨…⟩ þangat til gengit] geck til *D* **45** er] *om. D* **46** voro] *om. D* **47** þa spurþi hann] *om. D* **48** sva] til *D* **49** qvat] sagde *D* **50** Seth] hann *D* **51** þa] *om. D* **52** of] um *D* **53** *post* siþir *add.* sem ætlad var *D* **54** fyrer] *om. D* **55** at þar var elldr brenna⟨n⟩di at banna manni] *om. D* **56** *ante* paradisar *add.* hlid *D* **57** hveriom at⟨gøngo⟩] inn ad ganga *D* **58** þar var elldr brenna⟨n⟩di at banna manni hveriom at⟨gøngo paradisar⟩] *conieci* posuit ignem ibi qui intercluderet paradisi ingressum *T* **59** englar] vardhald *D* **60** øllom] *om. D* **61** dioflom] Fiandanum *post* Fiandanum *add.* inn ad ganga i hlid paradísar *D* **62** øndom] *om. D* **63** synðogra] syndugum *D* **64** manna] mónnum *D* **65** þar var elldr … / … synðogra manna] cf. Petr. Com. *Hist. schol. Liber Genesis* 3:24 (47/37-39) **66** of] um *D* **67** for] ferdina *D* **68** mina] fyrir mer *D* **69** þa] oc *D* **70** *post* baþc *add.* fyrir mer *D* **71** til Drottens] *post* Drottens *add.* míns *D* **72** oc] *om. D* **73** syndisc] kom á móti *D* **74** þar] *om. D* **75** viþ mic] *om. D* **76** til þin] *incipit B* **77** af Drottni] *om. B* **78** Ec emc sendr til þinn af Drottni] Ec kom ad segia þier *D* **79** em] emc *B* er *D* **80** til þess] *om. D* **81** sia] lita *B ante* sia *add.* til ad *D* **82** um] *om. B post* um *add.* þad at *D* **83** hag] *emendavi lect. dub.* hug **84** hvers mans hag] syndugr eingin fari i paradísu *D* **85** enn] oc *D* **86** sva] þad *D* **87** Seth] *om. B D* **88** *ante* eigi *add.* ad *B D* **89** meþ tarom] *om. B* **90** viþsmiors] *om. D* **91** *ante* getr *add.* er þú um *D* **92** at] *om. D* **93** allsiucr] siukr *B D* **94** af] *om. D* **95** viþsmior] *om. B* þad *D* **96** hann] *om. D* **97** mun hann ⟨allz⟩ ecki] *conieci* nullo modo poteris *T* **98** hava] fara *D post* hava *add.* ne þu *B* **99** verþa] ero *B D post* eru *add.* upp *D* **100** *post* heþan *add.* í fra *B* **101** VMCCCC] VMCXXX *B* VMIII *D* **102** *ante* þa *add.* Enn *D* **103** Sunr] Son *D* **104** gøra heila] gręþa *B* **105** menn] *om. B* **106** dauþa] daudum *D* **107** oc] *om. D* **108** sialfr] *om. D* **109** Christus] Cristr *B D post add.* sá Herra *D* **110** onne] *om. B* vatne *post* vatne *add.* þvi er ⟨…⟩ heiter D **111** Iordon] Iordán *B* Jordan *D* **112** *post* stigr *add.* upp *B* **113** þa *om. D* **114** meþ viþsmiorve miscunnar ⟨sinnar⟩] *conieci* de oleo misericordie sue *T* **115** lata] *om. B* **116** *post* þa *add.* menn *D* **117** *post* man *add.* hann *D* **118** miscunnarsmior] miskunnarvidsmiór *D* **119** endrgetasc] endrberasc *B* endrberast *D* **120** Helgom] *emendavi* Helogom **121** verþa] *emendavi* verþr þa **122** endrgetnaðr] *om. B* **123** af vatne oc Helgom Anda verþa endrgetnaðr] *om. D* **124** at] til *B D* **125** eilifre] *corr.* eileifre **126** astsame] kersti *B* ástsamlegaste *D* **127** vilia] *om. B D* **128** mun hann ecki … / … under iarþrike] cf. *Vita Adae et Evae* (vers. 42) **129** mon hann] *om. D* **130** þa] þadan *D* **131** Adam] *om. D* **132** føþor] feþr *D* **133** *post* þinn *add.* allt *D* **134** i] til *D* **135** parad⟨is⟩] paradisum *B* paradísar *D* **136** tre⟨s⟩] tresisns *D post* tresins *add.* oc vidsmiors tresins *D*

XIX.2

Erende[1] þvisa[2] er[3] þa[4] hafði Seth męlt[5] fognuþo[6] et mesta[7] [8] aller[9] patriarchar.[10]

1 Erende] máli *D ante* máli *add.* Þessu *D* **2** þvisa] þetta *D* **3** *ante* er *add.* enn *D* **4** þa] *om. B* **5** męlt] sagt *D ante* sagt *add.* so *D* **6** fognuþo] urþo ⟨…⟩ allfegnir *D* **7** et mesta] *om. B* **8** et] *emendavi lect. dub.* ætter, exultatione magna *T* **9** aller] *om. D* **10** patriarchar] *om. B* forfeþr *D*

XX.1

Nu[1] þa oc er þeim[2] varþ[3] [4] at[5] þvisa[6] gleþi mikil sem von[7] var at[8] [9] er[10] sact at Satan iotunn[11] helvitis[12] høfðingi er[13] stundom er[14] meþ VII høfðom[15] enn[16] stundom meþ[17] III[18] enn stundom[19] i[20] drekalike þess[21] er[22] omorlegr[23] [er] oc[24] ogorlegr[25] oc illilegr[26] [27] a allar lunder[28] hefir[29] ða[30] þingat[31] viþ iotna[32] oc[33] viþ[34] diofla[35] oc[36] viþ[37] rikistroll[38] ⟨oc⟩ gørvoll þau[39] er[40] i helvite voro[41] [42] oc męlti sva.[43] Verit[44] [nu][45] buner[46] viþ[47] at taca[48] oc[49] gripa Iesum[50] er þvi[51] vændisc[52] at hann se[53] Guþs Sunr [enn hann[54] er] þo maþr oc[55] merki ec[56] at[57] þvi at[58] hann qvidde dauþa.[59] Enn[60] þa⟨t⟩[61] er sa maþr er[62] [mer] hevir mioc[63] a[64] mot[65] gingat[66] [67] oc veret[68] enn grimmaste[69] avallt[70] oc marga[71] menn[72] [er ec] hafða blinda[73] gørva[74] ⟨oc hallta⟩ oc biuga oc[75] licþra[76] oc[77] oþa[78] þa grøddi hann[79] meþ [orþi sino].[80] [81]

1 Nu] Siþan *B* **2** Nu þa oc er þeim] *om. D* **3** *ante* varþ *add.* oc *D* **4** oc er þeim varþ] var þeim *B* **5** at] þat *B* þar *D* **6** þvisa] þesso *B om. D* **7** von] van *B* **8** at] þa *B* **9** sem von var at] *om. D* **10** *ante* er *add.* þad *D* **11** iotunn] *om. B D* **12** helvitis] heims *B* **13** *ante* er *add.* sa *D* **14** *post* er *add.* þar *B* **15** meþ VII høfðom] *om. D* **16** enn] eþa *B* **17** stundom meþ] *om. B* **18** *post* III *add.* hỏfdum *D* **19** enn stundom] *om. B* **20** *post* i *add.* hreþiligo *B* **21** þess] *om. B* **22** er] oc *B* sem *D* **23** omorlegr] oforlegr *D* **24** oc] *om. D* **25** ogorlegr] *om. D* **26** illilegr] *emendavi* illegre, illr *D* **27** er oc ogorlegr oc illilegr] *om. B* **28** Satan iotunn helvitis … / … a allar lunder] cf. Ap. 12:3 **29** *ante* hefir *add.* Hann *D* **30** ða] *om. D* **31** þingat] þing átt *post* átt *add.* bæde *D*

32 viþ iotna] *om. B* **33** oc] *om. B* **34** viþ] *om. D* **35** *post* diofla *add.* helvitis *B* **36** oc] *om. B* **37** viþ] *om. B* **38** rikistroll] *om. B D* **39** gorvoll þau] alla illsku anda *D* **40** er] þá *D* **41** voro] eru *D* **42** oc viþ rikistroll oc gørvoll þau er i helvite voro] *om. B* **43** sva] *om. B* **44** Verit] Vere þer *B D* **45** nu] *om. B D* **46** buner] albúner *D* **47** viþ] *om. D* **48** at taca] *om. B* **49** oc] *om. B* **50** *post* Iesum *add.* þann *D* **51** þvi] *om. B* **52** vændisc] callasc *B* vænist *D* **53** at hann se] *om. B* **54** hann] *om. D* **55** oc] sannlega *D* **56** *post* ec *add.* þad helst *D* **57** at] á *D* **58** at] er *B* **59** *post* dauþa *add.* sínom *D* **60** Enn] Enda *D* **61** þa⟨t⟩] þar *B* **62** *post* er *add.* ávallt *D* **63** mioc] *om. D* **64** a] at *B* i *D* **65** mot] moti *B D* **66** gingat] gingit *B* **67** hefir ⟨…⟩ gingat] stód *D* **68** veret] var *D* **69** *post* grimmaste *add.* viþ mig *D* **70** avallt] *pream. post* sa maþr er *D* **71** marga] mína *D* **72** *post* menn *add.* þa *B D ante* þa *add.* alla *D* **73** blinda] blindad *D* **74** gørva] giórt *D* **75** oc] *om. B D* **76** licþra] *om. B* **77** oc] edr *D* **78** ec hafða blinda gørva ⟨oc hallta⟩ oc biuga oc licþra oc oþa] *conieci* ego cecos claudos curuos leprosos et uexatos feci *T* **79** *post* hann *add.* strax *D* **80** sino] einu *D* **81** marga menn … / … meþ orþi sino] cf. Mt. 10:8 et 11:5

XX.2

Enn þeir[1] ⟨męlto⟩ oc[2] svaraþo[3] honom.[4] Eigi mondom ver vita at[5] sva se[6] sem þu
segir.[7] Enn þat vitom[8] ver[9] oc[10] kunno⟨m⟩ þat[11] sia at engi[12] hevir þu þann[13] til
handa [oss] spanet[14] Drottenn[15] er[16] sva[17] hafi ⟨haft⟩[18] þinn[19] crapt oc[20] rike[21]
niþrbrotet oc lamet[22] avalt [sem] sia[23] er þu segir nu fra þat[24] at eitt øþro[25] orð
hafi[26] męlt.[27] Enda[28] hy[ggiom] ver[29] þat oc leiþom[30] þeim[31] atqveþom[32] fyrer
þer[33] um[34] þar[35] er hann er[36] at hann[37] mon[38] [almattegr vera] i god⟨d⟩omenom[39]
at[40] engi mon mega[41] honom er i he⟨i⟩mi[42] er[43] slicr [sem hann er[44] i] mann-
dominom.[45] Þa[46] męlti[47] hofðinge myrcranna.[48] Hvat[49] ive[50] þer[51] umb[52] oc[53]
[hræþez][54] at[55] gripa þenna mann Iesum er beþi[56] er[57] ⟨ovin⟩ minn[58] oc yðvar.[59]
53r Þar [53r] [er[60] ec freistaða[61] hans[62] oc vacþa ec upp[63] Gyþinga lyð til[64] fiand-
scapar viþ hann oc buet[65] tre til crossfestingar ⟨honom⟩[66] oc] blandet v[insyr]o
til dryckiar[67] spiot hevi ec[68] hvessa latet til[69] [70] at [leggia] a[71] honom oc [nu]
mun[72] all[scamt][73] til unz[74] ⟨at⟩[75] hann mun andasc[76] oc mun ec[77] hann þa[78] [hin-
gat leiþa][79] at hann liggi[80] beþi under[81] yðr[82] oc mer.

1 þeir] dióflar *D* **2** męlto oc] *om. B D* **3** þeir ⟨męlto⟩ oc svaraþo] *conieci* respondens Inferus dixit *T* **4** honom] *om. B post* honom *add.* þegar *D* **5** at] nema *B* **6** se] sen *B* være *D* **7** sem þu segir] *om. B* **8** vitom] *om. B D* **9** vitom ver] *emendavi bis scr.* vitom vitom **10** oc] *om. B D* **11** þat] *om. B* ad *D* **12** engi] aungvann *D* **13** *post* þann *add.* hingad *D* **14** spanet] dreget *B D* **15** Drottenn] *om. B D* **16** er] at *D* **17** *post* sva *add.* opt hafi *D* **18** ⟨haft⟩] *om. B* **19** þinn] þann *D ante* þann *add.* at *D* **20** oc] ad so opt hafe *D* **21** *post* rike *add.* þitt *D* **22** oc lamet] *om. B D* **23** sia] sá *D* **24** þat] *om. B D* **25** øþro] *om. B D* **26** *post* hafi *add.* þess *D* **27** męlt] talad *post* talad *add.* ad menn yrde heilir og þú mátt ecki vidr *D* **28** Enda] *om. B* Oc *D* **29** ver] *om. D* **30** leiþom] hugleidum *D* **31** þeim] *om. D* **32** atqveþom] *om. D* **33** þer] *om. D* **34** um] umb *B om. D* **35** þar] *om. B* þad *D* **36** er hann er] sem mælt er *D* **37** hann] sa *B* **38** mon] mune *D* **39** god⟨d⟩omenom] goddomi *B* **40** at] *ante* at *add.* svo *D* **41** mega] vera *post* vera *add.* vid *D* **42** i he⟨i⟩mi] *om. B D* **43** er] *om. B* oc *D post* oc *add.* engin mun vera *D* **44** sem hann er] *om. B D* **45** manndominom] manndomi *B* **46** þa] *om. B D* **47** męlti] spurþi *B* **48** hofðinge myrcranna] Satan *B D* **49** Hvat] Hvart *B D* **50** ive] ifisc *B* hafi *D* **51** þer] er *B* **52** umb] ad segia *D* **53** oc] *om. D* **54** *post* hræþez *add.* þier þá *D* **55** *ante* at *add.* er *B* **56** beþi] *foramen in cod. B* **57** *post* er *add.* enn meste *D* **58** minn] *foramen in cod. B* **59** þenna mann Iesum er beþi er ⟨ovinn⟩ minn oc yðvar] *conieci* illum Ihesum adversarium meum et tuum *T om. B* **60** Þar er] *om. D* **61** freistaða] hefe freistad *post* freistad *add.* miǫg opt á marga vega oc feck eg alldre fang *D* **62** hans] á honom *D* **63** vacta ec upp] eggiat *B D post* eggiat *add.* eg hefe *D* **64** til] *om. B post* til *add.* samþickis vid mig til *D* **65** buet] er ętlat *B* hefe feingid *D ante* feingid *add.* eg nú *D* **66** til crossfestingar ⟨honom⟩] *conieci* ad crucifigendum eum *T* **67** blandet vinsyro til dryckiar] *om. B D* cf. Mt. 27:34 **68** *post* ec *add.* nú *D* **69** *post* til *add.* ad *D* **70** hevi ec hvessa latet til] *om. B* **71** a] í sídu *D* **72** mun] er *B post* mun *add.* oc *D* **73** allscamt] skamt *D* **74** unz] þess *D post* þess *add.* at *D* **75** ⟨at⟩] *om. B post* at *add.* bidia *D* **76** andasc] deyia *B* **77** *post* ec *add.* nú *D* **78** þa] *om. D* **79** leiþa] spenia *B post* leiþa *add.* til þess *D* **80** liggi] *foramen in cod. B*, *post* liggi *add.* her jafnan *D* **81** *post* under *add.* fótum *D* **82** yðr] yðar *D*

XX.3

Þeir[1] svoroþo.[2] Sagþer eigi þu ðat[3] [umb[4] þenna[5] mann[6] [7] at hann] hefði hotvetna[8] gørt[9] meþ orþe sino[10] oc[11] þat[12] heilt gørt[13] [er þu meitt[14]] hafðir[15] oc
drepit.[16] Enn þat[17] vitom[18] ver at hann hevir[19] menn[20] marga[21] d[auþa[22] af] ðer
teket þa[23] er[24] af[25] oss varo halldner. Eþa[26] hverr[27] var[28] sa[29] enn[30] orðsterci[31] er[32]
Lazarum[33] callaþe[34] heþan enn[35] ver helldom hann[36] her IIII[37] [38] daga aþr i
⟨dauþa⟩[39] bøndom[40] ⟨oc⟩ [var] hann þegar þa[41] kycr[42] a iarþriki[43] allr a[44] brauto[45]
fra oss.[46] Satan hofðinge dauþans[47] [48] svaraþi.[49] Iesus var sa.[50] Enn[51] þeir[52] svoroþo[53] þa sva.[54] Þess sveriom ver fyrer[55] þic[56] oc[57] [crapta þina] oc vara ⟨þar⟩
meþ at þu leiþer[58] hann eigi[59] hingat at[60] þvi at þa er ver heyrþom boþorþ[61] hans
þa varþ oss[62] ollom[63] viþ felmt[64] [65] oc[66] sculfo ða[67] þrelar[68] varer[69] aller[70] oc allar[71] smiþior orar[72] oc for sva fiarri umb[73] at ver męttim[74] Lazaro geta[75] halldet[76]
oc[77] nęsta[78] hvivetna[79] sciotara kastaþe[80] [honom[81] ⟨i[82] iorþ⟩[83] upp[84]] kyco⟨m⟩.[85]
Vissom[86] ⟨ver⟩ þat þa sem[87] nu[88] at inn[89] Almakti[90] Guþ[91] er [i manni] þeim[92]
innan[93] oc[94] mun[95] comenn til þess hingat i heim[96] at[97] [leysa menn af][98] syndom
oc leyþa[99] til lifs guþdoms sins.[100] Þar hverf ec [nu[101] fra] fyrst[102] er[103] þeir[104]
Satan[105] røddoz[106] viþ. Enn[107] ec tec[108] fra þvi at[109] segia [er þa][110] gørþisc enn[111]
fleira til[112] stormerkia.[113] *Þat var mioc i þat [mund døgra er][114] himenenn op-* Ap.
naþisc. Þa[115] com[116] fram fyrst[117] hestr hvitr enn[118] hofðinge[119] sa[120] reiþ hesti 19:11–16
þeim[121] er[122] morgom hlutom[123] er[124] gofgari[125] enn[126] gørvaster[127] aller aþrer.[128]
Augo[129] hans voro[130] se⟨m⟩ elldz[131] logi. Hann hafði[132] [coron]o a høfþi[133] þa
er[134] morg sigrsmerki matte[135] of[136] syna.[137] Hann hafði cleþi[138] þat umb
aunnor[139] [140] uta⟨n⟩ er[141] bloþ[stocet] var. A cleþi[142] hans yfer mioþmenni[143]
voro[144] orþ þessi[145] riten.[146] [Rex regum et Dominus dominantium.[147] Hann var
solo] biartare.[148] Hann leidde[149] eptir ser[150] [151] her[152] [mikinn[153] oc[154] aller
þeir[155] er[156] honom] fylgþo riþo[157] hestom[158] hvitom[159] oc voro[160] aller cleddir[161]
silki[162] [hvito[163] oc voro] lioser mioc.[164] [165] Sa inn ricsti[166] allvaldr [leit þa[167] til[168]
Iorsalaborgar[169] oc męlti.[170] Gilldra] su er at Iorsolom er gørr[171] verþi[172]

Miþ[garþzormi at scaþa].[173] Hann[174] fal þa[175] øngul[176] þann[177] er[178] hurvenn[179]
53v [var[180] agni[181] oc eigi sia m[53v]atte i [ęzl]ino þvi[182] er i gilldrona[183] var lagit oc
sva[184] vaþinn[185] gat[186] hann[187] folget[188] svat[189] eigi[190] of[191] matte[192] sia.[193] Þa[194]
bauþ hann nøcqverom dyrlingom[195] sinom at[196] fara fyrer ser oc gøra vart viþ[197]
como sina[198] til helvitis.

1 *post* Þeir *add.* dióflarner *D* **2** *post* svoroþo *add.* hónum *D* **3** ðat] svo *B D* **4** umb] frá *D* **5** þenna] þessum *D* **6** mann] manne *D* **7** umb þenna mann] *om. B* **8** hotvetna] allt þad *D* **9** hefði ⟨...⟩ gørt] *om. D* **10** meþ orþe sino] *om. D* **11** hotvetna gørt meþ orþe sino oc] *om. B* **12** þat] þa *D* **13** heilt gørt] greddi *B D* **14** meitt] meidder *D* **15** hafðir] *om. B D* **16** drepit] dræper *D* **17** þat] þo *D* **18** vitom] gruno *B* **19** hevir] hafi *B* **20** menn] mann *B om. D* **21** marga] *om. B* **22** dauþa] dauþan *B* **23** þa] þeir *D* **24** er] her *D* **25** af] med *D* **26** Eþa] Edr *D* **27** hverr] hvór *D* **28** var] er *B* **29** *post* sa *add.* yckar *D* **30** enn] er *D* **31** orðsterci] orþrammi *B* sterkare *D post* sterkare *add.* vard *D* **32** er] um *D* **33** *post* Lazarum *add.* oc *D* **34** *post* callaþe *add.* hann *D* **35** enn] er *B om. D* **36** hann] hónom *D* **37** her] *om. B* **38** IIII] VI *D ante* VI *add.* i *D* **39** ⟨dauþa⟩] *om. D* **40** ver helldom hann her IIII daga aþr i ⟨dauþa⟩ bøndom] *conieci* quem ego tenebam mortuum *T* **41** þa *om. D* **42** kycr] kvittr *D post* kvittr *add.* er hann var kominn *D* **43** iarþriki] iorþo *B post* iarþriki *add.* enn þá *D* **44** allr a] oc *B* **45** brauto] braut *B* **46** er Lazarum callaþi ... / ... brauto fra oss cf. Io. 11:38-43 **47** dauþans] dauda *D* **48** hofðinge dauþans] *om. B* **49** svaraþi] sagþi *B D* **50** *post* sa *add.* segir hann *D* **51** Enn] *om. B D* **52** þeir] ohreiner andar *D* **53** svoroþo] męlto *B* **54** þa sva] *om. B D* **55** Þess sveriom ver fyrer] Vier bidium *D* **56** þic] *om. B* **57** oc] *om. B D* **58** leiþer] spenir *B* **59** eigi] *emendavi* engi, egi *B* ecke *D* **60** at] *om. D* **61** boþorþ] *emendavi* boþorþom, call *B* ord *D post* ord *add.* oc kenningar *D* **62** oss] vor lídr *D* **63** ollom] all *D* **64** felmt] *emendavi* flemt **65** viþ felmt] hræddr vid *post* vid *add.* ord edr mál hans *D* **66** *post* oc *add.* þar med *D* **67** ða] þar med *D* **68** þrelar] lęyni *B* **69** varer] *bis scr.* var var *B* **70** allar] aull *B* **71** allar] *om. B* **72** orar] *om. D* **73** umb] vid *D* **74** męttim] *om. D* **75** geta] veita *B* giætum á *D* **76** halldet] a hǫlld *B* **77** oc] þviat *B D* **78** nęsta] *om. B D* **79** hvivetna] hvervetna *D post* hvervetna *add.* upp frá oss heilum *D* **80** kastaþe] hvarf *B* skaut *D* **81** honom] hann *B post* hann *add.* heþan oc gecc B **82** i] oc *D* **83** ⟨i iorþ⟩] *conieci* ipsa terra *T* a iorþo *B* **84** upp] *om. B post* upp *add.* þegar *D* **85** kycom] kvikr *B post* kvikr *add.* scilia *B* **86** Vissom] Þeckiomsc *B* Mæltum *D* **87** þat þa sem] *om. B* **88** nu] *om. B* satt var *D* **89** inn] *om. B* **90** Almakti] *om. B* Máttugare *D* **91** Guþ] Iesus *B* **92** þeim] þessum *D* **93** innan] *om. D* **94** er i manni þeim innan oc] *om. B* **95** mun] man *B post* mun *add.* hann vera bæde Gud oc madr oc *D* **96** heim] heimin *D* **97** comenn til þess hingat i heim at] *om. B* **98** af] frá *B D* **99** leyþa] *emendavi* leisa, perducentur *T* **100** sins] *om. D* **101** fra] *om. B* **102** fyrst] *om. B* þessu mále *D* **103** er] *om. B* **104** þeir] þeira *B* **105** Satan] Andscota *B* **106** røddoz] ręþom *B* **107** Enn] Nu *B* **108** tec] mun *B post* tec *add.* nu *D* **109** fra þvi at] *om. B* **110** þa] *om. D* **111** enn] *om. D* **112** til] fra *B* **113** stormerkia] stormerkiom *B post* stormerkiom *add.* þeim *B post* stormerkia *add.* er vor Herra Jesus Kristr sinde sina dírd etc *D* **114** er] at *B* **115** Þa] Þar *B D* **116** com] rann *B ante* rann *add.* oc *D* **117** fyrst] *om. B D* **118** enn] *om. B* **119** hofðinge] maþr *B post* maþr *add.* higgiligr *B* kongr *D* **120** sa] *om. B post* sa *add.* er *D* **121** hesti þeim] *om. B* **122** er] *om. D* **123** morgom hlutom] *om. B* **124** er] var *B D* **125** gofgari] *foramen in cod. B* vegligri *B* gófuglegre *D* **126** enn] oc *B* **127** gørvaster] tigoligri *B om.* vænne *D* **128** aller aþrer] hveriom *B* allt annad *D* **129** *ante* augo *add.* Enn *D* **130** *post* voro *add.* svo *D* **131** elldz] a ęlldi *B om. D* **132** hafði] bar *B* **133** *post* høfþi *add.* sier þá er ytarleg var á syndom *D* **134** þa er] *om. D* **135** *post* matte *add.* hann *D* **136** of] *om. B D* **137** *post* syna *add.* á sier *D* **138** cleþi] særdann *post* særdann *add.* fót sinn *D* **139** *post* aunnor *add.* føtt *B* **140** þat umb aunnor] *om. D* **141** *ante* er *add.* þad *D* **142** a cleþi] *om. D* **143** mioþmenni] enni ⟨…⟩ midiu *D* **144** voro] var *D* **145** orþ þess] *om. D* **146** riten] ritaþ *D* **147** Rex regum et Dominus dominantium] Kongur konga og Drottin drottna *D* **148** biartare] *foramen in cod. B* **149** leidde] hafde *D* **150** eptir ser] *om. D* **151** Hann leide eptir ser] *om. B* **152** her] einglaher *D* **153** mikinn] ovigr *B* hinn megtugasta *D* **154** oc] *om. D* **155** aller þeir] riddara *B* **156** er] oc *B* **157** riþo] hofþo *B* **158** hestom] hestar *B* **159** hvito] hvita *B* **160** voro] *om. B D* **161** cleddir] *om. B* skríddir *D* **162** silki] sniavi *B* **163** hvito] hvitari *B* **164** mioc] sem sól *D em. secundum Vuglata* angelum stantem in sole Ap. 11:17 **165** oc voro lioser mioc] *om. B* **166** ricsti] riki *B D* **167** þa] *om. B* **168** til] at *B om. D* **169** Iorsalaborgar] Ierusalem *B* **170** mǫlti] *foramen in cod. B post* mǫlti *add.* sva *B* **171** gørr] reist *D* **172** *post* verþi *add.* af *D* **173** scaþa] *corr.* bana *B post* scaþa *add.* giǒr *D* **174** Hann] Oc *B* kongurinn *D ante* kongurinn *add.* Sídann *D* **175** þa] *om. B* þar *D* **176** *post* øngul *add.* sinn *D* **177** þann] sa *B ante* þann *add.* í *D post* þann *add.* er hann atte *D* **178** er] enn *B* **179** hurvenn] hvarsi *B* hvervetna var hvassare *D* **180** var] er leynisc í *B* **181** agni] agino *B* **182** oc eigi sia mate i ęzlino þvi] *om. B* **183** i gilldrona] *corr.* i gilldrono, i gilldro *B* **184** sva] *om. B* **185** var agni oc eigi sia matte i ęzlino þvi er i gilldrona var lagit oc sva vaþinn] *om.* D **186** gat] verþi *B* var *D* **187** gat hann] *om. B* **188** folget] folginn *B post* folget *add.* í med Guds krapte *D* **189** svat] at *D* **190** eigi] einginn *D* **191** of] *om. B D* **192** mate] megi *B* **193** *post* sia *add.* nema kongrinn einn Allsvaldande Gud *D* **194** Þa] Eftir þad *D* **195** dyrlingom] einglum *D* **196** at] *emendavi* oc **197** *post* viþ *add.* þangad *D* **198** sina] hans *D*

XXI.1

Nu scal þar til mals[1] taca er ec[2] hvarf[3] aþr[4] fra at þa[5] er[6] þeir[7] Satan[8] røddoz viþ[9]
at[10] þeir heyra[11] er englar helgir[12] colluþo[13] sva hátt[14] at dynia[15] þotti umb[16] allt
oc mǫlto[17] sva.[18] *Tollite portas principes*[19] *vestras*[20] *et elevamini porte eternales* Ps.
et introibit Rex Glorie.[21] [22] Þa mǫlto[23] helvitis buar[24] viþ[25] Satan. Far a braut nu[26] 24 (23):7
or[27] sætum varom[28]. Ef þu matt[29] þa[30] berstu[31] nu hart[32] viþ[33] Dyrðar
Konong`enn´.[34] Ecki villdom[35] ver viþ hann eiga.[36] Þeir[37] raco[38] þa[39] braut[40]
høfði⟨n⟩gia sinn[41] or helvite.[42] Þa[43] er Satan[44] com ut[45] þa[46] sa hann[47] [48]
engla⟨liþ⟩[49] mikit[50] vera[51] comet[52] til helvitis enn Guþ eigi.[53] ⟨Hann for þa[54]
eigi⟩[55] til fundar viþ ða[56] oc[57] [58] sneide[59] hann þar[60] hia.[61] Þa[62] bra[63] hann[64] ser[65]
i drecalike oc gørdiz þa[66] sva mikill at hann þottesc[67] liggia mundo[68] umb[69]
heimenn allan utan.[70] [71] Hann[72] sa þau[73] tiþende[74] ⟨er[75] gørdoz⟩ at Iorsolom at
Iesus Christus[76] var þa[77] i andlati[78] oc[79] for[80] ⟨hann⟩[81] þangat[82] þegar[83] oc[84] ætlaþi[85] at[86] slita[87] ondina þegar[88] fra honom.[89] Enn[90] er hann com þar[91] oc[92] [93]
hugþez[94] [95] gløpa[96] mundo[97] hann[98] oc hafa[99] meþ ser[100] þa beit[101] øngullinn[102]
goddomens[103] hann[104] enn[105] crossmarkit fell a hann ovann oc varþ hann[106] þa[107]
sva veiddr se⟨m⟩ fiscr a øngle eþa mus under treketti[108] [109] eþa sem[110] melracki
i gilldro[111] [112] eptir þvi sem fyrer var spat.[113] Þa[114] for til[115] Dominus Noster[116] oc
batt hann[117] enn[118] qvade[119] til[120] engla[121] sina[122] at varþveita hann.[123] Enn[124] nu
tek[125] ec[126] þar[127] til mals[128] at[129] segia[130] þat[131] hvat[132] þeir hava[133] til tekit[134] [135]
i[136] helvite[137] siþan er Satan for ut.[138] Rikesdioflar[139] i helvite[140] mǫlto viþ

⟨smiþio⟩kappa[141] [142] sina. Teket er[143] greyper[144] oc[145] byrgget[146] nu[147] hliþen[148] ꝍll[149] oc føret[150] fyrer[151] iarngrinðr[152] oc[153] iarnbranda[154] oc verezc[155] hart[156] [157] oc standit[158] viþ vel[159] at er[160] verþet[161] eigi upptekner[162] eþa þat[163] verþi af yðr tekit[164] er er[165] hafet a halldet[166] her til.[167] [168]

1 mals] *om. B* **2** ec] ver *B* **3** hvarf] hvurfom *B* **4** aþr] aþan *B D* **5** þa] þar *D* **6** at þa er] *om. B* **7** þeir] þeira *B* **8** Satan] Sathans *B* **9** røddoz viþ] viþręþo *B* **10** at] þá *D* **11** heyra] heyrdo *B* **12** helgir] Guþs *D* **13** *post* colluþo *add.* miög *D* **14** hátt] *om. B* **15** dynia] scialfa *B D post* dynia *add.* oc skiálfa *D* **16** umb] *om. B* undir *D* **17** *post* męlto *add.* Guds einglar *D* **18** sva] *om. B* **19** principes] *incipit C* princeps *D* **20** vestras] venit *post* venit *add.* þad þíder so take þeir upp hlidin hófdinginn kemr oc þar mun inn ganga Kóngr Dírdarinar *D* **21** *post* glorie *add.* Þetta vers þydiz sva ꝍ vara tungu. Takit þier hlid hofdíngiar ydrir ok hefit upp hlid eirlig ok man inn ganga Konungr Dyrdar *C* **22** et elevamini porte eternales et introibit Rex Glorie] *om. D* **23** męlto] mælte *D* **24** buar] bórn *D* **25** viþ] oc *D* **26** nu] þu *B C* **27** far a braut nu or] fórum nú í burtu af *D* **28** varom] *iter. sup. l.* \`or´, *post* varom *add.* fyrst oc sógdu vid Satan *D* **29** ef þu matt] *om. C* **30** þa] oc *B C om. D* **31** berstu] berst *C* **32** hart] *om. D* **33** viþ] a mot *B* **34** Dyrðar Konong \`enn´] Konong Dyrðarinnar *C post* Dyrðarinnar *add.* ok *C* Kóngr Dírdarinnar *D* **35** villdom] villdi *B* vilium *D* **36** *post* eiga *add.* sódgu þeir. Hann svarar aungvu. Þá flicktust þeir ad hónum *D* **37** Þeir] *om. B* oc *D* **38** raco] rezk *B* **39** þa] *om. D* **40** braut] *om. B C* burt *D* **41** høfði⟨n⟩gia sinn] Sathan *B* hann *D post* hann *add.* edr dróu í *D* **42** or helvite] *om. B* **43** Þa] Enn *C* Oc *D* **44** Satan] hann *D* **45** *post* ut *add.* úr Helvíti *D* **46** þa] oc *B* **47** hann] *om. B* **48** Þa er Satan com ut þa sa hann] *om. B* **49** engla⟨liþ⟩] cum angelis suis *T* engligaflocka *B* englaflocka *D ante* engliga *add.* mot sa *B post* engla⟨liþ⟩ *add.* hit mesta *C* **50** mikit] hit mesta *C* mikin *D* **51** vera] *om. B D* **52** comet] coma *B D* **53** *post* eigi *add.* sialfan *D* **54** ⟨þa⟩] *om. D* **55** ⟨eigi⟩] ecke *D* **56** *post* ða *add.* einglana *D* **57** ⟨Hann for þa eigi⟩ til fundar viþ ða oc] *om. B* **58** oc] helldr *C D* **59** sneide] snere *D* **60** þar] þeim *B* þvert *D* **61** hia] í burt *D post* í burt *add.* frá þeim oc kallade hátt *D* **62** þa] oc *B D* **63** bra] brást *D* **64** hann] *om. B D* **65** ser] *om. D* **66** gørdiz þa] hugdiz at vera *C* giördist hann *D* **67** þottesc] hugþisc *B om. C* **68** mundo] megia *D* **69** umb] um *D* **70** umb heimen allan utan] i hring um all helviti *C* **71** Þa bra hann ser … / … heimen allan utan cf. Ap. 12:9 **72** *ante* hann *add.* Þá *D* **73** þau] þa *D* **74** tiþende] atburde *D* **75** *post* er *add.* þa *B* **76** Christus] *om. D* **77** þa] *om. C* **78** andlati] liflati *C post* andlati *add.* sinu a krossenum helga *D* **79** oc] þa *D* **80** for] flo *B* **81** ⟨hann⟩] *post* hann *add.* matti *C* Satan *D* **82** *post* þangat *add.* til *B* **83** þegar] *om. D* **84** *post* oc *add.* þótte hónum nu allt vel á horfast *D* **85** ætlaþi] villdi *B* hugdiz *C* **86** at] *om. B C* **87** slita] slęgia *B post* slita *add.* mundu *C* **88** þegar] *om. B C D* **89** honom] Iesu *C* **90** *post* enn *add.* þa *B C* **91** þar] *om. C* **92** com þar oc] *om. B* **93** Enn er hann com þar oc] Þá kom svo fyrer hónum ad hann *D* **94** hugþez] villdi *B* þóttist *D* **95** er hann com þar oc hugþez] *om.* B **96** gløpa] *foramen in cod. B* gleipt *D* **97** mundo] *om. B D* **98** hann] *foramen in cod. B* Iesum *C* hana *post* hana *add.* i kvid illsku sinnar *D* **99** *post* hafa *add. C* **100** ser] *om. B post* ser *add.* enn *D* **101** *post* beit *add.* hann *B* **102** øngullinn] aungul *B* **103** goddomens] guddómsins *D* **104** hann] hans *B* Satan *D* **105** enn] oc *D* **106** hann] Satan *D* **107** þa] *om. C* **108** eþa mus under treketti] *om. B* **109** treketti] fellu *post* fellu *add.* enn þad vard *D* **110** sem] *om. B C* **111** eþa sem melrakki i gilldro] *om. D* **112** Hann sa þau tiþende … / … melrakki i gilldro cf. Aug. *Sermo 265D* (*MiAg*, 662/8-19). **113** spat] sagt *D* **114** þa] ad þessu næst *D* **115** til] *om. B D* **116** Dominus Noster] Drottin *B post* Drottin *add.* til helvítis *D* Var Drottin *C* **117** hann] þar *post* þar *add.* óvin alls mannkyns fiandan *D* **118** enn] oc *D* **119** qvade] bauþ *B* **120** til] *om. D* **121** engla] englom *B* **122** sina] *om. B* **123** *post* hann *add. rubricam* Her seghir hvern vidbunat dioflarnir hofdu *C*

124 Enn] *om. C D* **125** tek] skal *B om. D* **126** ec] er *D* **127** tek ec þar] er fra þvi *C* **128** til mals] *om. C* **129** ec þar til mals at] *om. B* **130** segia] taka *D* **131** þat] *om. C D* **132** þat hvat] *foramen in cod. B* fra atburþom *B* **133** hava] hofduz *C* **134** til tekit] *om. C* **135** þeir hava til tekit] þeim er nęstir voro *B* **136** i] at *C* **137** þeir hava til tekit i helvite] ad helvitís búar tóku til i helvíte ad *D* **138** siþan er Satan for ut] *om. B post* ut *add.* úr helvíte sem fyrre sagde þa er einglarner komu þar ad *D* **139** rikedioflar] rikisþursar *B* **140** i helvite] *om. B* **141** kappa] *foramen in cod. B* **142** ⟨smiþio⟩kappa] smidiur oc kappa *D* **143** Teket er] *foramen in cod. B* Taki þer *B C* **144** greyper] grimir *B om. C* **145** Teket er greyper oc] Hina greipusti *D* **146** brygget] *foramen in cod. B* **147** nu] *om. D* **148** hliþen] hliþ *B* **149** *post* æll *add.* ramliga *B* **150** føret] setit *C D* **151** oc føret fyrer] meþ *B* **152** iarngrinðr] iarnhurþom *B* **153** *post* oc *add.* latiþ *B* **154** iarnbranda] *foramen in cod. B* slagbranda *B post* slagbranda *add.* viþ *om. D* **155** veresc] veret *C* **156** hart] *foramen in cod. B* **157** oc verezc hart] *om. D* **158** standit] stande þier *D* **159** *post* vel *add.* oc fast *D* **160** er] þer *C* þeir *D* **161** er verþet] þær sieu *D* **162** upptekner] uppgorvir *B* uppnæmar *D* **163** þat] liþ *B* **164** eþa þat verþi af yðr tekit] *om. D* **165** er] þer *C* **166** halldet] athallda *C* **167** er er hafet a haldet] *om. B D* **168** her til] *om. B C D*

XXI.2

Guþs helgir[1] er þeir[2] heyrþo[3] þetta[4] þa[5] męlto[6] þeir sva[7] viþ[8] [9] ðær illar vættir.[10] Ps.
[11] *Tollite portas*[12] *at*[13] *Dyrþar Konongr`enn´ megi*[14] *her*[15] *inn ganga.*[16] Þa toc 24(23):7
David konongr oc spamaþr[17] [18] viþ Guþs menn hatt[19] at męla. Þat var[20] þa[21] er
ec lifða[22] oc ⟨vasc⟩[23] callaþr konongr i Austrvexrike[24] at ec spaða[25] yðr[26] þetta.[27]
Confitemini[28] *Domino*[29] *⟨misericordie eius⟩*[30] *et inuocate nomen*[31] *eius et*[32] *mi-* Ps.
rabilia[33] *eius*[34] *⟨filiis hominum⟩*[35] *que fecit*[36] *quia contriuit portas ereas*[37] *et* 107(106):
uectes ferreos confregit.[38] *Suscepit eos de via iniquitatis eorum.*[39] Þa męlti 15–17
Ysaias spamaþr.[40] Veiztu at[41] ec spa⟨ða⟩[42] sva[43] fyrer.[44] Þa er ec vasc[45] a iorþo[46]
54r [47] at *dauþir*[48] [54r] *mundo upprisa. Enn*[49] *fagna þeir*[50] *er*[51] *i grofom væri.*[52] Is. 26:19
Dauþi[53] [oc helviti] myndi sigre tyna.[54]

1 *post* helgir *add.* menn *C add.* einglar *D* **2** er þeir] *om. B* **3** *post* heyrþo *add.* hial *B* **4** þetta] þeira *B post* þetta *add.* mælt *D* **5** þa] oc *B* **6** męlto] kóll⟨udu⟩ *D* **7** sva] *om. D* **8** viþ] *om.* C á *D* **9** þeir sva viþ] *om. B* **10** ðær illar vættir] fiandr *B* dióflana *D post* dióflana *add.* oc sógdu *D* **11** viþ ðær illar vættir] *om. C* **12** Tollite portas] Lucit upp hliþom *B* Latit upp hlidin *C D* **13** *ante* at *add.* þvi *D* **14** megi] mun *D* **15** her] *om. C D* **16** *post* ganga *add.* um þau *D* **17** spamaþr] spamenn *D* **18** oc spamaþr] *om. B* **19** viþ Guþs menn hatt] *om. D* **20** þat var] *om. C D* **21** *post* þa *add.* sagdi hann *C* **22** er ec lifða] er ec var lifs *C* **23** ⟨vasc⟩] varc *B* var *C D* **24** Austrvexrike] *corr.* Austrkexrike, Skede *D post* Skede *add.* so *D* **25** spaða] sagda *C* **26** yðr] *om.* C **27** yðr þetta] oc mælte *D* **28** Confitemini] Confiteantur *B* Játe þier *D* **29** Domino] Drottinn *D* **30** ⟨misericordie eius⟩] *conieci* misericordie eius *T* miscunnar *D* **31** et inuocate nomen] *om. B C D* **32** eius et] *om. D* **33** mirabilia] undarlega hlute *D* **34** eius] *om. D* **35** ⟨filiis hominum⟩] *conieci* filiis hominum *T* vid sonu mannanna *D* **36** que fecit] *om. B C* hann giórer *D* **37** quia contriuit portas ereas] þviad hann braut hlid sterkleg *D* **38** et uectes ferreos confregit] *om. B* oc lamde lok⟨u⟩r járnlegar *D* **39** Suscepit eos de via iniquitatis eorum *post* eorum *add.* Þersi vers þydaz sva a vára tungu. Iati þer Drottni ok miskunn hans þviat hann gerdi dasamliga luti sonum manna þviat hann ⟨braut hlid⟩ eirlig ok lamdi lokur iarnligar *C* hann tók af gnótt illsku þeirra *D* **40** spamaþr] propheta *B* spámann *D* **41** at] hvad *D* **42** spa⟨ða⟩] sagþa *B C D* **43** sva] *om. D* **44** fyrer] *om. C D* **45** vasc] var *C D* **46** *post* iorþo *add.* fyrre *D* **47** vasc a iorþo] lifþda *B* **48** *post* dauþir *add.* menn *D* **49** Enn] Oc *C* **50** þeir] þeim *C* **51** er] sem *C* **52** væri] lęgi *B C D* **53** *ante* dauþi *add.* Enn *D* **54** Dauþi oc helviti myndi sigre tyna] cf. 1 Cor. 15:55

XXI.3

Guþs helgir[1] er þeir heyrþo orþ ⟨þetta⟩[2] Y[saias[3] spamanz][4] cølluþo[5] acafliga[6] a
helviti⟨s⟩ folk.[7] Latet[8] er[9] upp nu[10] [hliþen][11] enn[12] ella[13] verþi[14] þer[15] ofrike
borner.[16] Þa hafa[17] þeir i annat sinn[18] heyrþa[19] rødd[20] sva[21] micla[22] at scialfa[23]
þotte helvite[24] allt.[25] *Tollite portas principes*[26] *vestras.*[27] Hofuðdioflar[28] er[29] Ps. 24
þeir[30] heyrþo tysvar[31] utan[32] callað[33] at upp scyldi luca[34] ⟨hliþen⟩[35] þa[36] brugþoz[37] (23):7
þeir[38] viþ ocunner[39] oc svoroþo.[40] *Quis est iste Rex Glorie*[41] *Dominus fortis et* Ps. 24
potens Dominus potens in prelio.[42] [43] Þa[44] męlti[45] David.[46] Ec kenni orþ þau[47] er (23):8
þar ero[48] męlt[49] af þvi at[50] ec spaða þetta[51] af[52] Helgom Anda.[53] Nu[54] mun[55] ec[56] Ps. 24
segia[57] yþr[58] [59] *Dominus*[60] *fortis*[61] *et*[62] *potens*[63] *Dominus*[64] *potens*[65] [66] *in prelio.*[67] (23):8–1
Ipse est[68] *Rex Glorie*[69] *quia*[70] *prospexit*[71] *de excelso*[72] *sancto suo*[73] *Dominus*[74] *de* Ps. 102
celo[75] *in terram*[76] *aspexit ut audiret gemitus compeditorum ut solueret filios* (101):21
interemptorum. Lioter oc saurger[77] latet[78] upp hliþen[79] at Rex Glorie[80] of[81]
comesc[82] hingat.[83]

1 Guþs helgir] Heilager einglar Guds *D* **2** þetta] þessi *B D* **3** Ysaias] *om. B* Esaiæ *D* **4** spamanz] *om. B C add.* þa *D* **5** *post* cølluþo *add.* þeir þess *D* **6** acafliga] ákaflegar *D* **7** folk] bua *B* **8** Latet] Lukiþ *B C* **9** er] *om. B C D* **10** nu] *om. B C D* **11** hliþen] hurþom *B* **12** enn] *om. B C D* **13** ella] ellegar *D* **14** verþi] munoþ *B D* **15** þer] er *B* **16** borner] þola *B* kenna *D* **17** hafa] *om. C* **18** hafa þeir i annat sinn] *om. D* **19** heyrþa] heyrt *B* heyrdu *C D post* heyrdu *add.* helvítis búarner *D* **20** rødd] call *B* **21** sva] *om. D* **22** micla] ogorligt *B post* micla *add.* oc so hvella *D* **23** scialfa] lypta *B* **24** helvite] helvitis *B om. D* **25** allt] *om. B post* allt *add.* er svo sagde *D* **26** principes] princeps *D* **27** vestras] *om. B* venit *D post* venit *add.* Nú þá *D* **28** hofuðdioflar] hofþíngiar helvitis *B C* stórdiǫflar *D* **29** er] *om. B* **30** þeir] *om. B D* **31** tysvar] *om. D* **32** utan] *om. B C D* **33** callað] kvatt *C* **34** at upp scyldi luca ⟨hliþen⟩] *om. B D* **35** ⟨hliþen⟩] *conieci* portas *T* **36** þa] oc *B om. D* **37** brugþoz] biuggust *D* **38** þeir] *om. B* **39** ocunner] ócunnom *B* i virkinu *D* **40** svoroþo] spurþo *B C* mæltu *D* **41** Quis est iste Rex Glorie] Hverr er sia Konongr Dyrþar *B D post* Glorie *add.* Hverr er þersi Koungr Dyrdar. Þa svaradu englarnar *C* **42** Dominus fortis et potens Dominus potens in prelio] *om. B D* **43** *post* prelio *add.* Þersi ord þydaz sva. Drottinn styrkr ok mattugur Drottinn mattugur i orostu *C* **44** Þa] *om. B* **45** męlti] svarade *D* **46** *post* David *add.* konungr *C D* **47** þau] þesse *D* **48** ero] voru *C D* **49** męlt] *foramen in cod. B* **50** af þvi at] oc þvi *D* **51** ec spaða þetta] *om. B D* **52** af] *om. D* **53** Helgom Anda] *om. D* **54** Nu] *om. D* **55** mun] man *C* **56** ec] *corr.* oc Drottinn *C* **57** segia] kynna *B* sigra *C* **58** yþr] *foramen in cod. B om. D* **59** oc segia yþr] *om. C* **60** Dominus] Drottinn *C D post* Drottinn *add.* er *D* **61** fortis] styrkr *C D* **62** et] oc *C* **63** potens] mattugr *C D* **64** Dominus] oc *C* **65** potens] auflugr *C* **66** Dominus potens] *om. D* **67** in prelio] i orostu *C D* **68** Ipse est] *om. B* Hann er *C* **69** Rex Glorie] *om. B D* Konungr Dyrdar *C* **70** quia] þat *C* **71** prospexit] hann leit *C* **72** de excelso] af hæd *C* **73** sancto suo] sini heilagri *C* **74** Dominus] *om. C* **75** de celo] af himni *C* **76** in terram] in terras *B* a iordina *C desinit C* **77** saurger] greypir *B* **78** latet] lykit *B* **79** hliþen] durom *B* **80** Rex Glorie] Konongr Dyrþar *B C* **81** of] *om. B* **82** comesc] gangi *B* **83** Ut audiret gemitus compeditorum ut solveret filios interemptorum. Lioter oc saurger latet upp hliþen at Rex Glorie of comesc hingat] *om. D*

XXII.1

Þa [1] er[2] David hafði[3] þetta[4] mȩlt[5] þa com Konongr Dyrþar[6] at[7] helvitis virki.[8] Hann[9] braut þegar[10] borg[11] helvitis oc gørþi[12] a hliþ miket. Hann hevir vitraz[13] i manz[14] asiono meþ liose miclo[15] svat[16] myrcr helvites[17] hafa þa horfit.[18] Hverr[19] goðr[20] maþr hevir[21] þa[22] losnat[23] [24] or þvi[25] bandi[26] sem bundinn var.[27] Sva micell[28] craptr[29] oc gnýr[30] hevir at gørzc[31] viþ þat er sva sciot[32] reð[33] ⟨hann⟩[34] um[35] brotet[36] helvites[37] [38] at dioflar[39] aller[40] toco at falma[41] oc at scialva.[42] Oc þa þegar brat eptir[43] er þeir sa Christum[44] þar ganganda[45] Guð þeira[46] þa[47] hafa þeir til kagat[48] þangat[49] aller[50] oc mȩlto þetta.[51] Yfer hevir þu nu oss stigit allhart hevir þu nu til raþit[52] oc[53] til sótt at hneyckia[54] oss.[55] [56] Se þar[57] undr ⟨oc⟩[58] endime.[59] ⟨Hann⟩ syndisc lagr oc litell[60] oc i þrels like[61] veginn[62] a crossi[63] oc niþrgravinn.[64] Enn[65] nu er⟨t⟩ þu[66] her comenn[67] leysir bundna oc[68] leysir hotvetna. Slict ett sama allar[69] helvites[70] fylor[71] toco sva umb at mȩla.[72] [73] Hvaþan er⟨t⟩ þu Ihesus[74] maþr[75] sva styrcr[76] oc sva[77] rikr maþr[78] oc sva[79] lióss[80] oc sva synðalauss. Sa heimr iarþlegr[81] er under oss hevir lengi[82] veret scattgilldr.[83] Hevir[84] oss slican dauþascatt fyrr alldrege[85] goldet. Ofraþarmaþr[86] er sia er sva hugfullr er at[87] fer[88] iver qvalar varar at hann[89] hrøþisc[90] eigi oc[91] gripr[92] menn[93] or bondom.[94] [95] Muna[96] þat nu at sa[97] Iesus[98] mune[99] her nu[100] vera[101] comenn er Satan hofðingi varr qvaz einn myndo raþa ⟨øllom⟩ heime[102] [103] eftir hans[104] dauþan.[105]

1 Þa] *foramen in cod. B* Enn *D* **2** er] *foramen in cod. B* **3** hafði] lauk *B* **4** þetta] sino *B* **5** mȩlt] mali *B* **6** Dyrþar] Dírdarinnar *D* **7** at] *foramen in cod. B* **8** virki] byrgi *B* dyrum *D* **9** hann] oc *B D* **10** þegar] *om. B* **11** borg] byrge *D* **12** borg helvitis oc gørþi] *om. B* **13** hevir vitraz] syndisc *B* vitradist *D* **14** i manz] viþ *D* **15** miclo] *foramen in cod. B* **16** *post* svat *add.* óll *D* **17** myrcr helvites] *foramen in cod. B* hvergi scugga *B* **18** hafa þa horfit] bar á *B* hórfu *post* hórfu *add.* Svo ad *D* **19** Hverr] Enn *B* **20** goðr] Guds *D* **21** hevir] *foramen in cod. B* **22** þa] *om. B* **23** losnat] leystr *B* **24** hevir þa losnat] losnade *D* **25** þvi] *om. B D* **26** bandi] baundom *B D* **27** sem bundinn var] *om. B D* **28** *post* micell *add.* Guds *D* **29** craptr] otti *B* **30** oc gnýr] *om. D* **31** hevir at gørzc] varþ fiandom *B* giórdist *D* **32** sva sciot] á ȩno auga *B* **33** reð] bragþi *B* **34** ⟨hann⟩] Drottinn Iesus *B* **35** um] *om. B* **36** brotet] braut *B* **37** helvites] helvíti *B ante* helvíti *add.* i allt *B* **38** viþ þat er sva sciot reð ⟨hann⟩ um brotet helvites] *om. D* **39** dioflar] þeir *B* **40** aller] *om. B D* **41** toco at falma] falmoþo *post* falmoþo *add.* af hrezlo *B* fólnudu *D* **42** at scialva] scutosc hingat oc þingat *post* þingat *add.* undan geislom hans *B* oc skulfu *D* **43** oc þa þegar brat eptir] *om. B D* **44** Christum] Jesum *D* **45** ganganda] *emendavi* gangandan **46** ganganda Guð þeira] *om. B* inn ganga í búdernar *D* **47** þa] oc *B* **48** hafa þeir til kagat] caugoþo *B post* caugoþo *add.* oframliga *B* kólludu þeir aller *D* **49** þangat] til hans *B* **50** aller] *om. B* **51** þetta] *om. B D* **52** til raþit] *om. B* **53** oc] *om. B* **54** hneykkia] scȩlfa *B* **55** *post* oss *add.* blauþir ero ver nu viþ ornir oc scemþar fullir *B* **56** Yfer hevir þu nu oss stigit allhart hevir þu nu til raþit oc til sótt at hneyckia oss] Almáttugur ertu yfer oss oc enn mæltu þeir *D* **57** þar] þier *D* **58** ⟨oc⟩] *om. D* **59** endime] þetta *D* **60** oc litell] *om. D* **61** like] ásiano *B* **62** veginn] festr *B* **63** *post* crossi *add.* sem þiofar *B* **64** niþrgravinn] i jórþ grafinn *D* **65** Nu] *om. B* **66** þu] hann *D post* hann *add.* svo *D* **67** *post* comenn *add.* heill oc lifandi oc rikr sem Guþ *B add.* ad hann *D* **68** leysir bundna oc] *om. D* **69** allar] allt *B* **70** helvites] fianda *B* **71** fylor] lið *B* **72** toco sva umb at męla] spurþi *B* **73** Slict ett sama allar helvites fylor toco sva umb at męla] *om. D* **74** þu Ihesus] *om. D* **75** *ante* maþr *add.* þesse *D* **76** sva styrcr] oflogr *B* **77** sva] *om. B* **78** sva] *om. B* **79** sva] *om. B* **80** oc sva rikr maþr oc sva lióss] *om. D* **81** *ante* iarþlegr *add.* sem *D* **82** lengi] *om. D* **83** scattgilldr] *om. D* **84** *ante* hefir *add.* Oc *D* **85** fyrr alldrege] *om. D* **86** maþr] þrekmaþr *B* **87** sva hugfullr er at] *om. B* **88** fer] stigr *B* **89** hann] *om. B* **90** hrøþisc] ottasc *B* **91** oc] at *B* **92** gripr] hialpa *B* **93** menn] monnom *B* **94** or bondom] *om. B* **95** Ofraþar maþr er sia … / … or bondom] *om. D* **96** Muna] Mun eigi *D* **97** sa] *om. D* **98** Iesus] *foramen in cod. B post* Iesus *add.* af Nazareth *D* **99** mune] sie *D* **100** nu] *om. B D* **101** vera] *om. B D* **102** heime] *om. D* **103** ⟨øllom⟩ heime] *conieci* totius mundi *T* **104** hans] *emendavi* hann **105** dauþan] dauþa *D*

XXII.2

54v [54v] [Þa] toc Dominus[1] Rex Glorie[2] at troþa niþr[3] hofðingi⟨a⟩[4] dauþans[5] [6] oc[7] batt hann [meþ[8] elldligom] bondom ⟨crapta[9] sinna⟩[10] [11]. Enn hann heimte[12] Adam[13] til sinnar birte.

1 Dominus] Drottinn *B post* Drottinn *add.* til *D* **2** Rex Glorie] Iesus Christus *B om. D* **3** *post* niþr *add.* enn *B* **4** *post* hofþ⟨i⟩ngia *add.* myrkra *B* **5** dauþans] dauþanom *B* **6** hofþ⟨i⟩ngia dauþans] Dióflana *D* **7** oc] *om. B* enn *post* enn *add.* hann greip til hins gamla Diófuls oc *D* **8** meþ] *om. D* **9** ⟨crapta⟩] veldins *D* **10** ⟨sinna⟩] sins *D post* sins *add.* so hann komst aldre þadan meir *D* **11** ⟨crapta sinna⟩] *conieci* sua potentia *T* **12** heimte] leiddi *B* dró *D* **13** Adam] *foramen in cod. B*

XXIII.1

Þa [toco] helvites buar ⟨at męla⟩[1] [2] viþ høfðingia[3] sinn[4] meþ ⟨a⟩socun micille[5] [6] oc avitoþo[7] hann.[8] Heyrþo qvaþo þeir glaz oddvite[9] oc[10] dauþa[11] ioforr[12] þrihofða⟨þ⟩r Bee⟨l⟩zebub[13] hlegenn af englom.[14] Til hvers var þer at heita oss friþendom viþ[15] hingatspaning[16] hans.[17] Allovisliga[18] hevir þer[19] umb raþiz[20]. Þat[21] ma nu of sia[22] at[23] Christus[24] fer her[25] nu[26] oc[27] rekr[28] a braut[29] meþ liose guþdoms[30] sins dauþa myrcr[31] oc braut[32] byrgi[33] var[34] øll[35] oc[36] leiþer[37] hann[38] hertecna heþan[39] oc[40] [41] þa marga[42] er vaner varo[43] at stynia[44] sarliga[45] under varom[46] pislom[47] oc[48] førisc nu sva[49] hotvetna or at[50] [51] nu[52] muna mannkyn[53] hans[54] coma siþan. Nu[55] cø⟨m⟩r[56] þat viþ[57] at þeir[58] dramba[59] viþ[60] oss er[61] alldregi matto[62] glaþer verða[63] oc taca oss[64] ogn[65] at[66] bioþa.[67] Heyrþo Satan ioførr helvitis[68] oc[69] allz illz[70] hvi[71] varþ ðer þat[72] fyrer nu[73] [74] at spenia hann[75] [76] ⟨hingat⟩[77] [78] at[79] nu er þess[80] at[81] van[82] at her verþet[83] gratr ne[84] stynr[85] i dauni[85] siþan[87] þeim enom micla[88] er þu atter ⟨i⟩ saure oc i fylo[89] oc gleþi[90] allri þeiri[91] er þu[92] hafðir her fingit[93] fyrer afbrigþartreet[94] hevir[95] þu[96] gørsamliga tynt fyrer crosstre oc mun øll gleþi[97] þin[98] fyrerfaraz[99] er þu villder[100] sialfan[101] Dyrþar Konong eggia[102] lata at mote þer.[103] [104] Of[105] grunnuþect[106] er þin[107] orþet.[108] Hafa[109] raþit a þann er sva var syndalauss oc spanet hann hingat enn nu[110] scyll-der[111] þu lata her nøþegr laust allt þat er þu vill eigi.[112] [113]

1 ⟨at mę̨la⟩] *om. B* **2** Þa toco ⟨...⟩ ⟨at mę̨la⟩] *conieci* Tunc suscipiens ⟨...⟩ dixit *T* **3** *post* høfðingia *add.* myrkra *B* **4** sinn] *emendavi* sinom *om. B* sinn *D* **5** micille] *om. D* **6** meþ ⟨a⟩socun micille] *conieci* cum nimia increpatione *T* **7** avitoþo] ascellingom *B* ávitun *D* **8** hann] *om. B D* **9** glaz oddvite] *om. D* **10** oc] *om. B D* **11** dauþa] dauþans *D* **12** ioforr] scilfingr *B* vesalingr *D* **13** Bee⟨l⟩zebub] *om. D* **14** hlegenn af englom] *post* englom *add.* oc hrøptr af monnom *B* oc dáradr af einglum *D* **15** viþ] oc *D* **16** hingatspaning] híngadkomu *D* **17** hans] Cristz *B* Guds sonar *D* **18** Allovisliga] Allvesallega *D* **19** þer] þu *D post* þu *add.* nu *D* **20** raþiz] rádid *D* **21** þat] her *B D ante* her *add.* þvíad *D* **22** ma nu of sia] *om. D* **23** at] *om. D* **24** Christus] Jesus *D* **25** her] yfir *B* post yfir *add.* fylgsni *B* **26** nu] *om. D* **27** nu oc] *om. B* **28** rekr] tekr *D* **29** a braut] ór *B* i burtu *post* burtu *add.* hedan *D* **30** guþdoms] crapz *B* **31** dauþa myrcr] *om. B D* **32** braut] hefir lamit *B* **33** byrgi] dyflizor *B* **34** var] *emendavi lect. dub.* varar **35** øll] *emendavi lect. dub.* allar *om. B* **36** oc] *om. B* **37** *post* leiþer *add.* ut bunna enn leysir *B* **38** hann] *om. B* **39** heþan] *om. B* **40** oc] *om. B* **41** oc braut byrgi var øll oc leiþer hann hertecna heþan oc] *om. D* **42** marga] *om. B* **43** vaner varo] *om. B* **44** at stynia] þoldo *B* **45** sarliga] sarar *B* **46** under varom] *om. B* **47** pislom] pislir *B* **48** oc] *om. B* **49** nu sva] *om. B* **50** at] stað *B* **51** er vaner varo at stynia sarliga under varom pilsom oc førisc nu sva hotvetna or at] er stódu under vorum bardaga sárlega haldner *D* **52** nu] oc *D* **53** mankyn] friþir menn *B* mankynid *D* **54** hans] her *B D ante* her *add.* eigi *D* **55** Nu] *om. D* **56** *post* cø⟨m⟩r *add.* oc *B D* **57** viþ] framm *D* **58** þeir] *ante* þeir *add.* dauþir oc herteknir *B add.* dauder menn *D* **59** dramba] *ante* dramba *add.* mono *B* voro *D* **60** viþ] yfir *B* af *D* **61** er] sem *D post* sem *add.* ad *D* **62** matto] *om. D* **63** verða] vera *B* urdu *D* **64** taca oss] *om. B* **65** ogn] riki *B* **66** at] *om. B* **67** oc taca oss ogn at bioþa] þá fagna þeir nú *D* **68** ioførr helvitis] *om. B* under rót *D* **69** oc] *om. B D* **70** *post* illz *add.* orkandi *B add.* oc helvítis upphafa sógdu þeir dióflarner *D* **71** hvi] *post* hvi *add.* óvitrlíga *B* þvi *D* **72** þat] *om. B* **73** nu] *om. D* **74** fyrer nu] *om. B* **75** spenia hann] *emendavi* spenian **76** hann] þann *B post* hann *add.* hingad til þessa eins *D* **77** *post* ⟨hingat⟩ *add.* er þu hefþir ecki í mott *B* **78** at spenia hann ⟨hingat⟩] *conieci* huc perduxisti *T* **79** at] *om. B D* **80** þess] *om. B D* **81** at] *om. B* **82** van] aurvent *B* **83** verþet] verde *D* **84** ne] oc *D* **85** stynr] sút *D* **86** i dauni] ad aude *D* **87** siþan] *post* siþan *add.* anstygþ *B om. D* **88** *post* micla *add.* mistum *D* **89** ⟨i⟩ saure oc i fylo] *om. D* **90** i dauni þeim enom micla er þu ater ⟨i⟩ saure oc i fylo oc gleþi] *om. B* **91** *post* þeiri *add.* oc ohrę̨si oc leíþendom *B* **92** *post* þu *add.* ádr *D* **93** hafðir her fingit] fect *B* **94** her fingit fyrer afbrigþartreet] þviad af brigdum þínum *D* **95** *ante* hefir *add.* þa *B* **96** *post* þu *add.* nu *B* **97** gleþi] virþing *B* **98** þin] vor *D* **99** fyrerfaraz] farasc *B* tínast *D* **100** villder] *foramen in cod. B* **101** sialfan] *om. B* **102** eggia] *emendavi lec. dub.* heggia **103** *post* þer *add.* oc oss *B* **104** er þu vilder sialfan Dyrþar Konong eggia lata] *om. D* **105** Of] *om. B D* **106** grunnuþect] grimmilegt *D* **107** þin] þier *D* **108** *post* orþet *add.* þo at *B add.* þer þitt til bragd *D* **109** hafa] *emendavi* hvafa, *ante* hafa *add.* At *B* **110** sva var syndalauss oc spanet hann hingat enn nu] þic rupplar sva *B* **111** scylder] scylir B **112** lata her nøgreþ laust allt þat er þu vill eigi] nu marga vanda oc sę̨kia lata lausa *B* **113** hafa raþit a þann ... / ... er þu vill eigi] *om. D*

XXIII.2

Eptir þetta er sact at[1] Konongr Dyrþar[2] męlti viþ helvites bua[3] alla[4] saman.[5] Nu scal[6] Satan her eptir[7] vera[8] i stað[9] Adams[10] oc barna hans[11] rettlatra minna.[12]

1 Eptir þetta er sact at] Siþan *B* **2** Konongr Dyrþar] Kóngr Dírdarennar *D* **3** helvites bua] myrkra hofþingiana *B* Satan *D* **4** alla] *om. D* **5** saman] *om. B D* **6** skal] skaltu *D* **7** eptir] *om. D* **8** vera] *om. B* **9** stað] stadinn *D* **10** Adams] *foramen in cod. B* **11** hans] *foramen in cod. B post* hans *add.* oc *D* **12** rettlatra minna] *foramen in cod. B* allra manna *D post* manna *add.* þá þagnade Satan illsku fullr *D*

XXIV.1

Enn[1] þa retti Guþ ⟨Drottinn⟩[2] hønd sina[3] oc męlti sva.[4] Comet[5] er[6] til min nu[7]
aller ⟨helgir⟩[8] þeir[9] er hafa[10] scilning mina.[11] Vitet[12] er þat[13] at Diofull oc[14]
Dauþi[15] er[16] nu[17] fyrerdømþr.[18] Þa sømno⟨þo⟩z aller[19] saman oc costuþo at[20]
renna[21] til handa Domino[22] Nostro.[23] Þa toc Dominus[24] [i] hønd ena høgri
Adams[25] oc męlti sva.[26] Friþr se þer meþ øllom børnom þinom rettlatom mi- Ps. 30
nom. Adam fell til fota Domino[27] oc męlti.[28] [29] *Exaltabo te Domine quoniam* (29):
suscepisti IV[30] vers søng[31] hann[32] af þeim[33] salm[34] framan.[35] [36] [Slict it] sama[37] 2–5
sungo[38] aller helgir oc[39] fello til fota Domino[40] ⟨oc męlto⟩[41]. Iamt[42] hefir þu
55r comet oc ennt þat er þu hezt [55r] oc þu[43] spaþer[44] fyrer løg oc[45] spamenn[46] at
leysa oss[47] oc heim allan[48] fyrer crossdauþann[49] ⟨þinn⟩[50] [51] oc niþrstigning til
var[52] oc[53] coma[54] oss[55] til[56] dyrþar[57] meþ metti þinom fra helvite[58] oc[59] marki
cross[60] þins at oss drottne eigi siþan dauþi.[61]

1 Enn] *om. D* **2** Enn þa retti Guþ ⟨Drottinn⟩] *conieci* Et extenends Dominus *T* **3** sina] *formanen in cod. B post* sina *add.* til mannligra flo\c/ka *B add.* ena hægre *D* **4** sva] *om. B D* **5** Comet] Kome *D* **6** er] þer *D* **7** nu] *formanen in cod. B om. D* **8** aller ⟨helgir⟩] *ante corr.* aller ęttir *B D, conieci* sancti Dei omnes *T* **9** þeir] þær *D* **10** hafa] hafit *B* **11** *post* mina *add.* oc *D* **12** Vitet] *formanen in cod. B* **13** er þat] *om. D* **14** *post* oc *add.* svo *D* **15** Dauþi] *formanen in cod. B* Dauden *D* **16** er] eru *D* **17** nu] *om. D* **18** fyrerdømþr] fyrirdæmder *D* **19** *post* aller *add.* helger menn *D* **20** costuþo at] *om. B D* **21** renna] runnu *B D* **22** Domino] Drottni *B D* **23** Nostro] Orom *B D* **24** Dominus] Drottin Iesus *B* **25** þa toc Dominus i hønd ena høgri Adams] *om. D* **26** sva] *om. B D* **27** Domino] Drottni *B* **28** męlti] oc saung þetta *B* **29** Friþr se þer ⟨…⟩ oc męlti] *om. D* **30** *ante* IV *add.* me oc *D* **31** søng] súngu *D* **32** hann] *om. D* **33** þeim] þessum *D* **34** *post* salm *add.* þetta þídir svo. Eg mun fagna þier Drottin oc upp hefia mun eg þig i lofe Drottins. Þvi ad þú tókst mig og oc ei gladder þu óvine mína yfer mier úr helvíte oc helian giarde þu mig frá nídrstigendum i heilar gróf. Sínge þier Drottne lof helgir menn oc játe þier hann i minning hans heilagleiks *D* **35** framan] *om. D* **36** IV vers søng hann af þeim salm framan] usque sanctitatis eius *B* **37** Slict it sama] Þa *B D* **38** sungo] *om. B D* **39** oc] *om. D* **40** Domino] Drottni *B D* **41** ⟨oc męlto⟩] *conieci* dicebant *T* **42** Iamt] *om. B D* **43** hezt oc þu] *om. B D* **44** spaþer] sagder *post* sagder *add.* oss *D* **45** løg oc] *om. B D* **46** spamenn] spámannsins *post* spámannsins *add.* munn. enn þad er *D* **47** *post* oss *add.* frá dióflinum *D* **48** allan *om.*

D **49** dauþan] *om. D* **50** ⟨þinn⟩] sins *B* **51** fyrer crossdauþann ⟨þinn⟩] *conieci* per crucem tuam et per mortem crucis *T* **52** var] þess *D* **53** oc] at *B D* **54** coma] taka *D* **55** oss] *om. B* **56** til] frá *D* **57** dyrþar] fagnaþa paradi⟨sar⟩ *B* vondum andskota *D* **58** helvite] helvitis *post* helvitis *add.* qvalom *B* **59** oc] *om. B* **60** cross] sigrs *B* **61** meþ meti þinom fra helvite oc marki cross þins at oss drottne eigi siþan dauþi] oc leida oss til fullsælu *D*

XXIV.2

Þa gørþi[1] siþan[2] Dominus[3] crossmarc ifer[4] Adam oc øllom[5] helgom[6] oc[7] toc[8] i
hønd Adams[9] oc ⟨ste⟩ upp[10][11] or helvite[12] meþ her[13] miclom[14] oc fylgþo Drottne[15]
aller helgir.[16] Þa męlti[17] David[18] hátt oc søng[19] þetta.[20][21] *Cantate Domino canti-* Ps. 98
cum nouum[22] ⟨*quia mirabilia fecit*[23] oc II vers søng af þeim salm en nęsto⟩.[24] (97): 1–2
Sva[25] syngo[26] aller ⟨helgir⟩[27] meþ honom[28] oc qvaðo[29] amen[30] ⟨oc męlto þetta.[31] Ps. 150
Hec est gloria omnibus sanctis eius. Alleluia⟩.[32] (149):9

1 gørþi] blęzaþi *B* **2** siþan] *om. D* **3** Dominus] Drottinn *B D* **4** crossmarc ifer] *om. B* **5** øllom] alla *B* **6** helgom] helga *B post* helgom *add.* mónnum *D* **7** oc] þa *B* **8** *post* toc *add.* Guþ *B* **9** Adams] Adami *B* Adam *D* **10** upp] *om. D* **11** ⟨ste⟩ upp] *conieci* ascendit *T* **12** or helvite] til paradisar *B* **13** her] hann *B D* **14** miclom] *om. B D* **15** fylgþo Drottne] med hónum *D* **16** *post* helgir *add.* menn *D* **17** męlti] sang *B* kallade *D* **18** *post* David *add.* konongr *B* **19** søng] mælte *D* **20** þetta] *om. D* **21** oc søng þetta] *om. B* **22** Cantate Domino canticum nouum] Synge þier nyan lofsóng D **23** ⟨quia mirabilia fecit⟩] *conieci* quia mirabilia fecit *T* Hann giórde undarlega hlúte heila *D* **24** ⟨oc II vers af þeim salm enn nęsto⟩] *conieci* giórde oss hin hægre hónd hans oc heilagr armleggr hans kunnugt giórde Drottinn hiálpræde sitt í augliti heidinna þióda mun hann sína oss rettlæti sitt *D* **25** sva] *om. D* **26** syngo] svaroþo *B D* **27** aller ⟨helgir⟩] *conieci* ombibus sanctis *T* **28** meþ honom] *om. B D* **29** qvaðo] sógdu *D* **30** amen] *add.* amen. Já já já *D* **31** ⟨oc męlto þetta⟩] *conieci* dicentes *T* Oc enn mæltu þeir *D* **32** ⟨Hec est gloria omnibus sanctis eius. Alleluia⟩ *conieci* Hec est gloria omnibus sanctis eius. Alleluia *T* Dírd se óllum helgum hans. Amen. Alleluia *D*

XXIV.3

Eptir þetta callaþi[1] Abbacuc spamaþr.[2] [3] *Ætlaþer ðu heilso þioð*[4] *þinne*[5] *at leysa* Hab. 3:13
valaþa[6] *ðina.* Enn[7] aller helgir[8] svoroþo[9] oc męlto.[10] *Lofaþr se sa er cømr in* Ps. 118
nomine[11] *Domini*[12] *oc*[13] *leysti Guþ*[14] *oss at eilifo.*[15] [16] Sva męlti oc Micheas[17] (117): 26–7
spamaþr.[18] *Hver e r guþ slicr sem Vor Guþ. Þu recr braut*[19] *illzcor varar oc stigr* Mi. 7:
iver synþer varar[20] *oc helldr vitne reiþe þinnar*[21] *i gegn illom.*[22] *Þu*[23] *ert viliandi* 18–19
miscunn[24] ⟨*oc snyr*⟩ *til var*[25] *dauðir*[26] *þu*[27] *allar illzcor varar oc allar synðer*
varar[28] i minni⟨n⟩g[29] dauþa[30] þins ⟨sva sem[31] þu svarþir[32] feþrom vorom⟩.[33] [34] Þa Ps. 48
svaroþo[35] aller helgir. *Sia er Guþ var at eilifo of verolld verallda*[36] ⟨*mon hann* (47):15
rikia i verolld⟩.[37] *Þa qvaþo aller*[38] *amen.*[39] Þa toco aller spamenn[40] at syng\va/[41]
sín orþ er þeir fylgþo Domino[42] Nostro.[43] [44]

1 callaþi] męlto *B* **2** spamaþr] propheta *B* **3** Eptir þetta callaþi Abbacuc spamaþr] *om. D* **4** þioð] þioðar *B* **5** *post* þinne *add.* til *D* **6** valaþa] útvalda *D* **7** Enn] *om. D* **8** *post* helgir *add.* menn *D* **9** *post* svoroþo *add.* Amen amen amen etc *D* **10** oc męlto] *om. B D* **11** in nomine] í nafni *B D* **12** Domini] Drottins *B D post* Drottins *add.* Guþs *B* **13** oc] er *B* **14** Guþ] *om. B* **15** at eilifo] amen *B* **16** oc leysti Guþ oss at eilifo] *om. D* **17** Micheas] Helias *D* **18** spamaþr] propheta *B* **19** recr braut] ert sa er bráut rac *B* brautst *D* **20** oc stigr iver synþer varar] *om. D* **21** *post* þinnar *add.* þviat *B* **22** i gegn illom] *om. B* **23** *ante* þu *add.* Þviat *B* **24** miscunn] miscunnar *post* miscunnar *add.* þinne *D* **25** var] vorum *D* **26** dauðir] fedrum *D* **27** ⟨oc snyr⟩ ⟨…⟩ þu] *conieci* Ipse auertis *T* þú hiálpader *D* **28** oc allar synðer varar] om. *D* **29** i minni⟨n⟩g] í gliking *B om. D* **30** dauþa] dauþans *B* miskuns *D* **31** ⟨sva sem⟩] *om. D* **32** ⟨svarþir⟩] hiálpader *D* **33** *post* vorom *add.* af miskun þinne. Þá mælte Drottin. Þióned mier syner míner oc mun eg stirkia ydir *D* **34** ⟨sva sem þu svarþir feþrom vorom⟩] *conieci* sicut iurasti patribus nostris *T* **35** svaroþo] mæltu *D* **36** of verold veralda] *om. D* **37** ⟨mon hann rikia i verolld⟩] *conieci* reget nos in secula T *om. D* **38** Þa qvaþo aller] *om. B D* **39** *post* amen *add.* amen *B* **40** *post* spamenn *add.* hverr *B* **41** syng\`va′] *bis scr.* syng\`va′ syngva, lęsa *B* **42** Domino] Drottni *B* **43** Nostro] Órom *B* **44** Þa toco aller spamenn at syng\`va′ sin orþ er þeir fylgþo Domino Nostro] *om. D*

XXV

Guþ[1] baud Michael[2] archangelo[3] at ⟨fylgia⟩[4] Adam ⟨ok[5] ǫllu[6] helgum⟩[7] hans[8] [9] at leide[10] þa ⟨alla⟩[11] i paradisum[12] ⟨hina føgnuþ⟩.[13] Þa[14] runno[15] II[16] menn a móte þeim. Þa[17] spurþo spamenn[18] hverer ⟨veri[19] er[20] þið[21] hafit eigi daudir[22] verit[23] meþ oss i helviti helldr⟩[24] eroþ ⟨þið⟩[25] nu[26] til þegar[27] licamliger[28] i paradiso.[29] [30] Þa[31] svaraþe annarr.[32] Enoch he\`i′ti ec enn[33] ec[34] var meþ[35] Guþs orþi[36] hingat førþr[37] enn sa er[38] mer fylger[39] heiter Helyas er[40] Thesbites[41] er[42] callaþr[43]. Hann var hingat ekinn i ell⟨dl⟩igre kerro[44] oc[45] hofum við[46] enn[47] ecki[48] daet.[49] Við[50] scolom her[51] hirðer[52] ⟨vera⟩[53] [54] til þess unz[55] Antichristus er[56] uppi.[57] Enn þa[58] munom[59] viþ[60] ðanga⟨t⟩[61] coma[62] [63] oc[64] beriaz a mot[65] honom[66] meþ[67] Guþs iarteinom oc tacnom.[68] Hann[69] mon ocr lata vega[70] ⟨i⟩ Iorsalaborg.[71] Enn[72] eptir III daga[73] oc halfan fiorþa[74] verþom viþ meþ scyiom[75] ⟨i annat sinn⟩[76] uppnumner.[77]

1 Guþ] *ante* Guþ *add.* Enn *B iterum incipit C* Drottinn Várr *C* Drottinn *D post* Drottinn *add.* sídan *D* **2** Michael] Mic\`h′aeli *B* Michaele *C* **3** archangelo] engli *B* hofudengli *C D* **4** ⟨fylgia⟩] *conieci* secuti sunt *T* **5** at ⟨fylgia⟩ Adam ⟨ok⟩] *om. B* **6** ǫllu] alla *B* **7** ⟨ok ǫllu helgum⟩] *conieci* et omnes sancti *T* **8** hans *emendavi* hann **9** at ⟨fylgia⟩ Adam ⟨ok ǫllu helgum⟩ hans] *om. D* **10** *ante* leide *add.* hann *D* **11** ⟨alla⟩] *conieci* omnes *T om. C* **12** paradisum] paradisar *B* paradísu *D* **13** ⟨hina føgnuþ⟩ *conieci* in gloria eternam *T* hína fornu *C om. D* **14** *ante* Þa *add. rubricam* Her segir fra Enok ok þeim Helias ok sem þeir komu þar *C* **15** runno] komu *D* **16** II] tveir *D* **17** þa] *ante* þa *add.* Enn *B D* þeir *C* **18** spamenn] þa *C* **19** *ante* veri *add.* þeir *B D* **20** er] þvi *D* **21** þið] it *B* **22** daudir] dáit *B* **23** verit] *om. B* **24** ⟨er þið hafit eigi daudir verit meþ oss i helviti helldr⟩] *conieci* uos qui nobiscum in inferis mortui nondum fuistis *T* **25** eroþ ⟨þið⟩] *conieci* estis *T* **26** nu] *om. B* **27** til þegar] *om. D* **28** *post* licamliger *add.* comnir *B* **29** paradiso] paradisum *B* **30** er þið hafit … / … i paradiso] cf. Gen. 5:18 et Heb. 11:5 **31** Þa] *om. D* **32** *post* annar *add.* þeira *B C* **33** enn] *om. B C* oc *D* **34** ec] *om. D*

35 meþ] viþ *C* **36** orþi] orþi *D* **37** førþr] leiddr *B* uppnuminn *post* uppnuminn *add.* oc sendr oc fæddr *D* **38** *post* mer *add.* med *C D* **39** fylger] er *C* fer *D* **40** er] oc *C* **41** Thesbites] Tespites *B* **42** er] var *B om. C* heiter *D* **43** callaþr] *om. D* **44** Helyas … / … i ell⟨dl⟩igre kerro] cf. IV Reg. 2:11 **45** oc] *om. C* enn *D* **46** við] ver *D* **47** enn] *om. B* einn veg *D* **48** ekki] *om. B D* **49** daet] dauþa bergt *B C* dauda tekid *D* **50** *ante* við *add.* þvi *D* **51** her] *om. B post* her *add.* enn *C* **52** hirðer] *om. B* vardveittir *C D* **53** ⟨vera⟩] lifa *B* **54** Við scolom her hirðer ⟨vera⟩] *conieci* reseruati sumus *T* **55** unz] er *C D* **56** er] verdr *D* **57** uppi] borinn *C post* uppi *add.* viskur *D* **58** Enn þa] *om.* B Þvi ad *D* **59** munom] skulum *B C* fórum *D* **60** viþ] *om. B* **61** ðanga⟨t⟩] i heiminn *C* þa *D* **62** coma] fara nidr *C post* fara *add.* til ydrar *D* **63** en þa munom viþ ðanga⟨t⟩ coma] *om. B* **64** oc] at *D* **65** a mot] viþ *B C D* **66** honom] hann *B C D* **67** meþ] at *D* **68** iarteinom oc tacnom] fyrirætlan *D* **69** Hann] Gud *D ante* hann *add.* Enn *C D* **70** vega] vegna *D ante* vega *add.* verda fyrer hónum *D* **71** Iorsalaborg] Ierusalem *B D* **72** En] Oc *D* **73** *post* daga *add.* lidna *C* **74** oc halfan fiorþa] *om. D* **75** *post* scyiom *add.* frá mónnum *D* **76** ⟨i annat sinn⟩] *conieci* iterum *T om. C D* **77** *post* uppnumer *add.* fra mónnum *D*

XXVI

Þat var[1] þa[2] er þeir[3] Enoch oc Elyas rødosc[4] slict[5] við[6] oc[7] Guþs helgir[8] at[9] þar[10]
com at gangande ⟨einn⟩[11] maþr[12] allosęlligr[13] sa[14] hafði[15] crossmarc[16] a herþom
ser.[17] ⟨Þa[18] er[19] Guþs helgir sa þenna mann⟩[20] þeir[21] spurþo[22] [23] hverr hann[24]
væri.[25] ⟨Oss synisc sem[26] þu muner[27] illvirke[28] veret hava[29] eþa hvi genger at[30]
þu bersc[31] crossmark⟩.[32] [33] Hann[34] svaraþi.[35] Ec[36] var illvirke[37] oc geyrþa ec[38]
hotvitna[39] illt a iorþo.[40] Enn[41] Gyþingar[42] crossfesto[43] mic[44] meþ Cristi.[45] Enn
þat var[46] þa[47] er ec sa undr þau er urþu[48] at[49] ec þotomc vita[50] at Cristr[51] myndi
vera[52] Scapare allrar scepno.[53] Toc[54] ec af þvi[55] at[56] biþia[57] [58] ⟨hann⟩ mer[59] mis-
55v cunnar [55v] oc męlta[60] ec sva.[61] *Minnztu mín[62] Drottinn er[63] þu cømr i riki þitt.* Lc. 23:42
Hann[64] toc vel male mino þa[65] þegar[66] oc[67] męlti[68] sva.[69] *Vist[70] segi ec þer[71] i dag* Lc. 23:43
verþr þu[72] meþ mer i paradiso. Þa gaf hann mer þetta crossmarc[73] oc męlti.[74] Ef
angelus[75] sa er vørþr[76] er paradisar[77] bannar þer inngøngo[78] þa syndo[79] honom
crossmarc ⟨þetta⟩[80] oc[81] seg[82] honom þat[83] at Iesus Christus sa er[84] nu[85] [86] er[87]
crossfestr[88] hafe[89] ⟨þic⟩ þangat[90] sent.[91] [92] Nu gørða ec sva[93] at[94] [95] ec męlta[96]
viþ[97] ⟨englenn⟩ paradisar vorþ[98] [99] [100] sem mer var boþet.[101] Hann[102] lauc þegar[103]
upp fyrer[104] mer[105] paradisar hliþ[106] oc leidde mic inn[107] til hegri handar[108] oc
męlti.[109] Her scolom[110] biþa litla[111] stund þviat Adam faþer allz manncyns[112]
man hingat[113] coma bratt[114] meþ børnom sinom ⟨helgom[115] oc⟩ rettlatum[116] [117]
Crisz Drottens[118] in⟨s⟩ crossfesta.[119] [120] Þa[121] er høfuðfeþr[122] oc[123] spamenn hey-
rðo þetta er illvirkenn[124] sagði[125] [126] þa[127] toco aller[128] senn[129] at męla.[130] Lofaþr
ser[131] þu Almattegr Guþ[132] er sva miscunnsamr ert at ðu veitter overþum[133] ⟨ey-
lifa sælu um allar alldir. Amen⟩.[134]

1 þat var] *om. B C D* **2** þa] oc *C* enn *D* **3** þeir] *om. D* **4** rødosc] redo *B* taladu *C* ræddu *D* **5** slict] þetta *C D* **6** við] umb *B C* um *D* **7** oc] *om. B D* **8** helgir] helga *B post* helga *add.* menn *C* fólk *D* **9** at] *om. B* þá *D* **10** þar] þa *B* **11** ⟨einn⟩] *om. B* **12** ⟨einn⟩ maþr] *conieci* alius uir *T* **13** allosęlligr] otirligr *B* **14** sa] hann *D* **15** sa hafði] hafandi *C* **16** crossmarc] cross *B* **17** ser] *om. B* **18** Þa] *om. D* **19** er] *om. B* enn *D* **20** ⟨sa þenna mann⟩] *om. B D* **21** þeir] þa *B C om. D* **22** *post* Guþs helgir *add* menn *D* **23** ⟨Þa er Guþs helgir sa þenna mann⟩ þeir spurþo] *conieci* Uidentes autem sancti omnes dixerunt ad eum *T* **24** hann] sa *B* þenna mann *C* **25** hverr hann væri] ad nafne *D* **26** sem] *om. B* **27** muner] *om. B* **28** illvirke] odygligr *B* **29** veret hava] *om. B* **30** at] er *B* **31** bersc] ber *B* **32** crossmark] cross *B post* cross *add.* a herþom *B* **33** ⟨Oss synisc sem þu muner illvirke veret hava eþa hvi genger at þu bersc crossmark⟩] *conieci* Uidentes autem sancti omnes dixerunt ad eum. Quis es tu anime quia uisio tua latronis est? *T om. D* **34** *ante* hann *add.* Enn *D* **35** svaraþi] sagde *D* **36** *ante* Ec *add.* segir ek ydr at *C post* ec *add.* heite Dismas enn eg sege ydr satt ad *D* **37** illvirke] þiofr *B* **38** ec] *om. C* **39** hotvitna] mart *B D ante* mart *add.* mikid oc *D* **40** a iorþo] *om. D* **41** Enn] oc var fyrir þad *D* **42** Gyþingar] *om. D* **43** crossfesto] crossfestr *D* **44** mic] *om. D* **45** Cristi] Iesu *B C D* **46** þat var] *om. B* þa vid þat *C om. D* **47** þa] þat *C om. D* **48** urþi] *foramen in cod. B* gerþuz *B C D* **49** at] þa *B D* **50** vita] scilia *B* **51** Cristr] Iesu *B C D* **52** vera] *om. D* **53** *post* scepno *add.* svo oc ad hann munde vera lausnare oc grædare alls mannkyns oc heims oc *D* **54** Toc] *om. B* **55** af þvi] þa *C D* **56** at] *om. B* **57** biþia *post* biþia *add.* hann *C D* **58** Toc ec af þvi at biþia] baþ ec *B* **59** biþia ⟨hann⟩ mer] *conieci* deprecatus sum eum *T* **60** męlta] *foramen in cod. B* **61** sva] þetta *B* **62** minnztu mín] miskunna þu mer *C* **63** er] *om. D ante* er *add.* þa *C D* **64** *ante* hann *add.* Enn *C* **65** *ante* þa *add.* oc *C* **66** þa þegar] *om. B D* **67** oc] *om. D* **68** *post* męlte *add.* vid mik *C* **69** sva] *om. B C* **70** Vist] Sat *B* **71** *post* þer *add.* ad *D* **72** verþr þu] skaltu *C D post* skaltu *add.* vera *D* **73** cross] *om. B* **74** oc męlti] *post* męlti *add.* sva *B om. C* **75** angelus] engill *C D* **76** vørþr] *om. D* **77** paradisar] i paradísu *D* **78** *post* inngøngo *add.* þar *D* **79** syndo] syn *D* **80** crossmarc ⟨þetta⟩] *conieci* signum istud *T* **81** Ef angelus sa er vørþr er paradisar bannar þer inngøngo þa syndo honom crossmarc oc] *om. C* **82** *post* seg *add.* þú *D* **83** þat] *om. C D* **84** er] sem *post* sem *add.* Gud⟨s⟩ son er *D* **85** nu] *om. D* **86** sa er nu] *om. B* **87** er] enn *B* var *D* **88** crossfestr] crossfesti *B* **89** hafe] hefir *C* ad hann *D* **90** þangat] hingat *B C* **91** sent] sende *D* **92** hafe ⟨þic⟩ þingat sent] *conieci* transmisit te ad me huc *T* **93** sva] eptir þvi sem mer var kent *B* **94** gørða ec sva at] *om. C* **95** Nu gørða ec sva at] Enn er *D* **96** *post* oc *add.* þetta *C* **97** at ec męlta viþ] *om. B* **98** vorþ] *emendavi* vorþr **99** paradisar vorþ] *om. B D* **100** viþ ⟨englenn⟩ paradisar vorþ] *conieci* ad angelum custodem paradysi *T* **101** sem mer var boþet] *om. B D* **102** *ante* hann *add.* Þá *D* **103** þegar] *om. D* **104** fyrer] *om. B* **105** fyrer mer] *om. C D* **106** paradisar hliþ] paradisu oc *D* **107** *post* inn *add.* híngad *D* **108** handar] *emendavi lect. dub.* hogdar *post* handar *add.* iafntit *B add.* ser *C* **109** męlti] sagde *D* **110** scolom] scalltu *B post* scalltu *add.* nu *C post* scolom *add.* vid *D* **111** *post* lita *add.* þa *B* **112** faþer allz manncyns] *om. C* **113** hingat] her *C* **114** bratt] *om. C* skiótlega *D* **115** ⟨helgom⟩] ỏllum *D* **116** *post* rettlatum *add.* mỏnnum *D* **117** ⟨helgom oc⟩ rettlatum] *conieci* sanctis et iustis *T* **118** *post* Drottens *add.* Chrisz *C* **119** in⟨s⟩ crossfesta] *om. B* **120** Chrisz Drottens in⟨s⟩ crossfesta] *om. D* **121** Þa] Enn *C D* **122** høfuðfeþr] fedr *C om. D* **123** oc] *om. D* **124** illvirken] þiofr *B* **125** sagði] męlti *B* **126** er illvirkenn sagði] *om. D* **127** þa] *om. B* **128** aller] *ante* aller *add.* þeir *C* þeir *D* **129** senn] *emendavi* sennt *post* senn *add.* sva *C* **130** at męla] mæltu *D* **131** ser] se *B* **132** Guþ] Drottin minn *post* minn *add.* Almáttugr Skapare *D* **133** *post* overþum *add.* eylifa sælu um allar alldir *C ante* overþum *add.* líkn oc lausn *D post* overþum *add.* Sídann leidde Gud allsvaldande alla sinn hóp edr flock til eilífs sætis oc paradísar vistar þar sem ad er lopt listelegt oc liós ævarannlegt aller heilager Guds sungu þá lof Gude ad eilífu allra alda *D* **134** ⟨eylifa sælu um allar alldir. Amen⟩] *conieci* in pascua delectationis et in uitam eternam. Amen. *T om. B*

XXVII.1

Karinus[1] oc Leutius[2] fundosc[3] eigi i grofom sinom eftir uppriso Crisz af[4] dauþa.[5] Helldr[6] hafa þeir uppriset[7] meþ honom oc marger aþrer[8] sem sva[9] segir[10] i Guþspiollom.[11] Mt. 27:52
⟨*Et multa corpora sanctorum qui dormierant surrexerunt. Oc margir likamir heilagra dauþra*[12] *manna er sofnat hofþo*[13] *riso upp*⟩.[14] [15]

1 Karinus] Marinus *C ante* Marinus *add. rubricam* Fra Karinus ok Leutius *C* **2** Leutius] *emendavi* Leuntius *post* Leutius *add.* synir Simeonis *C D post* Simeonis *add.* hins Rettlata *C* **3** *ante* fundosc *add.* þeir *D* **4** af] oc *C* **5** af dauþa] *om. D* **6** Helldr] Oc *D* **7** hafa ⟨...⟩ uppriset] risu upp *D* **8** *post* aþrer *add.* helger menn *D* **9** sva] *om. D* **10** segir] ritiþ er *B C* **11** Helldr hafa þeir ... / ... i Guþspiollom cf. Mt. 27:52 **12** dauþra] *om. D* **13** *post* hofþo *add.* fyrer *D* **14** riso upp] upprisu *D post* uppriso *add.* Kristi risu upp med hónom *D* **15** ⟨Et multa corpora sanctorum qui dormierant surrexerunt⟩] *trasp. hic post cap. XVII.1 et em. secundum Vulgata* non sunt ibi corpora eorum sed resurrexerunt *T om. B D*

XXVII.2

Karinus oc Leutius[1] voro senir[2] [3] siþan i borg[4] Arimathia[5] at[6] Iosephs[7] oc rito[8] þenna[9] þott niþrstigningar Criz[10] af[11] ðviat[12] þeir villdo ecki viþ menn[13] męla oc leto bocena coma[14] i hendr[15] [16] Nicodemo oc Iosep⟨h⟩ enn þeir[17] reþo[18] upp ⟨fyrer⟩ \`oðrom´.[19] [20] Enn[21] morgom mannzøll⟨drom⟩[22] siþar comsc at boc þeire[23] Theodosius keisere[24] sonr[25] Archadii. Hann[26] hafði meþ sér i Miclagarþ oc let þar uppraþa[27] oc varþ þar[28] monnom[29] alldat[30] umb.[31] Per omnia ⟨Benedictus Deus in⟩ secula seculorum.[32] [33] Amen.

1 Leutius] *pro* Leucius **2** senir] *emendavi lect. dub.* sendir **3** voro senir] vitrudust *D* **4** *post* borg *add.* þeiri er heitir *C* **5** Arimathia] *emendavi* Arimachia **6** at] *om. B D* **7** Iosephs] Ioseph *B* **8** rito] skrifdu *C* ritudu *post* ritudu *add.* þar *D* **9** þenna] *foramen in cod. B* **10** Criz] Drottins *D* **11** af] *om. D* **12** ðviat] þvi *D* **13** *ante* menn *add.* adra *D* **14** leto bocena coma] sendu bókina þessa *D* **15** *post* hendr *add.* þeim *C* **16** i hendr] til handa *D* **17** þeir] þesser *D* **18** reþo] lasu *B* hafa lesit *C* lietu upplesa *D post* upplesa *add.* sídann *D* **19** \`oðrom´] *iter. in marg.* **20** fyrer oðrom] *om. C* **21** *post* Enn *add.* þar eptir *D* **22** *ante* mannzøll⟨drom⟩ *add.* árum oc *D* **23** þeire] þann *C* **24** keisere] biskup *D post* keisere *add.* oc *A lectio dub. expunxi, add.* hann var *C* **25** sonr] *emendavi lect. dub.* oc sendi **26** hann] oc *B C D* **27** uppraþa] upplesa *C D* **28** þar] þvi *C post* þar *add.* þvi *D* **29** *ante* monnom *add.* óllom *D* **30** alldat] dat *B* altídt *D post* altídt *add.* oc fyrer þessa nú skráda jarteikn er Gud vilde veita oss oc ollum mǫnnum rett kristum. Þa skilim vier so segia *D* **31** alldat umb] nytt um dasemdir *C post* dasemdir *add.* Almattigs Guds *C* **32** in secula seculorum] *om. B* um allar alder *D* **33** Per omnia ⟨Benedictus Deus in⟩ secula seculorum] *om. T* Dírd sie Gude Fødr oc Syne oc Helgum Anda oc svo sem hún var ad upphafe er enn nú oc iafnann oc um allar alder. Amen. *D*

Niðrstigningar saga

The Younger Redaction

(E Copenhagen, Den Arnamagnæanske Samling, AM 238 fol. V)

XVIII.3

1r [1r] *Þessi er Son minn elskuligr vidur þann er mier likadi vel* ok for eg firir Mt.
asionu hans ok steig eg nidur til ydar til þess at segia ydur at sialfur Guds Son 3:16–17
upprennandi af hifna hæd mun skiott koma ok vitia ydar ok allra sina vina þeira er sitia i myrk⟨r⟩um ok i skugga daudans.[1]

1 ok for eg … / … i skugga daudans cf. Lc. 1:76–9

XIX.1

Ok þa er Adam fadir vor heyrdi þat sagt at Iesus er skridur[1] i Iordan gladdiz hann geysi miog ok leit til Seth sonar sins ok mællti vid hann. Heyrdu son minn sagdi hann ber fram ok boda hofudfedrum alla hluti þa er þu heyrdir af Mikaele hofudeingli þa er eg senda þik til paradisar hlids at þu skylldir bidia Drottin at hann sendi engil ⟨sinn⟩[2] ok gæfi þer vidsmiorh af myskunnartre at eg smyrda likama minn þa er eg var siukur. Þa geck Seth fram ok sagdi til hofudfedrum ok spamanna ok mælti sva. Eg Seth þa er eg kom til hlida paradisar eg sa[3] elld brennanda sa er bannade hveriu sem einum manne ingaungo ok einglar Guds vardveittu þessi hlid bædi firir dioflu⟨m⟩ ok syndugum monnum[4] ok þar sem eg stod vard eg miog gagnhræddur ok bad eg til Drottins med miklum otta. Þa syndiz mier Mikael eingill ok mællti vid mik. Eg er sendur til þin af Drottni. Eg er skipadur yfir mannlegum likama. Enn eg segi þer Seth med sonnu. Eigi þarf þu at starfa med ervidi eda tarum bidia sakir vidsmiors myskunnartres at þu smyrir fodur þinn Adam at betridz likams sott hans þviat med aungum hætti mattu taka þetta vidsmiorh nema æfstum dogum okomins tima þa er adur ˋfyllaz´[5] VMCXXX ara. Þa mun koma yfir jord hinn elskulegsti Guds Son Christus at vekia upp likame⟨r⟩ daudra manna.[6] Oc þa er hann sialfur kemr mun hann skira i vatni ok Helgum Anda þa mun hann smyria alla þa er æ hann trua med vidsmiǫrvi sinnar myskunnar ok mun þetta myskunnar vidsmior vera til enˋd´urgetningar[7] þeim er fa muno af vatni ok Helgum Anda i eilift lif. Þa mun nidurstiga til jardar enn elskuligsti Sonur Guds Christus[8] ok mun þa inleida fodur þinn Adam i paradisum til miscunartress.

1 skridur] *emendavi* skirdur **2** engil ⟨sin⟩] *conieci* angelum suum *K* **3** eg sa] *bis scr.* **4** Eg sa elld brenanda … / … ok syndugum monnum cf. Petr. Com. *Hist. Schol. Liber Genesis* 3:24

(47/37) **5** `fyllaz´ ] *iter. in marg.* **6** likame⟨r⟩ daudra manna] corpora mortorum *K* **7** `d´] *iter. in marg.* **8** med aungum hætti … / … Sonur Guds Christus cf. *Vita Adae et Evae* (vers. 42)

XIX.2

Ok þa ⟨er⟩[1] allir hofudfedur ok spamenn heyrdo þessa hluti framsagda af Seth þa fognudo þeir med mikille gledi.

1 Ok þa ⟨er⟩] Et cum *K*

XX.1

Ok þa er allir helgir glaudduz meþ fagnade þa kom til þeira helvitís hofdíngi leidtogi daudra i liking hrædilegs dreka ok miog auskurlegs sa er stundum syndiz þeim med VI hofdum enn stundum med III ⟨enn⟩ stundum i manzliki.[1] Hann hliodadi med harri roddu til hevítis ok sagdi. Bu þig sialfur med allri. Kanstu at taka vid Jesu sa er sialfan sik dyrkar ok segiz vera Christus Son Guds enn hann er madur þviat hann ottaz daudan svo mælande. *Hrygg er aund min* Mt.
allt til dauda[2] ok margar illgiordir fyndi hann i moti mier ok marga græddi 26:38
hann med ordi sínu þa er eg giorda blinda hallta krepta likþra ok kvalda meinsemdum.[3]

1 helvitís hofdíngi … / … i manzliki cf. Ap. 12:3–5 **2** hann ottaz daudan svo mælande. Hrygg er aund min allt til dauda] timnes mortem dicens. Tristis est anima mea usque ad mortem *K T om. A B C D* **3** ok margar illgiordir … / … kvalda meinsemdum cf. Mt. 10:8 et 11:5

XX.2

Þa svaradi helviti ok sagdi til Satans hofdingia. Hverr er sua mattugur i orde ok se hann þo madur ok ottaz dauda þviat alla mattuga jardar hofdingia hefi eg halldit undir mino vallde þa er þu fluttir nu yndir orpna med þinom styrk. Enn ef þu ert mattugur hverr er þessi `madur´ [1] Jesus er ottaz dauda ok stendur þo i moti þier ok þinu valldi. Ef hann ⟨er⟩ þvi likur i manndomi mattugur ok styrkur sannliga segi þer almattugur er hann þa i guddome ok eingi mun þa mega i moti standa hans styrk ok mætti ok ef hann segir sig hrædaz[2] dauda þa vill hann leyna guddoms mætti sinum ok eigi mun þat vera um eilifar veralldir. Þa svarar Satan helvitis hofdinge ok mællti. Hvi efar þu eda ottaz at taka þenna Iesum er bædi gioriz minn ok þinn mo⟨t⟩staudumadur þviat eg freistada hans ok vakta upp lyd hans Gydinga flock med ofurkappe ok reidi i mot honum. Hvesta eg spiot ok frameggia [1v] di eg at legia a sidu honum gallsuro blandada eg at gefa honum i þosta dryck.[3] Eg bio tre at krossfesta hann ok nu er miog nalægur daudi hans ok mun eg leida hann til þin ok min yfirkomin.

1 \`madur´] *add. in marg.* **2** hrædaz] *bis scr.* hræddan hrædaz **3** Gallsuro … / … i þosta dryck cf. Mt. 27:34

XX.3

Þa svarade helvíti ok mælti. Þu sagdir mier at þessi er sa sialfur er dauda menn dro fra mer. Enn margir eru þeir er eg hiellt i valldi er fra mer voru gripnir af þeir[1] lifdo æ jordu er hver er þersi Jesus er med ædi sínu ok gudligom bænum kallar dauda menn til lifs almattigur er hann er sa er dro \`af´[2] mier dauda menn þa er eg hugdumz mattuliga hallda mundo undir minu vallde. Mun eigi þessi sa vera er leysti Ladarum[3] sa er i grauf la IIII daga þann er eg hellt daudan i mino vallde ok gallt hann lifanda firir ord síns almattar.[4] Þa svarar Satan hofdíngi dau\`d´ans[5] ok segir sva. Þersi sialfur er sa Iesus ok þa er hann sagdi þetta heyrde helviti ok sagdi til hans. Særi eg firir krapta þina ok mina at eigi leidir þu hann híngat til min þviat þa er ek heyrda styrkan matt ordz hans þa vard ek miog gagnhræddur med skialfanda otta ok allir helvitis þionar med mier urdo skialfir. Ok eíge matta ek hallda Ladarum[6] med aullum styrk ok fliotleik mínum ok spratt hann upplifandi ok heill ok sialf jord su er hiellt daudligan likama Ladari[7] gallt hann lifanda ok firir þvi veit ek at sa madur er þessa alla hluti matti giora hann er styrkur i valldi mattugur i manndomi grædari allz mannkyns ok hann mun leysa þa er byrgdir eru i grimre myrkvastofu ok stridligum synda baundum ok leida til lífs sins guddoms. *Þar var ok i þat mund dægra ok þen-* Ap.
nan tíma at himenn opnadiz. Þa kom fram fyst hestur hvitur enn sa kongur er 19:11–17
reid hesti þeim er maurgum hlutum er fridari ok fegri enn allir adrir ok tigolegri. Augu hans voru sem eldz loge. Hann hafdi koronu þa áá hofdi er morg sigurmerke synde. Hann hafdi þat klædi um onnur utan er blodstocket[8] *var.* ÁÁ *kledi hans yfir miodmenne voru þessi ord ritud. Kongur konga ok Drottinn drottna. Hann leiddi med sier her hinn mesta. Þeir* ⟨*er*⟩ *honum fylgdu ridu hvitum hestum ok voru klæddir silke hvito liosir hardla.* Sa hinn rikazti allvalldur leit þa til Jo⟨r⟩salaborgar ok mælti. Gilldra su er at Jorsolum er ⟨gorr⟩ verdi Midgardzorme at skada. Hann fal aungul sin i æzlíno þvi er i gilldruna var lagt ok sva gat hann vadinn folginn at eigi matti um sia. Þa baud hann nockrum sinum elskuligum vínum at þeir skyllde fyrir fara ok boda til kvomo hans.

1 af þeir] *pro* er þeir **2** \`af´] *add. in marg.* **3** Ladarum] *pro* Lazarum **4** er leysti Ladarum … / … ord sins almattar cf. Io. 11:38-43 **5** \`d´] *add. in marg.* **6** Ladarum] *pro* Lazarum **7** Ladari] *pro* Lazari **8** blodstocket] *emendavi* blodstocken

XXI.1

Enn þa er þau tauludo med sier sem firir sagt Satan hofdingie ok helvíte þa vard
hvell rodd mikellar reidar þrumo ok andlekt kall sva mælanndi. Heyrit hofdíngiar helvítes. *Lukit upp hlid*: *Ydur ok hefiz upp eilif hlid ok mun i⟨nn⟩ganga* Ps. 24
Kongur Dyrdar. Ok þa er helvite heyrdi þess ord þa sagdi þad til Satans hofdin- (23):7
gia sins. Far þu brott heidan ok fly skiott ut af mínum sætum. Enn ef þu ert
mattugur bardaga madur þa berstu vid Dyrdar Kongín þviat hvat áá eg at skyll-
da med honum. Ok eptir þat rak þad Satan hofdíngia sinn ut af sætum sinum.
Enn þa er Satan var brott rekinn leit hann utalligan fiolda himnesks folks ok
herlids enn eigi sa hann þa Dyrdar Kongin þar kominn ok villdi hann þo eigi
moti þeim ganga. Helldur hneigdi hann sik fra augliti þeira. Þa likti hann sik i
mynd ogurligs dreka þeim er jafnat er at mikeleik vid Midgard⟨z⟩orm sa er sagt
⟨er⟩ at ligi um allan heiminn.[1] Hann sa þa takn þau er voru i Jorsalaborg ⟨at⟩
Drottinn Varn ⟨var⟩ i andlati ok jamskiott.[2]

1 þa likti hann … / … um allan heimin cf. Ap. 12:9 **2** *desinit E*

TRANSLATIONS

Niðrstigningar saga

The Older Redaction

(A Copenhagen, Den Arnamagnæanske Samling, AM 645 4to)

PROLOGUE

"The Story of the Descent." The [two] brothers Carinus and Leucius, sons of Simeon the Elder, relate about Christ's Descent into Hell in their book that they wrote on how Christ had freed Adam and all the others from Hell. And although this is scarcely considered in comparison to what is written about it in other holy writings, there is nothing related here, which may be doubtful. The book is called "The Deeds of the Saviour." People say that Nicodemus, the disciple of the Lord, composed it.

XVIII.1

"We had been placed," they said, "in a place that seemed like a field. There was Adam and all the patriarchs and prophets, and it was misty and dark as usual. Then something memorable and remarkable occurred: suddenly there shone over us all a fair and bright light as if from the sun. Then Adam, the father of all mankind, and all the patriarchs and prophets began to rejoice greatly and said this: 'This light shines from God, who has promised us that He would send His light.' Then the prophet Isaiah called out and said, 'This light is from
God, just as I said when I was alive on earth and said this: "*Land of Zabulon* Mt.
and land of Nephtali, by the way of the sea, beyond the Jordan, Galilee of the 4:15–16

Gentiles. The people who sat in darkness have seen great light, and a light has downed on those living in the region of the shadow of death." Now that light has come over us, as I prophesied it would come, for truly we sit in the darkness of Hell. But now we may all see and rejoice greatly at this light.'"

XVIII.2

"Then our father Simeon came walking to the place where a multitude of people had all gathered together and said with great joy to the friends of God, 'Glorify Our Lord, Jesus Christ, for I took Him in my arms when he was a child and carried Him into church when I was urged by the Holy Spirit and I sang this: "*Now you dismiss*," until the end.' All the saints of God rejoiced greatly at Lc. 2:29
this message."

XVIII.3

"Then came a man walking, whom they did not recognize. This man was accomplished and dressed in such a manner as if he had come from the desert. They asked that man his name and if he had anything new to say. He was called John: 'And I was the voice crying from the desert and the forerunner of the Son of God on earth to give knowledge to people that it was the Son of God who had come there for them in order to help those who wished to receive it. And when I saw Him come to find me, the Holy Spirit urged me, and I said this:
"*Behold the Lamb of God*," until the end. Then I baptized Him in the river Io. 1:29
Jordan and *I saw the Holy Spirit descending upon Him in the shape of a dove.* Mt.
And behold, I heard *a voice from Heaven saying*, "*This is my Beloved, in whom* 3:16–17
I am pleased." And now I can say this to you, that I have preceded Him here to announce to you that very shortly the Son of God Himself shall come down here from Heaven to visit those of us who sit in the darkness of Hell.'"

XIX.1

"Then it occurred that when our first-created father Adam heard about this, when this man John departed from the world, that Jesus was baptized in the Jordan, that he [Adam] became very joyful and turned towards his son and said this to him: 'Seth, Son, tell the patriarchs and the prophets about what you heard the archangel Michael tell you, when I sent you to Paradise to seek and beseech this of Our Lord, whether he would be willing to send His angel to bring you from there the oil, which begets from the olive tree of mercy, so that my body might be anointed with it when I was sick, in order to receive healing.' Then, when Seth had come to the place where the patriarchs and the prophets were, he addressed them and begun to say this: 'It occurred,' said Seth, 'when I travelled on my father's errand, that I came at last to the gates of Paradise. There were two things before me: there was burning fire to deny any man entrance to Paradise, and angels to guard it against all devils and the souls of sinful men. When my passage was to be obstructed, I halted and prayed to the Lord, and the archangel Michael appeared to me and said this to me: "I am sent to you from the Lord. I am set up to see to each man's condition and you should be told this, Seth: you do not need to pray with tears for the oil that begets in Paradise, to give it to your father, although he is very sick, for in no way shall he have the oil from there until five thousand and four hundred years have passed. Then shall come upon earth the Beloved Son of God, Christ Himself, and He shall give health to many sick men, and raise some from the dead, and Christ Himself shall be baptized in the river Jordan. And when He shall rise from the water, He shall anoint with the Oil of Mercy all those who believe in Him, and that Oil of Mercy shall regenerate from the water among them, and the Holy Spirit shall be regenerated unto eternal bliss. It shall also happen that the Beloved Son of God, Jesus Christ, shall willingly descend unto earth, and shall lead Adam, your father, into Paradise to the tree of mercy."'"

XIX.2

"At this message announced by Seth, all the patriarchs rejoiced greatly."

XX.1

"And now, while among them there was such a great joy, as might be expected, it is said that the giant Satan, the Prince of Hell, who sometimes has seven heads and sometimes three, and sometimes is in the shape of a dragon, which is horrible, terrible, and awful in all respects, convened the giants, the devils, the mighty trolls, and all of those who were in Hell, and said this: 'Prepare yourself now to take and seize Jesus, who boasts that He is the Son of God, and nevertheless He is a man, and I have noticed it because he feared death. And yet He is that man who has opposed me greatly and has always been most cruel to me, and many men whom I made blind, lame, crippled, lepers, and mad, He cured with His word.'"

XX.2

"And they spoke and replied to him: 'We do not know that things are as you say, but we know and can see, O Lord, that you have drawn no one to us like the one about whom you speak now, He who has always destroyed and thrashed your might and power. Therefore, we believe and say to you that He must be almighty in divinity and no one in the world, who is as He is in humanity, can withstand Him.' Then the Prince of Darkness said, 'Why do you doubt and fear to seize this man Jesus, who is both my enemy and yours? For I tempted Him and aroused the Jewish people to hostility against Him, and prepared the wood for His crucifixion, and blended vinegar to drink, and have had a spear sharpened to thrust into Him. Now very shortly He shall die, and I shall bring Him here, so that He may be submitted to both you and me.'"

XX.3

"They replied: 'Did you not say about that man that He could achieve anything with His word, and healed what you had injured or slain? We know that He has taken from you many dead men who were held by us. But who was the one so strong in words that called Lazarus here? Before that, we had held him here in the bonds of Death for four days, and then he was instantly alive on earth far away from us.' Satan, the Prince of Death, replied, 'That was Jesus.' Then they replied thus: 'We abjure you by your powers and ours that you do not bring Him here, for when we heard His commandments, we all became terrified, and all of our servants and all our smithies trembled, and by no means could we hold Lazarus, who almost at once was cast up onto earth alive. As for now, we know that the Almighty God is within that man and will have to come here into the world to release men from sins and bring them to the life of His divinity.' Now I shall turn away from when Satan and Hell talked first, and begin to relate the most wondrous events that occurred next. *It was at that point of the day* Ap.
that Heaven opened, and there came forth first a white horse and the prince 19:11–16
who rode that horse was in many respects more noble than the most accomplished of all others. His eyes were like blazing fire. He had a crown on his head where many tokens of victory could be seen. He had a vestment above the others that was spattered with blood. On His vestment, around the waist, these words were written: King of kings and Lord of lords. He was brighter than the sun. He led a great army, and all those who followed Him rode white horses, and all were dressed in white silk and were very bright. Then He, the most powerful supreme ruler, looked towards Jerusalem and said, 'May the trap that is made in Jerusalem harm the Midgard Serpent.' He then lowered a hook, in which was enclosed a bait that could not be seen into the carrion that was lain in the trap and, done that, He concealed it in such a way that it could not be seen. Then He ordered some of His saints to go before Him and announce His arrival in Hell."

XXI.1

Now the story will be resumed from where I previously turned away. "While Satan and the others were talking to each other, they heard that the holy angels called out so loudly that everything seemed to resound like thunder and said this: '*Lift up your gates, O princes, and be lifted up, O eternal gates, and the* Ps. 24
King of Glory will come in.' Then the inhabitants of Hell said to Satan, 'Depart (23):7
now from our seats. If you can, fight hard with the King of Glory. We do not want to deal with Him.' Then they expelled their Prince out of Hell. When Satan came out, he saw that a great host of angels had arrived to Hell, but not God. He [Satan] did not go to meet them and rather passed them by. Then he transformed himself into the shape of a dragon and grew to such a stature that it seemed he could lie around the whole world. He saw those events that occurred in Jerusalem, that Jesus Christ was breathing His last, and immediately travelled there and intended to tear away His soul at once from Him. But when he came there and thought he could swallow Him and carry Him away, the hook of divinity bit him, and the sign of the cross fell down on him, and he was caught like a fish on a fishhook, a mouse in a mousetrap, or an arctic fox in a snare, according to what was previously prophesied. Then Our Lord went to him and bound him, and ordered His angels to guard him." Now I shall begin to relate about what had happened in Hell after Satan had left. "The mighty devils in Hell said to the smithy champions: 'Take, O cruel ones, and shut all the gates, and bring forth iron grates and iron bars. Oppose sternly and withstand well, so that you will not be seized, and the captives whom you have held here will [not] be taken from you.'"

XXI.2

"When the saints of God heard this, they said to those evil spirits, '*Lift up* Ps. 24
your gates, so that the King of Glory may come in.' Then the king and prophet (23):7
David began to call out loudly to the men of God: 'It occurred, when I lived and
was called king in the Eastern kingdom, that I prophesied this to you: "*Confess* Ps. 107
to the Lord His mercy, proclaim His name and the marvels that He has done to (106):
the sons of men, for He has worn down the gates of bronze and broken the bars 15–16
of iron. He has taken them up from the way of their iniquity."' Then the prophet Isaiah said: 'Do you know that I have prophesied this when I was alive on earth
that "*the dead would rise up and those who were in* [*their*] *graves would re-* Is. 26:19
joice. Death and Hell shall lose victory."'"

XXI.3

"When the saints of God heard this word of the prophet Isaiah, they called out vehemently to the people of Hell: 'Now open up your gates, otherwise you will be conquered through oppression.' Then they heard a second time such a great
voice that all Hell seemed to quake: '*Lift up your gates, O princes*.' When the Ps. 24
chief devils heard twice shouted that the gates should be opened, they reacted (23):7
with ignorance and replied, '*Who is the King of Glory, the Lord strong and* Ps. 24
mighty, the Lord mighty in battle?' Then David said: 'I recognize those words (23):8
that are being spoken there, for I prophesied this through the Holy Spirit, and I
will tell you: "*The Lord strong and mighty, the Lord mighty in battle, He is the* Ps. 24
King of Glory, who looked down from the height of His sanctuary. The Lord (23):8–10
Himself from Heaven looked down upon earth to hear the groans of those who Ps. 102
had been fettered and free the children of those who had been afflicted." O hid- (101):
eous and filthy ones, open up the gates so that the King of Glory may come in.'" 21–2

XXII.1

"When David had said this, the King of Glory came to the stronghold of Hell, destroyed at once the fortress of Hell and opened up a large gate. He revealed Himself in the shape of a man with such a great light that the darkness of Hell vanished, and every good man was then freed from the bond binding him. Such great power and din has occurred with it, and so quickly He destroyed Hell, that all the devils began to flinch and tremble. And then, immediately after that, when they saw Christ their God walking there, they all bent forward and stared in that direction, and said this: 'Now you have overcome us. Now you have forcefully attacked us and sought to confound us. Be this a wonder and an abomination. He seemed low and little in the body of a servant, slain on the cross and interred. And now you have come here to loose the bonds and free everything.' In a similar way, all the foul ones of Hell began to speak thus: 'Whence are you, Jesus, so strong and so powerful a man, so bright and so sinless? That earthly world, which has for so long paid tribute to us, has never before paid us with such a tribute of death. He is a mighty hero so full of courage that He overcomes our torments and does not fear them and seizes men from bonds. Is it not so now, that Jesus has now come here, of whom Satan our Prince said would alone rule the entire world after His death.'"

XXII.2

"Then the Lord, the King of Glory, began to trample down the Prince of Death and bound him with the blazing bonds of His powers and drew Adam to His brightness."

XXIII.1

"Then the inhabitants of Hell began to talk with their Prince with great reproach and rebuked him: 'Listen,' they said, 'O chief of perdition and Prince of Death, three-headed Beelzebub and scorn of angels. Why did you make fair promises to us about His drawing hither? You have spoken very unwisely. It can now be seen that Christ comes here and drives away with the light of His divinity the darkness of Death and breaks all our enclosures, and He leads all the captives away from here and also many [others] who were accustomed to groaning sorrowfully under our torments, and now everything withholds, for His offspring shall come hereafter. Now it happens that those who could never be joyful are haughty towards us and begin and threaten us. Listen, O Satan, Prince of Hell and of all evil, why did you have to draw Him here so that now it is likely that here there will be no more groaning or crying? In that great stench, which you owned, in dirt and in filth, and your delight in that which you had acquired from the tree of prevarication, you have lost completely through the wood of the cross, and now all your delight shall perish, for you wanted to provoke the King of Glory Himself against yourself. Very thin-witted is your word to have attacked the One who is so sinless, and to have drawn Him here, and now you will be forced to relinquish everything you do not wish to.'"

XXIII.2

"After this, it is said that the King of Glory spoke to the inhabitants of Hell all together: 'Now and hereafter shall Satan be here in the place of Adam and his sons, my righteous ones.'"

XXIV.1

"Then God the Lord stretched out His hand and said this: 'Come to me now, all saints who have my understanding. Know that the Devil and Death are now condemned.' Then they all gathered together and cast themselves running towards the hands of Our Lord. Then Our Lord took Adam's right hand and said this: 'Peace be with you and all your sons, my righteous ones.' Adam fell at the

feet of the Lord and said: '*I will exalt you, O Lord, for you have lifted*,' and Ps. 30
sang four more verses from that psalm. Likewise, all the saints sang and fell at (29):2–5
the feet of the Lord and said, 'You have come and fulfilled what You had promised us and prophesied through the law and the prophets, to free us and the entire world through Your death on the Cross, and Your descent to us, You have come to us from Hell through [Your] glory, with Your power and through the sign of the cross, so that Death does not dominate us any longer.'"

XXIV.2

"Thereafter, the Lord made the sign of the cross over Adam and all the saints, and taking Adam by the hand, He ascended from Hell with a great army, and
all the saints followed the Lord. Then David spoke loudly and sang this: '*Sing* Ps. 98
to the Lord a new song, for He has done marvels.' And he sang two verses from (97):1–2
the next psalm. Thus all the saints sang with him and said amen, and said this: '*This glory is to all his saints. Alleluia*.'"

XXIV.3

"Thereafter, the prophet Habakkuk cried out, '*You destined the salvation of* Ps. 150
Your people and to free your poor ones.' And all the saints replied and said: (149):9
'*Blessed be He who comes in the name of the Lord. God has freed us to eternal* Hab.
life.' The prophet Micah also said, '*Who is a god like Our God*? *You take away* 3:13 Ps. 118
our iniquities and overcome our sins and hold witness of Your anger against (117):
the evil. You are willingly in mercy and turn away from our deaths and put to 26–7
death all our iniquities and all our sins in memory of Your death, as You prom- Mi. 7:19
ised to our fathers.' Then all the saints replied, '*He is Our God unto eternity*, Ps. 48
throughout eternal ages. He shall rule in eternity.' Then they all said amen and (47):15
all the prophets began to sing their words as they followed Our Lord."

XXV

"God ordered the archangel Michael to accompany Adam and all His saints, and to lead them all into the joy of Paradise. Then two men ran towards them and the prophets asked them who they were: 'For you have not been dead with us in Hell, and on the contrary are now physically in Paradise?' Then one of them replied, 'I am called Enoch, and I was brought here with The Word of God, and the one who follows me here is named Elias and is called the Thesbite, who was driven here in a blazing chariot, and we have not died yet. We shall be hidden here until the Antichrist comes and then we shall come to that place and fight against him with the miracles and divine signs of God. He shall slay us in Jerusalem, but after three days and a half, we shall be taken up once more into the clouds.'"

XXVI

"Then it occurred that when Enoch and Elias were talking thusly to each other and to the saints of God, there came forth a most joyless man who had a sign of the cross on his shoulders. When the saints of God saw that man, they asked [him] who he was: 'You seem to us as if you might have been a malefactor, and why is it that you are carrying a sign of the cross?' He replied, 'I was a malefactor and worked all sorts of evil on earth, and the Jews crucified me with Christ. And it occurred, when I saw the wonders which were worked, that I seemed to understand that Christ might be the Creator of all creation. Therefore
I began to beg Him for mercy, and I said this: "*Remember me, O Lord, when*
You come into Your kingdom." At that time He took well my speech and said, Lc. 23:42
"*Verily, I say to you, that today you shall be with me in Paradise*." Then He Lc. 23:43
gave me the sign of the cross and said, "If the angel who is a guard of Paradise forbids you the entrance, then show him this sign of the cross, and say to him this, that Jesus Christ, who is now crucified, has sent you there." Next I did so, I talked to the angel of Paradise, as I was ordered. Then he opened up the gates of Paradise before me and led me to the right-hand side and said, "Here we shall wait a little while, for Adam, father of all mankind, shall come soon with his sons, the saints and righteous of Christ the Lord crucified." When the patriarchs and the prophets heard what the malefactor said, then they all began to say: "Blessed be you, Almighty God, who are so merciful that you grant mercy to the unworthy."'"

XXVII.1

"Carinus and Leucius were not found in their graves after the resurrection of Christ from the dead. On the contrary, they have resurrected with Him and
many others as it is said in the Gospels: '*And the bodies of the saints who had* Mt. 27:52
fallen asleep resurrected. And the bodies of the holy dead men who slept had resurrected.'"

XXVII.2

"Carinus and Leucius were later seen near Arimathea, the city of Joseph, and wrote this section of text about Christ's Descent, for they did not talk to men, and let their book come into the hands of Nicodemus and Joseph, and they read it aloud before others. And many generations later, their book came to the Emperor Theodosius, son of Arcadius. He had it with him in Constantinople and had it read aloud and people were very impressed by it. Blessed be in every way Our Lord, throughout endless ages. Amen."

Niðrstigningar saga

The Younger Redaction

(E Copenhagen, Den Arnamagnæanske Samling, AM 238 fol. V)

XVIII.3

"*This is my Beloved Son in Whom I am well pleased.* And I have travelled before His countenance and I have descended to you in order to tell you this, that the Son of God Himself, raising from the height of Heaven, shall soon come to visit us and all His friends who sit in the obscurities and in the shadow of Death." Mt. 3:16–17

XIX.1

"And when our father Adam heard saying that Jesus is baptized in the River Jordan, he rejoiced exceedingly, and looked towards his son Seth and said to him, 'Listen, my son,' he said, 'Deliver your speech and proclaim to the patriarchs all the things which you have heard from the archangel Michael, when I sent you to the gate of Paradise, so that you might beseech the Lord that He should send His angel and give you the Oil of Mercy from the tree of mercy so that I could anoint my body when I was sick.' Then Seth went forth and spoke to the patriarchs and prophets and said this: 'I, Seth, when I arrived to the gates of Paradise, I saw burning fire which forbade the entrance to each and every man and the angels of God who guarded this gate both against the devils and the sinful men. And as I halted, I became very frightened, and I prayed to the Lord with great fear. Then the archangel Michael appeared to me and spoke to me: "I am sent to you from the Lord. I am appointed over the human body and verily I tell you this, Seth: you do not need to toil with labour or tears beseeching for the Oil of Mercy so that you [may] anoint your father to improve the sickness of his body, for in no way you can take that oil until the very days of the future come, before five thousand hundred and thirty years shall be completed from now. Then shall come upon earth the Beloved Son of God, Christ, to waken the bodies of the dead men. And when He Himself comes, He shall baptize in water and the Holy Spirit. Then He shall anoint with the oil of His mercy all of those who believe, and that Oil of Mercy shall regenerate among those who shall receive it from the water and unto eternal life. Then the Beloved Son of God, Christ, shall descend unto earth, and shall lead Adam, your father, into Paradise to the tree of mercy.'""

XIX.2

"And when all the patriarchs and the prophets heard this thing announced by Seth, they all rejoiced with great joy."

XX.1

"And while all the saints rejoiced with joy, the Prince of Hell, the guide of the dead, in the shape of a dreadful and very hideous dragon, who sometimes appears to them with seven heads and sometimes with three in the shape of a man, screamed with a loud voice to Hell and said, 'Prepare yourself with all the others. Can you receive Jesus who boasts Himself and says that He is Christ,
the Son of God? And [yet] He is a man for He fears death, saying: "*My soul is* Mt.
afflicted, all unto death," and found so many misdeeds against me, and many 26:38
whom I have made blind, lame, crippled, lepers, and tormented with tortures, He cured with His word.'"

XX.2

"Then Hell replied and said to Prince Satan, 'Who is so powerful in words even though He is a man and fears death? For I have held under my power all the mighty princes of the earth, whom you now carry subject with your strength. But if you are mighty, who is this man Jesus who fears death and yet opposes you and your power? If He is so powerful and strong in humanity, truly I tell you, He is almighty in divinity and no one can oppose His strength and might. And if He says He fears death, then He wants to conceal the divinity of His might and it shall not be throughout endless ages.' Then Satan, the Prince of Hell, replied and said, 'Why do you doubt or fear to take that man Jesus, who acts as both my adversary and yours? For I tempted Him and aroused the Jewish people with excessive zeal and wrath against Him. I have sharpened the spear and egged on to thrust Him. I have blended gall to give Him as a drink for His thirst. I have built the wood to crucify Him and now His death is very close, and I will lead Him subject to you and me.'"

XX.3

"Then Hell replied and said, 'You told me that He is the same who drew the dead away from me. And there are many whom I have held subject here, who were taken from me when alive on earth. Who is this Jesus who with His disposition and through divine prayers calls dead men to life, the Almighty who is the one who drew away the dead from me when I thought I would have held them under my power? Is He not the one who freed Lazarus, who had lain in a grave for four days, whom I held dead in my power, and He returned alive through the word of His omnipotence?' Then Satan, Prince of Hell, replies and says, 'So that is Jesus.' And when he said this, Hell heard these things and said to him, 'I adjure you through your powers and mine not to lead Him to me, for when I heard the strong might of His Word I became very frightened with trembling fear, and all the servants were shaken with me. And I could not hold Lazarus with all my strength and fleetness, and he sprang up whole and alive, and the earth itself, which held the mortal body of Lazarus, returned him alive. And, therefore, I know that this man who was able to do all these things is strong in power and mighty in humanity, saviour of all mankind, and He shall free those who are enclosed in the grim dungeon by the severe bonds of
sins and lead them to the life of His divinity.' *Then at that point of the day, and* Ap.
at that time, Heaven opened, and there came forth first a white horse and the 19:11–17
Prince who rode that horse is in many respects more handsome, fair, and lordly than all others. His eyes were like blazing fire. He had a crown on His head, which displayed many tokens of victory. He had a vesture above the others, which was imbrued with blood. On His vesture, over the waist, these words were written: King of kings and Lord of lords. He led with Him a great army. Those who followed Him rode white horses, and all were dressed in white silk and were very bright. Then the most powerful supreme ruler looked towards Jerusalem and said: 'The trap that is in Jerusalem shall harm the Midgard Serpent.' He then lowered His hook into the carrion that was lain in the trap, and done that, He concealed it in such a way that it could not be seen. Then He ordered some of His beloved friends to precede Him and announce His arrival."

XXI.1

"And while they, Prince Satan and Hell, were talking to each other as previously said, there occurred a shrilling voice of a great clap of thunder and a
spiritual cry: '*Open the your gates, and be lifted up, O eternal gates, and the* Ps. 24
King of Glory will come in.' And when Hell heard these words, he said this to (23):7
Satan, his Prince: 'Depart from this place quickly and flee from my seats. And

if you are a mighty warrior, then fight with the King of Glory, for what keeps me bound in duty to Him?' Thereafter he expelled Satan, his Prince, out of his seats. And when Satan was expelled, he looked at the multitude of the heavenly folk and troops, but he did not see that the King of Glory had arrived there and, nevertheless, did not want to go towards them and rather escaped from their countenance. Then he took the shape of an awful dragon, whose largeness is compared to that of the Midgard Serpent, about whom it is said that it lies around the whole world. Then he saw those signs that occurred in Jerusalem, that Our Lord was breathing His last, and immediately."

Bibliography

Primary Sources

Agnesar saga. In *Heilagra manna sögur*, vol. 1, 22.

Agǫtu saga. In *Heilagra manna sögur*, vol. 1, 7–13.

Alciato, Andrea. *Emblematum liber*. Augsburg: Heinrich Steyner, 1531.

Alexíss saga I. In *Heilagra manna sögur*, vol. 1, 23–7.

– In *AM 623 4to: Helgensagaer*, 47–53.

AM 623 4to: Helgensagaer. Edited by Finnur Jónsson. SUGNL 52. København: Jørgensen, 1927.

Andersen, Merete Geert. *Katalog over AM Accessoria 7. De latinske fragmenter*. Bibliotheca Arnamagnæana 7. Hafniæ: C.A. Reitzel Forlag, 2008.

Andersson-Schmitt, Margarete, Håkan Hallberg, and Monica Hedlund. *Mittelalterliche Handschriften der Universitätsbibliothek Uppsala: Katalog über die C-Sammlung*. Vol. 6, *Handschriften C 551–935*. Acta Bibliothecae Regiae Universitatis Upsaliensis 26. Stockholm: Almqvist & Wiksell International, 1993.

Andréss saga postola I. In *Isländska handskriften No. 465 4to*, 124–30.

– In *Postola sögur*, 349–53.

Astås, Reidar, ed. *Stjórn: tekst etter håndskriftene*. Vol. 2. Norrøne tekster 8. Oslo: Riksarkivet, 2009.

Augustine. *De Trinitate*. In *Patrologiae Cursus Completus, Series Latina*, vol. 42, cols. 819–1098.

– *Enarrationes in psalmos LI-C*. Edited by Eligius Dekkers and Johannes Fraipont. CCSL, vol. 39. Turnhout: Brepols, 1956.

– *In Iohannis Evangelium tractatus CXXIV*. Edited by Radbodus Willems. CCSL, vol. 36. Turnhout: Brepols, 1954.

– *Sermones ad populum*. In *Patrologiae Cursus Completus, Series Latina*, vols. 38–9.

– *Sermo* 265D. In *Patrologiae Cursus Completus, Series Latina Supplementum*, vol. 2, cols. 704–8. In *Miscellanea Agostiniana*, vol. 1, 659–64.

Barthólómeuss saga postola I. In *Isländska handskriften No. 645 4to*, 99–108.

– In *Postola sögur*, 757–62.

Belsheim, Johannes, ed. *Evangelium Palatinum: Reliquias IV Evangeliorum ante Hieronymum Latine translatorum / Ex codice Palatino purpureo vindobonensi quarti vel quinti p. Chr. saeculi et ex editione Tischendorfiana principe denuo.* Christianiae: Dybwad, 1896.

Biblia sacra iuxta Vulgatam versionem. Edited by Robert Weber, Boniface Fischer, Jean Gribmont, H.F.D. Sparks, and Walter Thiele. Stuttgart: Deutsche Bibelgesellschaft, 1969. 5th ed. revised by Roger Gryson. Stuttgart: Deutsche Bibelgesellschaft, 2007.

Bischoff, Bernhard. *Katalog der festländischen Handschriften des neunten Jahrhunderts (mit Ausnahme der wisigothischen)*. Vol. 1, *Aachen-Lambach*. Edited by Birgit Ebersperger. Wiesbaden: Harrassowitz, 1998.

Blasíuss saga. In *Heilagra manna sögur*, vol. 1, 256–64, 265–9.

A Book of Miracles: MS No. 645 4to of the Arna-Magnæan Collection in the University Library of Copenhagen. Edited by Anne Holtsmark. Corpus Codicum Islandicorum Medii Aevi 12. Copenhagen: Einar Munksgaard, 1938.

Brøndum-Nielsen, Johannes, ed. *Et gammeldansk digt om Christi opstandelse efter fragment Stockh. *A 115 (c. 1315)*. Det Kongelige Danske Videnskabernes Selskab, Historisk-filologiske Meddelelser 35, pt. 1. København: Munksgaard, 1995.

Bullitta, Dario, ed. and trans. *Páls leizla. The Vision of St Paul.* Viking Society for Northern Research Text Series. London: University College of London, forthcoming.

Byskupa sǫgur. Edited by Jón Helgason. Editiones Arnamagnæanæ, Ser. A, vol. 13, pt. 2. København: Reitzel, 1978.

Byskupa sögur. Vol. 2, edited by Ásdís Egilsdóttir. Íslenzk fornrit 16. Reykjavík: Hið Íslenzka Fornritafélag, 2002.

Carron, Helen, ed. and trans. *Clemens saga. The Life of St Clement of Rome.* Viking Society for Northern Research Text Series 17. London: University College of London, 2005.

Dansk biografisk Lexikon tillige omfattende Norge for tidsrummet 1537–1814. Edited by C.F. Bricka. 19 vols. København: Gyldendal, 1887–1905.

de Leeuw van Weenen, Andrea, ed. *The Icelandic Homily Book, Perg. 15 4° in the Royal Library Stockholm*, ÍH, Series in Quarto, vol. 3. Reykjavík: Stofnun Árna Magnússonar á Íslandi, 1993.

Diplomatarium Islandicum. Íslenzkt fornbréfasafn. Edited by Jón Sigurðsson. 16 vols. København: S.L. Möllers; Reykjavík: Hið íslenzka bókmentafélag, 1857–59.

Dolbeau, François, ed. "Vie latine de sainte Ame, composée au XIe siècle par Étienne, abbé de Saint-Urbain." *Analecta Bollandiana* 105 (1987): 25–63.

Elliott, J.K., trans. *The Apocryphal New Testament: A Collection of Apocryphal Christian Literature in an English Translation Based on M.R. James*. Oxford: Clarendon Press, 1993. Paperback ed. Oxford: Oxford University Press, 2005.

Finnur Jónsson, ed. *Jón Arason religiøse digte*. Det Kongelige Danske Videnskabernes Selskab. Historisk-filologiske meddelelser 2, pt. 2. København: Høst & Søn, 1918.

Floyer, John K., and Sidney G. Hamilton *Catalogue of Manuscripts Preserved in the Chapter Library of Worcester Cathedral*. Oxford: Printed for the Worcester Historical Society by James Parker, 1906.

Foote, Peter, ed. "A Fragment of Text in AM 235 fol." In *Twenty-Eight Papers Presented to Hans Bekker-Nielsen on the Occasion of His Sixtieth Birthday 28 April 1993*, 237–55. Odense: Odense University Press, 1993.

Gilson, Julius Parnell, ed. *The Mozarabic Psalter (ms. British Museum, Add. 30851)*. Henry Bradshaw Society 30. London: Harrison and Sons, 1905.

Gregory the Great. *Homiliae in evangelia*. Edited and translated by Raymond Étaix. Corpus Christianorum Series Latina, vol. 141. Turnhout: Brepols, 1999. *Patrologiae Cursus Completus, Series Latina*, vol. 76, cols. 1075–314.

Gregory of Nyssa. *Oratio Catechetica magna*. In *Patrologiae Cursus Completus, Series Graeca*, vol. 45, cols. 9–106.

Gryson, Roger, ed. *Vetus Latina. Die Reste der altlateinischen Bibel*. Vol. 12, pt. 1, *Esaias*. Freiburg im Brisgau: Herder, 1987.

Hallgrímur J. Ámundason, ed. "AM 655 XXVII 4to: Útgáfa, stafagerð, stafsetning." BA thesis. Reykjavík: Háskóli Íslands, 1994.

Hart, William E., and Ponsonby A. Lyons, eds. *Cartularium monasterii de Rameseia*, vol. 2. Cambridge Library Collection – Rolls. Cambridge: Cambridge University Press, 2012.

Haugen, Odd Einar, ed. "Niðrstigningar saga." In *Norrøne tekster i utval*. Edited by Odd Einar Haugen, 250–65. Oslo: Ad Notam Gyldendal, 1994.

Heilagra manna sögur. Fortællinger og legender om hellige mænd og kvinder. Edited by Carl R. Unger. 2 vols. Christiania: B.M. Bentzen, 1877.

Henningham, Eleanor Kellogg, ed. *An Early Latin Debate of the Body and Soul. Preserved in MS Royal 7 A III in the British Museum*. New York: New York University, 1939.

Hildebert of Lavardin. *Sermones de tempore*. In *Patrologiae Cursus Completus, Series Latina*, vol. 171, cols. 343–606.

Hofmann, Dietrich, ed. *Die Legende von Sankt Clemens in den skandinavischen Länder im Mittelalter*. Beiträge zur Skandinavistik 13. Frankfurt am Main: Peter Lang, 1997.

Homburger, Otto. *Die illustrierten Handschriften der Burgerbibliothek Bern. Die vorkarolingischen und karolongischen Handschriften*. Bern: Selbstverlag der Burgerbibliothek Bern, 1962.

Hreinn Benediktsson, ed. *Early Icelandic Script as Illustrated in the Vernacular Texts of the Twelfth and Thirteenth Centuries*. ÍH, Series in Folio II. Reykjavík: The Manuscript Institute of Iceland, 1965.

Hulme, William H., ed. *The Middle English Harrowing of Hell and Gospel of Nicodemus*. Early English Text Society 100. London: Paul, Trench, Trübner & Co., 1907.

Hungrvaka. In *Byskupa sögur*, vol. 2, 2–43.

Häring, Nikolaus, ed. "The *Eulogium ad Alexandrum papam tertium* of John of Cornwall." *Mediaeval Studies* 13 (1951): 253–300.

Indrebø, Gustav, ed. *Gamal norsk Homiliebok Cod. AM 619 4to*, Norsk historisk kjeldeskrift-institutt, Skrifter 54. Oslo: Jacob Dybwad, 1931.

Isländska handskriften No. 645 4to i den Arnamagnæanska samlingen på universitets-biblioteket i København i diplomatariskt aftryck. Edited by Ludvig Larsson. Lund: Gleerup, 1885.

Íslenzk miðaldakvæði. Islandske digte fra senmiddelalderen. Edited by Jón Helgason. 2 vols. København: Ejnar Munksgaard, 1936–8.

Íslenzkar æviskrár frá landnámstímum til ársloka 1940 (*1948–1976*). Edited by Páll Eggert Ólason, Jón Guðnason, and Ólafur Þ. Kristjánsson. 6 vols. Reykjavík: Hið íslenzka bókmenntafélags, 1948–76.

Izydorczyk, Zbigniew. *Manuscripts of Evangelium Nicodemi: A Census*. Subsidia Mediaevalia 21. Toronto: Pontifical Institute of Mediaeval Studies, 1993.

Jakobs saga postola (*ins eldra*) I. In *Postola sögur*, 513–29.

James, Montague R. *A Descriptive Catalogue of the Manuscripts in the Library of St John's College*. Cambridge: Cambridge University Press, 1912.

Jarðabók Árna Magnússonar og Páls Vídalíns. 2nd ed. Edited by Hið íslenska fræðafélag. 13 vols. Reykjavík: Sögufélag, 1980–90.

Jarteinabók Þorláks byskups in forna. In *Byskupa sögur*. vol. 2, 103–40.

Jarteinabók Þorláks byskups ǫnnur. In *Byskupa sögur*. vol. 2, 227–50.

Jón Helgason, ed. *Kvæðabók úr Vigur. AM 148 8vo*. Kaupmannahöfn: Híð íslenska fræðafélag, 1955.

– ed. *Niðrstigningarvísur*. In *Íslenzk miðaldakvæði. Islandske digte fra senmiddelalderen*, vol. 1, pt. 2, 212–38. København: Ejnar Munksgaard, 1936.

Jóns saga baptista II. In *Postola sögur*, 849–52, 873–85, 925–31.

Jóns saga postola III. In *Postola sögur*, 455–65.

Jørgensen, Ellen. *Catalogus codicum latinorum medii aevii Bibliothecae Regiae Hafniensis*. Hafniae: Prostat in Ædibus Gyldendalianis, 1926.

Kålund, Kristian. *Katalog over Den arnamagnæanske Håndskriftsamling*. 2 vols. København: Gyldendalske Boghandel, 1889–94.

Karl Jónsson, ed. *Saga Sverris konungs*. Fornmanna sögur 8. Kaupmannahöfn: Hin konúngliga norræna fornfræðafélag, 1834.

Katrínar saga I. In *Heilagra manna sögur*, vol. 1, 401–21.

Kim, Hack C., ed. *The Gospel of Nicodemus: Gesta Salvatoris. Edited from the Codex Einsidlensis, Einsiedeln Stiftsbibliothek, MS 326*. Toronto Medieval Latin Texts 2. Toronto: Pontifical Institute of Mediaeval Studies, 1973.

Klemming, Gustaf E., ed. *Klosterläsning. Järteckensbok, Apostla gerningar, Helga manna lefverne, Legender, [och] Nichodemi Evangelium efter gammal handskrift*. SSFS 22. Stockholm: Nordstedt & Söner, 1877–8.

Kross saga II. In *Heilagra manna sögur*, vol. 1, 301–8.

Latínubrót um Þórlaks byskups. In *Byskupa sögur*, vol. 2, 341–64.

Lombard, Peter. *Collectaneorum in Paulum continuatio: In Epistolam ad Hebræos, Caput* II. In *Patrologiae Cursus Completus, Series Latina*, vol. 192, cols. 414–24.

– *Sententiae in IV libris distinctae*. Edited by Ignatius Brady. Spicilegium Bonaventurianum 4–5. Grottaferrata: Editiones Collegii S. Bonaventurae Ad Claras Aqua, 1971–81.

– *The Sentences*. Translated by Giulio Silano. Toronto: Pontifical Institute of Mediaeval Studies, 2007–10.

Lowe, Elias A., ed. *Codices latini antiquiores. A Paleographical Guide to Latin Manuscripts Prior to the Ninth Century*. 11 vols. Oxford: Clarendon Press, 1963.

Marcel, Richard, ed. *Hippolytus Werke*. Vol. 1, *Kommentar zu Daniel*. Die griechischen christlichen Schriftsteller der ersten drei Jahrhunderte, Neue Folge 7. Berlin: Akademie Verlag, 2000.

Margrétar saga I. In *Heilagra manna sögur*, vol. 1, 474–81.

Maríu Saga. Legender om Jumfru Maria og hendes Jertegn. Vol. 1. Edited by Carl R. Unger. Christiania: Brögger & Christie, 1871.

Martinus saga byskups I. In *Heilagra manna sögur*, vol. 1, 554–74.

Masser, Achim, ed. *Dat ewangelium Nicodemi van deme lidende unses heren Ihesu Christi. Zwei mittelniederdeutsche Fassungen*. Texte des späten Mittelalters und der frühen Neuzeit 29. Berlin: E. Schmidt, 1978.

Masser, Achim, and Max Siller, eds. *Das Evangelium Nicodemi in spätmittelalterlicher deutscher Prosa. Texte*. Germanische Bibliothek, Reihe 4, Texte und Kommentar. Heidelberg: Carl Winter Universitätsverlag, 1987.

Mattheus saga postola. In *Postola sögur*, 797–841.

Meyer, Wilhelm, ed. "Vita Adae et Evae." In *Abhandlung der Philosophisch-philologischen Klasse der königlich bayerischen Akademie der Wissenschaften*, vol. 14, 185–250. Munich: Verlag der königlichen Akademie in Commission bei G. Franz, 1878.

Miscellanea Agostiniana. Vol. 1, *Sancti Augustini Sermones post Maurinos reperti*. Edited by Germain Morin. Rome: Tipografia poliglotta vaticana, 1930.

Mǫrtu saga ok Maríu Magðalenu II. In *Heilagra manna sögur*, vol. 1, 513–51.

Nicholas of Lyra. *Textus Biblie cum glossa ordinaria, et exposition Lyre litterali et morali, necnon additionibus ac replicis super epistolas ad Romanos*. Vol. 6. Basel, 1508.

Niðrstigningar saga I. In *Heilagra manna sögur*, vol. 2, 1–17.

Niðrstigningar saga II. In *Heilagra manna sögur*, vol. 2, 17–20.

Ordbog over det norrøne prosasprog. A Dictionary of Old Norse Prose. 3 vols. (*A-em*) and 12 indices. Edited by Helle Degnbol, Bent C. Jacobsen, James E. Knirk, Eva Rode, Christoper Sanders, and Þorbjörg Helgadóttir. København: Den arnamagnæanske Kommission, 1989. Available at http://onp.ku.dk/.

Overgaard, Mariane, ed. *The History of the Cross-Tree Down to Christ's Passion: Icelandic Legend Versions*. Editiones Arnamagnæane, ser. B, vol. 26. Copenhagen: Munksgaard, 1968.

Ólafur Halldórsson, ed. *Mattheus saga postula*. Reykjavík: Stofnun Árna Magnússonar á Íslandi, 1994.

Patrologiae Cursus Completus, Series Graeca. Edited by Jacques-Paul Migne. 161 vols. Paris: Migne, 1857–66.

Patrologiae Cursus Completus, Series Latina. Edited by Jacques-Paul Migne. 221 vols. Paris: Migne, 1884–55.

Patrologiae Cursus Completus, Series Latina Supplementum. Edited by Adalbert Hamman. 6 vols. Paris: Édition Garnier Frères, 1961.

Páls saga byskups. In *Byskupa sögur*, vol. 2, 297–332.

Páls saga postola I. In *Postola sögur*, 216–36.

Pettorelli, Jean-Pierre, ed. "La vie latine d'Adam et Eve." *Archivum latinitatis medii aevi* 56 (1998): 18–104.

Pétrs saga postola I. In *Isländska handskriften No. 645*, 74–90.

– In *Postola sögur*, 201–11.

Postola sögur. Legendariske fortællinger om apostlernes liv, deres kamp for kristendommens udbredelse samt deres martyrdød. Edited by Carl R. Unger. Christiania: B.M. Bentzen, 1874.

Pseudo-Augustine. *Sermo* CLX *De Pascha* II. In *Patrologiae Cursus Completus, Series Latina*, vol. 39, cols. 2059–61 [olim Augustine].

– *Sermo* CLX *De Pascha* II. In *Patrologiae Cursus Completus, Series Latina*, vol. 208, cols. 925–32 [olim Martin of Léon with the title *Sermo vicesimus quintus. De Resurrectione Domini*].

Romero-Posé, Eugenio, ed. *Sancti Beati a Liébana Commentarius in Apocalypsin*. Rome: Typis Officinae Polygraphicae, 1985.

Saga af Fídes, Spes, Caritas II. In *Heilagra manna sögur*, vol. 1, 372–6.

Schaff, Philip, and Henry Wallace, trans. *Nicene and Post-Nicene Fathers*, ser. 2. Vol. 5, *Gregory of Nyssa: Dogmatic Treatises*. Grand Rapids, MI: Christian Classics Etherial Library, 1982. Reprint, New York: Christian Literature Publishing Co., 1983.

Scrivener, Frederick H., ed. *Bezae Codex Cantabrigiensis, Being an Exact Copy in Ordinary Type, of the Celebrated Uncial Greco-Latin manuscript of the Four*

Gospels and Acts of the Apostles, Written Early in the Sixth Century, and Presented to the University of Cambridge by Theodore Bezae, A.D. 1581. Cambridge: University of Cambridge, 1864.

Sjau sofanda saga. In *Heilagra manna sögur*, vol. 1, 236–40.

– In *AM 623 4to*: *Helgensagaer*, 54–9.

Stefán Karlsson, ed. *Sagas of Icelandic Bishops*: *Fragments of Eight Manuscripts*. Early Icelandic Manuscripts in Facsimile 7. Copenhagen: Rosenkilde and Bagger, 1967.

Sylwan, Agneta, ed. *Petri Comestoris Scolastica Historia. Liber Genesis*. Corpus Christianorum Continuatio Mediaevalis 191. Turnhout: Brepols, 2005.

Thilo, Johann C., ed. *Codex apocryphus Novi Testamenti e libris editis et manuscriptis, maxime Gallicanis, Germanicis, et Italicis, collectus, recensitus et prolegomenis illustratus*. Vol. 1. Lipsiae: Sumptibus Frid. Christ. Guilielmi Vogel, 1832.

Thorpe, Benjamin, ed. *Libri Psalmorum versio antiqua Latina cum Paraphrasi Anglo-Saxonica, partim soluta oratione, partim metrice composita. Nunc primum E cod. MS. in Bibl. Regia Parisiensi adversato*. Oxford: E Typografico Academico, 1835.

Unterkircher, Franz. *Die datierten Handschriften der Österreichische Nationalbibliothek bis zum Jahre 1400*. 2 vols. Wien: Austrian Academy of Sciences Press, 1969.

von Tischendorf, Constantin, ed. *Evangelia Apocrypha. Adhibitis plurimis codicibus graecis et latinis maximam partem nunc primum cunsultis atque ineditorum copia insignibus*. Leipzig: Avenarius et Mendelssohn, 1853.

Widding, Ole, and Hans Bekker-Nielsen, eds. “A Debate of the Body and the Soul in Old Norse Literature.” *Mediaeval Studies* 21 (1959): 272–89.

Wolf, Kirsten, ed. “Saga af Fídes, Spes, Caritas.” *Gripla* 22 (2009): 56–61.

Wordsworth, John, ed. *The Gospel According to Matthew from St. Germain Ms. g1. Now Numbered Lat 11553 in the National Library at Paris*. Oxford: Clarendon Press, 1883.

Wordsworth, John, and Henry I. White, eds. *Nouum Testamentum Domini nostri Iesu Christi Latine secundum editionem sancti Hieronymi*. Vol. 1, *Quattor Euangelia*. Oxford: Clarendon Press, 1889–98.

Wright, David H., ed. *The Vespasian Psalter: British Museum, Cotton Vespasian A.I.*. With a contribution on the gloss by Alistair Campbell. Early English Manuscripts in Facsimile 14. Copenhagen: Rosenkilde and Bagger, 1967.

Þórlaks saga byskups in elzta. In *Byskupa sögur*, vol. 2, 47–99.

Secondary Sources

Aho, Gary L. “A Comparison of Old English and Old Norse Treatments of Christ’s Harrowing of Hell.” PhD diss. University of Oregon, 1966.

– “*Niðrstigningarsaga*: An Old Norse Version of Christ’s Harrowing of Hell.” *Scandinavian Studies* 41 (1969): 150–9.

Astås, Reidar. *Et bibelverk fra middelalderen. Studier i Stjórn I.* 2nd rev. ed. Tønsberg: Høgskolen i Vestfold, 2010. http://www-bib.hive.no/tekster/Astaas-2010-Et-bibelverk-fra-middelalderen.pdf.

Aulén, Gustaf. *Christus Victor: An Historical Study of the Three Main Types of the Idea of Atonement.* Translated by A.G. Herbert. London: SPCK, 1931. Reprint, New York: McMillan, 1969. Originally published as *Den kristna försoningstanken.* Stockholm: Svenska Kyrkans diakonistyrelses bokförlag, 1930.

Ásdís Egilsdóttir. "St. Þorlákr in Iceland: The Emergence of a Cult." *The Haskins Society Journal* 12 (2003): 121–32.

– "The Beginnings of Local Hagiography in Iceland: The Lives of Bishops Þorlákr and Jón." In *The Making of Christian Myths in the Periphery of Latin Christendom (c. 1000–1300)*, edited by Lars Boje Mortensen, 121–33. Copenhagen: Museum Tusculanum Press, 2006.

BeDuhn, Jason D. *Augustine's Manichaean Dilemma.* Vol. 2, *Making a "Catholic" Self, 388–401 C.E.* Divinations: Rereading Late Ancient Religion. Philadelphia: University of Philadelphia Press, 2013.

Beer, Rudolf. *Die Handschriften des Klosters Santa Maria de Ripoll.* Vol. 155, *Sitzungsberichte der Philosophisch-historischen Klasse der Kaiserlichen Akademie der Wissenschaften in Wien.* 3 Abhandlung. Wien: Akademie der Wissenschaften, 1907.

Bekker-Nielsen, Hans. "Nikodemusevangeliet." In *Kulturhistorisk Leksikon for nordisk middelalder*, vol. 12, cols. 308–10. København: Rosenkilde and Bagger, 1967.

– "The Victorines and Their Influence on Old Norse Literature." In *The Fifth Viking Congress, Tórshavn July 1965, Proceedings*, edited by Bjarni Niclasen, 32–6. Tórshavn: Føroya Fróskaparfelag, 1968.

Berchtold, Jacques. *Des rats et des ratières: anamorphoses d'un champ métaphorique de saint Augustin à Jean Racine*. Geneva: Librairie Droz, 1992.

Bischoff, Bernhard. *Die südostdeutschen Schreibschulen und Bibliotheken in der Karolingerzeit.* 2 vols. Leipzig: Otto Harrassovitz, 1974–80.

Bonnet, Guillaume. "Survivance du grec en occident au IXe siècle: une consultation à Laon." In *Survivances et métamorphoses*, edited by Hervé Duchêne, 263–78. Dijon: Université de Bourgogne, 2005.

Bradshaw, David. "The *Opuscula Sacra*: Boethius and Theology." In *The Cambridge Companion to Boethius*, edited by John Marenbon, 105–28. Cambridge: Cambridge University Press, 2009.

Bullitta, Dario. "*Crux Christi muscipula fuit diabolo.* Un sermone agostiniano dietro la cattura di Satana nella *Niðrstigningar saga*." In *Intorno alle saghe norrene*, edited by Carla Falluomini, 129–54. Seminario Avanzato in Filologia Germanica XIV. Alessandria: Edizioni dell'Orso, 2014.

– "The Old Swedish *Evangelium Nicodemi* in the Library of Vadstena Abbey: Provenance and Fruition." *Scandinavian Studies* 86 (2014): 268–307.

– "The Story of Joseph of Arimathea in AM 655 XXVII 4to." *Arkiv för nordisk filologi* 131 (2016): 47–74.

Böhm, Dorothee. "Von der Höllenfahrt Christi zu den Topo-Analysen des modernen Subjektgehäuses. Die Darstellung des Descensus Christi und ihr Nachleben in der bildenden Kunst des 20. Jahrhunderts." In *Höllen-Fahrten. Geschichte und Aktualität eines Mythos*, edited by Markwart Herzog, 131–50. Stuttgart: Kohlhammer, 2006.

Campbell, Jackson J. "To Hell and Back: Latin Tradition and Literary Use of the *Descensus ad Inferos* in Old English." *Viator* 13 (1982): 107–58.

Colish, Martia L. *Peter Lombard*. 2 vols. Brill's Studies in Intellectual History 41. Leiden: Brill, 1994.

Contreni, John J. "Three Carolingian Texts Attributed to Laon: Reconsiderations." *Studi medievali* 17 (1976): 797–813.

– *The Cathedral School of Laon from 850 to 930. Its Manuscripts and Masters.* Münchener Beiträge zur Mediävistik und Renaissance-Forschung 29. München: Arbeo-Gesellschaft, 1978.

Cormack, Margaret. *The Saints of Iceland. Their Veneration from the Conversion to 1400.* Subsidia Hagiographica 78. Brussels: Société des Bollandistes, 1994.

Cross, James E. "The Use of Patristic Homilies in the Old English Martyrology." *Anglo-Saxon England* 14 (1985): 107–28.

– "Saint-Omer 202 as the Manuscript Source for the Old English Texts." In *Two Old English Apocrypha*, 82–104.

Cross, James E., and Julia Crick. "The Manuscript: Saint-Omer, Bibliothèque Municipale, 202." In *Two Old English Apocrypha*, 10–35.

Curley, Michael. "John of Cornwall." In *Celtic Culture: A Historical Encyclopedia*, vol. 1, edited by John T. Koch, 1038. Santa Barbara: ABC-CLIO, 2006.

Dabley, Marcia A. "Patterns of Preaching in the Blickling Easter Homily." *American Benedictine Review* 24 (1981): 478–92.

Dendle, Peter J. *Satan Unbound: The Devil in Old English Narrative Literature.* Toronto: University of Toronto Press, 2001.

di Paolo Healey, Antonette. "Anglo-Saxon Use of the Apocryphal Gospel." In *The Anglo-Saxons: Synthesis and Achievement*, edited by James D. Woods and David A. E. Pelteret, 93–104. Waterloo: Wilfrid Laurier University Press, 1985.

Dubois, Jean-Daniel. "La représentation de la Passion dans la liturgie du Vendredi Saint: Les 'Actes des Pilate' et la liturgie ancienne de Jérusalem." In *Liturgie et anthropologie: Conférences Saint-Serge, XXVIe semaine d'études liturgiques, Paris, 27–30 juin 1989*, edited by Achille M. Triacca and Alessandro Pistoia, 77–89. Roma: C.L.V. Edizioni liturgiche, 1990.

Dumville, David N. "Liturgical Drama and Panegyric Responsory from the Eighth Century? A Re-examination of the Origin and Contents of the Ninth Century Section of the Book of Cerne." *Journal of Theological Studies* 23 (1972): 374–406.

Durrenberger, E. Paul, and Gísli Pálsson. *The Anthropology of Iceland*. Iowa City: University of Iowa Press, 1989.

Edward, Grant. *The Foundations of Modern Science in the Middle Ages. Their Religious, Institutional, and Intellectual Contexts*. Cambridge Studies in the History of Science. Cambridge: Cambridge University Press, 1996.

Gijsel, Jan. *Die unmittelbare Textüberlieferung des sog. Pseudo-Matthäus*. Verhandelingen van de Koninklijke Academie voor Wetenschappen, Letteren en Schone Kunsten van België. Klasse der Letteren, vol. 43, n. 96. Bruxelles: Paleis der Academiën, 1981.

Gschwantler, Otto. "Christus, Thor und die Midgardschlange." In *Festschrift für Otto Höfler zum 65. Geburtstag*, vol. 1, edited by Helmut Birkhan, Otto Gschwantler, and Irmgard Hansberger-Wilflinger, 145–68. Wien: Verlag Notring, 1968.

Gyllerup, Sophus M. "Skonning, Hans Hanssen." In *Dansk biografisk Lexikon*, vol. 16, edited by C.F. Bricka, 58–61. København: Gyldendal, 1902.

Haugen, Odd Einar. "Between Graphonomy and Phonology: Deciding on Scribes in AM 645 4to." In *Papers from the Tenth Scandinavian Conference of Linguistics*, vol. 1, edited by Victoria Rosén, 254–72. Bergen: Institutt for fonetikk og lingvistikk, Universitet i Bergen, 1988.

– ed. *Stamtre og tekstlandskap: Studiar i resensjonsmetodikk med grunnlag i Niðrstigningar saga*. 2nd rev. ed. 2 vols. PhD diss. Bergen: Nordisk institutt, Universitetet i Bergen, 1992.

– ed. "Soga om nedstiginga i dødsriket. Den norrøne omsetjinga av Nikodemus-evangeliet." *Agora* 2 (1994): 84–114.

– "The Development of the Latin Script I: in Norway." In *The Nordic Languages*, vol. 1, 824–32.

Haynes, Justin. "New Perspectives on the *Evangelium Nicodemi* Latin C: A Consideration of the Manuscripts on the Way to a Modern Critical Edition." *Apocrypha* 21 (2010): 103–12.

Hennecke, Edgar. *Handbuch zu den Neutestamentlichen Apokryphen in Verbindung mit Fachgelehrten*. Tübingen: Mohr Siebeck, 1904.

Hoffmann, Werner J. "The *Gospel of Nicodemus* in Dutch and Low German Literatures of the Middle Ages." In *The Medieval Gospel of Nicodemus*, 346–9.

Izquierdo, Josep. "The *Gospel of Nicodemus* in Medieval Catalan and Occitan Literatures." In *The Medieval Gospel of Nicodemus*, 133–64.

Izydorczyk, Zbigniew. "Introduction." In *The Medieval Gospel of Nicodemus*, 1–20.

– "The *Evangelium Nicodemi* in the Latin Middle Ages." In *The Medieval Gospel f Nicodemus*, 43–102.

– "The Latin Source of an Old French *Gospel of Nicodemus*." *Revue d'histoire des textes* 25 (1995): 265–79.

– "Two Newly Identified Manuscripts of *Sermo de confusione diaboli*." *Scriptorium* 43 (1989): 253–5.

– "The Unfamiliar *Evangelium Nicodemi*." *Manuscripta* 33 (1989): 169–91.

Izydorczyk, Zbigniew, and Dario Bullitta, "The Troyes Redaction of the *Evangelium Nicodemi* and Its Vernacular Legacy." In *Gnose et manichéisme. Entre les oasis d'Égypte et la Route de la Soie: Hommage à Jean-Daniel Bubois*, edited by Anna Van der Kerchove and Luciana G. Soares Santoprete, 571–617. Bibliothèque de l'École des Hautes Études, Sciences Religieuses 176. Turnhout: Brepols Publishers, 2016.

Izydorczyk, Zbigniew, and Jean-Daniel Dubois. "Nicodemus's Gospel Before and Beyond the Medieval West." In *The Medieval Gospel of Nicodemus*, 21–42.

Janssen, Johannes. *Geschichte des deutschen Volkes seit dem Ausgang des Mittelalters*. 8 vols. Freiburg in Brisgau: Herder, 1894.

Jón Helgason. "Bækur og handrit á tveimur húnvetnskum höfuðbólum á 18du öld." *Landsbókasafn Íslands Árbók 1983. Nýr flokkur 9. ár* (1983): 5–46.

Jón Hnefill Aðalsteinsson. *Under the Cloak: The Acceptance of Christianity in Iceland with Particular Reference to the Religious Attitudes Prevailing at that Time*. Acta Universitatis Upsaliensis. Studia Ethnologica Upsaliensia 4. Stockholm: Almqvist & Wiksell, 1978.

Jónas Gíslason. "Island (till 1700)." In *Ur nordisk kulturhistoria: Universitetsbesöken i utlandet före 1660*, edited by Mauno Jokipii and Ilkka Nummela, 119–140. Studia historica Jyväskyläensia vol. 22.1. Jyväskylä: Jyväskylän yliopisto, 1981.

Kirby, Ian J. *Bible Translation in Old Norse*. Université de Lausanne, Publications de la faculté des Lettres 27. Geneva: Librairie Droz, 1986.

Klausner, David N. "The *Gospel of Nicodemus* in the Literature of Medieval Wales." In *The Medieval Gospel of Nicodemus*, 403–18.

Kuhn, Hans. "The Emergence of a Saint's Cult as Witnessed by the *Jarteinabœkr Þorláks byskups*," *Saga-Book* 24 (1996): 240–54.

Kulturhistorisk Leksikon for nordisk middelalder. 22 vols. Edited by Hjeile Brendt, Johannes Brondsted, John Danstrup, Lis Jacobsen, Allan Karker, Olaf Olsen, Georg Rona, Peter Skautrup, and Niels Skyrum-Nielsen. København: Rosenkilde and Bagger, 1956–78.

Laistner, Max L.W. "*Rivipullensis* 74 and the *Scolica* of Martin of Laon." In *Mélanges Mandonnet. Études d'histoire littéraire et doctrinale du moyen age*, vol. 2, edited by Pierre Mandonnet, O.P., 31–7. Bibliothèque Tomiste XIV. Paris: Librairie Philosophique J. Vrin, 1930.

Langley, Kyle. "The *Niðrstigningarsaga*: Christ's Battle with the Miðgarðr Serpent." *The Colorado Historian. An Undergraduate Journal* (2011): 18–22.

Lima, Robert. "The Mouth of Hell: the Iconography of Damnation on the Stage of the Middle Ages." In *European Iconography East and West. Selected Papers of the Szeged International Conference. June 9–12, 1993*, edited by György E. Szónyi, 35–48. Symbola et Emblemata: Studies in Renaissance and Baroque Symbolism 7. Leiden: Brill, 1995.

Lobrichon, Guy. "Une nouveauté, les gloses de la Bible." In *Le Moyen Age et la Bible*, edited by Pierre Riché and Guy Lobrichon, 95–114. Bible des tous les temps 4. Paris: Beauchsene, 1984.

Lynch, Katherine E. "Satan Bound: The Devil and the Imagery of Physical Constraint in Early Medieval England." PhD diss. University of Wisconsin, 2010.

Maas, Paul. *Textual Criticism*. Translated by Barbara Flower. Oxford: Clarendon Press, 1958. Originally published as *Textkritik*, 3rd rev. ed. Leipzig: Teubner, 1957.

MacCulloch, John A. *The Harrowing of Hell: A Comparative Study of an Early Christian Doctrine*. Edinburgh: T. & T. Clark, 1930.

Magnús Már Lárusson. "Um Niðurstigningarsögu." *Skírnir* 129 (1955): 159–68.

Marchand, James W. "Leviathan and the Mousetrap in the *Niðrstigningarsaga*." *Scandinavian Studies* 47 (1975): 328–38.

Marenbon, John. "Carolingian Thought." In *Carolingian Culture: Emulation and Innovation*, edited by Rosamond McKitterick, 183–4. Cambridge: Cambridge University Press, 1984.

Marsden, Richard. *The Text of the Old Testament in Anglo-Saxon England*. CSAE 15. Cambridge: Cambridge University Press, 1995.

Marsh, David. *Renaissance Fables: Aesopic Prose by Leon Battista Alberti, Bartolomeo Scala, Leonardo da Vinci, Bernardino Baldi*. Tempe: Arizona Center for Medieval Renaissance and Studies, 2004.

Matter, E. Ann. "The Apocalypse in Early Medieval Exegesis." In *The Apocalypse in the Medieval Ages*, edited by Richard K. Emmerson and Bernard McGinn, 38–50. Ithaca: Cornell University Press, 1992.

Mazzaferri, Frederick D. *The Genre of the Book of Revelation from a Source-Critical Perspective*. Beihefte zur Zeitschrift für die neutestamentliche Wissenschaft 54. Berlin: de Gruyter, 1989.

McNamara, Martin. *The Psalms in the Early Irish Church*. Journal for the Study of the Old Testament, Supplement Series 165. Sheffield: Sheffield Academic Press, 2000.

The Medieval Gospel of Nicodemus. Texts, Intertexts and Contexts in Western Europe. Edited by Zbigniew Izydorczyk. MRTS 158. Tempe: Arizona Board of Regents for Arizona State University, 1997.

Meulengracht Sørensen, Preben. "Thor's fishing expedition." In *Words and Objects: Towards a Dialogue between Archeology and the History of Religion*, edited by Gro Steinsland, 257–78. Oslo: Norwegian University Press, 1986.

Meyer, Wilhelm. "Die Geschichte des Kreuzholzes vor Christus." *Abhandlung der Philosophisch-philologischen Klasse der königlich bayerischen Akademie der Wissenschaften*, vol. 16.2, 101–66. München: Verlag der königlichen Akademie in Kommission bei G. Franz, 1882.

Mogk, Eugen. *Geschichte der norwegisch-isländischen Literatur*. 2nd rev. ed. Strassburg: Trübner, 1904.

Monagle, Clare. *Christological Nihilism in the Twelfth Century: The Contested Reception of Peter Lombard's "Sententiae."* Turnhout: Brepols, 2007.

Morey, James H. "Peter Commestor, Biblical Paraphrase and the Medieval Popular Bible." *Speculum* 68 (1993): 6–35.

Morin, Germain. "Un sermon inédit de saint Augustine pour la fête de l'Ascension." *Revue bénédictine 41*, (1929): 134–43.

Mork, Endre. "Morphological Developments from Old Nordic to Early Modern Nordic: Inflexion and Word Formation." *The Nordic Languages* 2 (2005): 1128–48.

The Nordic Languages: An International Handbook of the History of the North Germanic Languages. 2 vols. Edited by Oskar Bandle, Kurt Braunmüller, Ernst Hakon Jahr, Allan Karker, Hans-Peter Naumann, Ulf Telemann, Lennart Elmevik, and Gun Widmark. Handbücher zur Sprach- und Kommunikationswissenschaft, vols. 22.1–2. Berlin: De Gruyter, 2002–5.

Ólafur Halldórsson. *Helgafellsbækur fornar*. Studia Islandica 24. Reykjavík: Heimspekideild Háskóla Íslands og Bókaútgafa Menningarsjóðs, 1966.

Paasche, Fredrik. *Norges og Islands litteratur inntil utgangen av middelalderen.* Edited by Anne Holstmark. Oslo: Aschehoug, 1957.

Pelham, Abigail. *Contested Creations in the Book of Job: The-World-as-It-Ought-and-Ought-Not-to-Be*. Biblical Interpretation Series 113. Leiden: Brill, 2012.

Pelle, Stephen. "Twelfth-Century Sources of Old Norse Homilies: New Evidence from AM 655 XXVII 4to." *Gripla* 24 (2013): 45–75.

Philippart, Guy. "Fragments palimpsestes latins du Vindobonensis 563 (Ve siècle?). Évangile selon S. Matthieu, Évangelie de l'Enfance selon Thomas, Évangile de Nicodème." *Analecta Bollandiana* 90 (1972): 390–411.

Quinn, Esther C. *The Quest of Seth for the Oil of Life*. Chicago: University of Chicago Press, 1962.

Raschellà, Fabrizio D. "Le traduzioni bibliche come testimonianza di storia della lingua islandese tra medioevo e prima età moderna." In *La Bibbia nelle letterature germaniche medievali. Atti del XXXIX Convegno dell'Associazione Italiana di Filologia Germanica, Venezia, 6–8 Giugno 2012*, edited by Marina Buzzoni, Massimiliano Bampi, and Omar Khalaf, 11–36. Venice: Edizioni Ca' Foscari – Digital Publishing, 2015.

Rashdall, Hastings. *The Idea of Atonement in Christian Theology*. London: MacMillan and Co., 1919.

Rella, Frank A. "Continental Manuscripts Acquired for English Centres in Tenth and Early Eleventh Century, A Preliminary Checklist." *Anglia* 98 (1980): 105–16.

Renz, Gabi. "Nicodemus: An Ambiguous Disciple? A Narrative Sensitive Investigation." In *Challenging Perspectives on the Gospel of John*, edited by John Lierman, 255–83. Wissenschaftliche Untersuchungen zum Neuen Testament 2, Reihe 219. Tübingen: Mohr Siebeck, 2006.

Richards, Mary P. *Texts and Their Traditions in the Medieval Library of Rochester Cathedral Priory*. Transactions of the American Philosophical Society 78. Philadelphia: The American Philosophical Society, 1988.

Rosemann, Philipp W. *Peter Lombard*. Great Medieval Thinkers. Oxford: Oxford University Press, 2004.

Roughton, Philip. "AM 645 4to and AM 652/630 4to: Study and Translation of Two Thirteenth-Century Icelandic Collections of Apostles' and Saints' Lives." PhD diss. University of Colorado, 2002.

– "Stylistics and Sources of the *Postola Sögur* in AM 645 4to and AM 652/630 4to." *Gripla* 17 (2005): 7–50.

Ruggerini, Maria E. "A Just and Riding God: Christ's Movement in the *Descent into Hell*." In *Myths, Legends and Heroes. Essays on Old Norse and Old English Literature in Honour of John McKinnell*, edited by Daniel Anlezark, 206–24. TONIS 5. Toronto: University of Toronto Press, 2011.

Russell, Jeffrey B. *The Devil: Perceptions of Evil from Late Antiquity to Primitive Christianity*. Ithaca: Cornell University Press, 1977.

Satran, David. "Deceiving the Deceiver. Variations on an Early Christian Theme." In *Things Revealed: Studies in Early Jewish and Christian Literature in Honor of Michael E. Stone*, edited by Esther G. Chazon, David Satran, and Ruth A. Clements, 357–64. Leiden: Brill, 2004.

Savage, John J. "The Medieval Tradition of Cerberus." *Traditio* 7 (1949–52): 405–10.

Schapiro, Meyer. "The Beatus Apocalypse of Gerona." In *Late Antique, Early Christian and Mediaeval Art. Selected Papers*, vol. 3, edited by Meyer Schapiro, 319–28. New York: George Braziller, 1979.

Schiller, Gertrud. *Ikonographie der christlichen Kunst*. Vol. 3, *Die Auferstehung und Erhöhung Christi*. Gütersloher Verlagshaus: Gerd Mohn, 1971.

Scott-Macnab, David. "St Augustine and the Devil's 'Mousetrap'." *Vigiliae Christianae* 68 (2014): 409–15.

Seip, Didrik Arup. *Nye studier i norsk språkhistorie*. Oslo: Aschehoug, 1954.

– *Palæografi B: Norge og Island*. edited by Johannes Brøndum Nielsen. Stockholm: Albert Bonnier. Nordisk kultur XXVIII: B. Oslo: A. Aschehoug; København: J.H. Schulz, 1954.

Shields, Hugh. "Bishop Turpin and the Source of Nycodemus gospel." *English Studies* 53 (1972): 497–502.

Skonning, Hans Hanssen. *Collegium Philosophorum Hedenske Philosophia eller Vijsdom Vdi huilcken findis adskillige, mærckelige oc værckelige Bedrifft, Ordsprog oc Tale, aff vjse Hedninge oc Philosophis foregiffuit, Aff adskillige Grædske oc Latinske Autoribus colligerit, oc vdi nogle visse Locos Communes, med sine observationibus oc Lærdomme, tilhobe skreffuit, oc vdi Danske Sprog forfærdiget*. Aarhus: Autoris tryckerij, 1636.

Spehr, Harald, ed. *Der Ursprung der isländischen Schrift und ihre Weiterbildung bis zur Mitte des 13. Jahrhunderts*. Halle: Max Niemeyer, 1929.

Stefán Karlsson. "The Development of the Latin Script II: In Iceland." In *The Nordic Languages* 1 (2002): 832–40.

– *The Icelandic Language*. Translated by Rory McTurk. London: Viking Society for Northern Research, 2004. Originally published as "Tungan." In *Íslensk Þjóðmenning*, vol. 6, *Munnmenntir og bókmenning*, edited by Frosti F. Jóhannesson, 1–54. Reykjavík: Þjóðsaga, 1989.

Strömback, Dag. *The Conversion of Iceland: A Survey*. Translated and annotated by Peter Foote. Viking Society for Northern Research Text Series 6. London: Viking Society for Northern Research, 1975.

Svanhildur Óskarsdóttir. "Universal History in Fourteenth-Century Iceland: Studies in AM 764 4to." PhD diss. London: University College of London, 2000.

Tamburr, Karl. *The Harrowing of Hell in Medieval England*. Cambridge: D.S. Brewer, 2007.

Thomas, David A. *Revelation 19 in Historical and Mythological Context*. Studies in Biblical Literature 118. New York: Peter Lang, 2008.

Timpanaro, Sebastiano. *The Genesis of Lachmann's Method*. Edited and translated by Glenn W. Most. Chicago: University of Chicago Press, 2005. Originally published as *La genesi del metodo del Lachmann*. 2nd rev. ed. Padova: Liviana, 1981.

Trovato, Paolo. *Everything You Always Wanted to Know About Lachmann's Method. A Non-Standard Handbook of Genealogical Textual Criticism in the Age of Post-Structuralism, Cladistics, and Copy-Text*. Storie e Linguaggi 7. Padova: libreriauniversitaria.it, 2014.

Turville-Petre, Gabriel. *Origins of Icelandic Literature*. Oxford: Clarendon Press, 1953.

Two Old English Apocrypha and Their Manuscript Source. The Gospel of Nicodemus and the Avenging of the Saviour Edited by James E. Cross. CSAE 19. Cambridge: Cambridge University Press, 1996.

Van Deusen, Natalie. "The Old Norse-Icelandic Legend of Saints Mary Magdalene and Martha." PhD diss. Madison: University of Wisconsin–Madison, 2012.

van Liere, Frans. "Biblical Exegesis Through the Twelfth Century." In *The Practice of the Bible in the Middle Ages. Production, Reception and Performance in Western Christianity*, edited by Susan Boynton and Diane J. Reilly, 157–78. New York: Colombia University Press, 2011.

von Dobschütz, Ernst. "Nicodemus, Gospel of." In *A Dictionary of the Bible*, vol. 3, edited by James Hastings, 544–7. New York: Charles Scribners' Sons, 1919.

Wawrykow, Joseph. "Peter Lombard." In *Augustine Through the Ages: An Encyclopedia*, edited by Allan D. Fitzgerald and J.C. Cavadini, 650–1. Grand Rapids: W.B. Eerdmans, 1999.

Wellendorf, Jonas. "Whetting the Appetite for a Vernacular Literature: The Icelandic Hungrvaka." In *Historical Narratives and Christian Identity on a European Periphery: Early History Writing in Northern, East Central, and Eastern Europe (ċ. 1070–1200)*, edited by Ildar Garipzanov, 123–42. Medieval Texts and Northern Culture of Northern Europe 6. Turnhout: Brepols, 2011.

Widding, Ole, Hans Bekker-Nielsen, and Laurence K. Shook. "The Lives of the Saints in Old Norse Prose: A Handlist." *Mediaeval Studies* 25 (1963): 294–337.

Wolf, Alois. "Sehweisen und Darstellungsfragen in *Gylfaginning*: Thors Fischfang." *Skandinavistik* 7 (1977): 1–27.

Wolf, Kirsten. "Om en 'tabt' islandsk oversættelse af Nikodemusevangeliet." *Arkiv för nordisk filologi* 107 (1992): 167–79.

– "The Influence of the *Evangelium Nicodemi* on Norse Literature: A Survey." In *The Medieval Gospel of Nicodemus*, 261–86. Reprint of "The Influence of the *Evangelium Nicodemi* on Norse Literature: A Survey." *Mediaeval Studies* 55 (1993): 219–42.

– "Pride and Politics in Late-Twelfth-Century Iceland: The Sanctity of Bishop Þorlákr Þórhallson." In *Sanctity in the North. Saints, Lives and Cults in Medieval Scandinavia*, edited by Thomas A. DuBois, 241–70. TONIS 2. Toronto: University of Toronto Press, 2008.

– *The Legends of the Saints in Old Norse-Icelandic Prose*. TONIS 6. Toronto: University of Toronto Press, 2013.

Wright, Charles D. "Apocryphal Lore and Insular Tradition in St Gall, Stiftsbibliothek MS 908." In *Irland und die Christenheit: die Kirche im Frühmittelalter. The Bible and the Missions*, edited by Proinséans Ní Chatháin and Michael Richter, 124–54. Stuttgart: Klett-Cotta, 1987.

– *The Irish Tradition in Old English Literature*. CSAE 6. Cambridge: Cambridge University Press, 1993.

Þór Magnússon, "Hrafnahrekkurinn. Sitt af hverju um refagildrur." In *Árbók hins íslenzka fornleifafélags 1980* (1981), 73–87.

Index of Scriptural Quotations

Index of Manuscripts

General Index

The present index covers all topics, titles of works, place names, personal names, and their respective epithets cited in the volume. Medieval and Icelandic people are indexed by their first name. To facilitate their localization, reference to the place names will be made exclusively through their modern provinces, regions, and countries of affiliation.

Toronto Old Norse and Icelandic Series

1 *Einarr Skulason's* Geisli*: A Critical Edition* edited and translated by Martin Chase
2 *Anglo-Saxon England in Icelandic Medieval Texts* by Magnus Fjalldal
3 *Sanctity in the North: Saints, Lives, and Cults in Medieval Scandinavia* edited by Thomas DuBois
4 *Snorri Sturluson and the* Edda*: The Conversion of Cultural Capital in Medieval Scandinavia* by Kevin J. Wanner
5 *Myths, Legends, and Heroes: Essays on Old Norse and Old English Literature in Honour of John McKinnell* edited by Daniel Anlezark
6 *The Legends of the Saints in Old Norse–Icelandic Prose* by Kirsten Wolf
7 *Essays on Eddic Poetry* by John McKinnell
8 *Into the Ocean: Vikings, Irish, and Environmental Change in Iceland and the North* by Kristjan Ahronson
9 *Egil, the Viking Poet: New Approaches to* Egil's Saga edited by Laurence de Looze, Jón Karl Helgason, Russell Poole, and Torfi H. Tulinius
10 *The Saints in Old Norse and Early Modern Icelandic Poetry* by Kirsten Wolf and Natalie M. Van Deusen
11 *Niðrstigningar saga: Sources, Transmission, and Theology of the Old Norse "Descent into Hell"* by Dario Bullitta

www.ingramcontent.com/pod-product-compliance
Lightning Source LLC
LaVergne TN
LVHW090158080826
844660LV00013B/863/J

* 9 7 8 1 4 4 2 6 9 7 9 9 7 *